CW01214855

THE LOTUS BOOK
Collectables

by William Taylor
with
Olav Glasius

Coterie Press Limited

THE LOTUS COLLECTABLES BOOK
A COMPLETE HISTORY OF LOTUS CARS MEMORABILIA

A COTERIE PRESS BOOK

First British Edition 2000

Published in the UK by Coterie Press Limited

115e Cleveland Street, London, W1T 6PU, England

Copyright © 2000 Coterie Press Limited

Text & Photographs Copyright © William Taylor

All Rights Reserved

No part of this book covered by the Copyrights hereon may be reproduced, stored in a database or retrieval system or copied in any manner whatsoever without written permission, except in the case of brief quotations embodied in articles or reviews. For information contact the publishers.

ISBN : 1 902351 01 0

Printed in Hong Kong

Reproduction in Malaysia

The Authors extend their special thanks for help in the preparation of this book to : Jo Taylor; Clive Chapman (Classic Team Lotus); Zoe Hardinge; Nigel Osborne; Jim Marsden; Simon Hadfield.

WRITTEN BY: **WILLIAM TAYLOR WITH OLAV GLASIUS**

ADDITIONAL WORDS BY: **DAVID LONG**

CREATIVE DIRECTOR: **WILLIAM TAYLOR**

EDITOR: **JAMES BENNETT**

EXECUTIVE EDITOR : **ZOE HARDINGE**

DESIGN: **PAUL COOPER**

PRINT : **COLORPRINT**

ORIGINATION BY : **GLOBAL COLOUR**

ALL COMMISSIONED PHOTOGRAPHY IS BY WILLIAM TAYLOR

THIS BOOK IS DEDICATED TO THE MEMORY OF JOHN DAWSON DAMER

CONTENTS

FOREWORD, BY **GRAHAM ARNOLD**.	5
INTRODUCTION BY **WILLIAM TAYLOR**.	6
and **OLAV GLASIUS**	7

1948-1959:	MARK I TO TYPE 17	10-39
1960-1969:	TYPE 18 TO TYPE 65	42-131
1970-1979:	TYPE 69 TO TYPE 81	134-171
1980-1989:	TYPE 81 TO TYPE 101	174-219
1990-2000:	TYPE 102 TO TYPE 118	222-249
ACBC:	ANTHONY COLIN BRUCE CHAPMAN	250-252

POSTSCRIPT BY **PATRICK PEAL**	253
INDEX	254-255
ACKNOWLEDGMENTS	256

CLUB LOTUS

FOREWORD

BY GRAHAM ARNOLD

I must congratulate William Taylor on putting this book together. His previous definitive publication, *'The Lotus Book'*, promoted him to the top position as the Lotus historian of record. This book confirms his status. Throughout the 1960s and for much of the '70s, as a poorly trained Commercial Artist and less-than-adequate copywriter, I wrote and designed almost every Lotus car and boat brochure and advertisement we produced. For more than ten years my priorities – and indeed my budgets – for such literature were minimal. Artistic, plastic covered extravaganzas, based on £1,000 a day photo shoots, were out of the question. I also followed a policy that I believe in today: that a bad salesman will give away lots of expensive brochures, a good salesman will get the order using a photocopied sheet. I also believe that really rave road tests will sell more cars than clever catalogues – look at the Elise, no Lotus ever has so captivated the press. It is my proud boast that our Road Test Preparation Team at Lotus turned out a succession of Lotus press cars so well that we never had a bad or even qualified road test report.

To quote Wayne Cherry, one time head of General Motors Styling Department in Europe, who said, to assembled Vauxhall dealers, 'If we design our cars to be beautiful, offer them against a reputation for performance, comfort, reliability, and economy, with good service, through good dealers; we won't need to advertise.' I relied on well-produced, two sided information sheets for each model. Stuart White and I photographing the cars down by the River Lea, complete with a duck or two. One day Colin said, 'No more ducks please Graham'. The next leaflet had no ducks so I proudly showed it to Colin saying, 'Look Colin, no ducks, just Swans!'. Colin hated my brochures even more than my advertising but as they say 'That was my responsibility as long as we got results – and didn't we just.'

Looking through the pages of this fine book I have been transported by nostalgia. It reminds me of some of my most enjoyable years because I can say, with a catch in my throat, 'I was there, I remember that, let me fill you in on the why and the where'. The first copy should be ceremoniously buried at the Lotus factory in a time capsule. My main regret is that I didn't save a hundred of every Lotus sales item as I now go to classic car shows and see my brochures being offered for £25 each. I could have supplemented my pension quite generously with some forethought.

INTRODUCTION

BY WILLIAM TAYLOR

The Lotus Book was an adventure. When I started in 1994 I had always been a Lotus fan, I had a couple of cars and the obligatory collection of memorabilia that most owners accumulate throughout their years of Lotus ownership. After The Lotus Book had been published and I continued to work on my goal to photograph one of every model ever produced, very quickly due to the success of the book, I realised that this would turn into a second edition dubbed 'Series 2', and again it took up most of time, just when I thought I could relax !

As I worked on The Lotus Book and met more and more of the owners and enthusiasts I realised that as well as the passion for the cars almost everybody, myself included, had their own collection of 'stuff'. Sometimes it seemed that there was more interest in collecting stuff than cars, I suppose thats understandable when it's a little easier to store your collection than it is several cars, although many people seem to do quite well at that also.

As I think almost everyone does, I thought I had a nice little collection, some quite interesting bits and pieces, but even while meeting people on The Lotus Book project I began to realise that there was so much more stuff out there than I ever thought was possible. Suddenly the idea came that I should do a companion book to the first just covering all this wealth of things related to Lotus. The more I researched the more amazing the amount of things I began to find, everything from books and brochures to models and toys, as well as all the more obscure things in between. There was just so much available for inclusion in the book, the big problem became how to put a limit on the amount of stuff to include. I wanted the book to show as much as possible, so I hope you will find some of the more unusual things interesting. I have tried to include some of the things that you won't have seen before but also some of the more popular and easily available items. My mission as before became to photograph and show as much as possible, with the same type of quality images and information but to make it above all else look good !

Again as on The Lotus Book I have been to some amazing places and met such interesting people in the making of this book and by taking almost all the photographs indoors at least I avoided the 'weather problems' I had encountered before. Over the two years it has taken, I have made yet more Lotus friends and decided to enlist one of them, Olav to help in producing the book, his wealth of knowledge and contacts throughout the Lotus world has helped immeasurably. I discovered a whole new world of Lotus 'stuff' and I hope you enjoy the book as much as I did making it.

INTRODUCTION

BY OLAV GLASIUS

I think most of you, interested in motor racing, have a hero. When I was around sixteen there was one incredibly good driver, Jim Clark. My hero. Winning not only in Formula 1, but also easily racing Formula 2 or with the famous Ford Cortinas. Lifting one front wheel, when sliding through corners, giving the big Galaxies a run for their money, whoever has seen it will never forget that sight.

My father died when I was three years old, but in those days my mother had a Cortina MK 1, a normal one of course not the Lotus one, but still in white. After long persuasion that it looked much more sporty I convinced her that the car needed green stripes. With a spraygun on the vacuum cleaner I transferred it into a Lotus Cortina lookalike and of course added the famous badges.

I still had no drivers license, in Holland you need to be 18, but she allowed me to drive it to the local garage where it was parked, half a mile from our house. I always took the opportunity before going to the garage to drive it around our small village, to improve my driving skill. Until one day I was already back home when the doorbell ran. My mother opened and a gentleman handed over a hubcap, telling her that her son cornered so fast that it had come off. That was for a long time the end of my driving her car.

When I was 18 – a birthday which in my opinion was a long time coming – my first car was a secondhand Ford Anglia, with the funny rear window. I painted it in Alan Mann's red and gold livery. Many more secondhand cars followed and I always dreamed about a Lotus Seven, but couldn't afford it. Instead I started to make a scratch built copy with original bodyparts – but I never finished the project. Many years later though I bought my first real Lotus, and it was indeed the Seven Series 3. After that many more followed ranging from Marks 6 to 8, 14, 27, 28, 47 to an Esprit Turbo. Now the collection counts around 15 cars and as a full blooded enthusiast I also started to collect books, brochures, paintings, toys, models, pedal cars, in fact everything to do with Lotus. There are more than 130 books about Lotus, but not a single one deals with these Lotus collectables. I always had the idea to solve that problem but when I met William Taylor, who was busy with the making of his, now famous book, I found the ideal partner in making it. We spent some lovely times in the making of this, and I hope you have the the same enjoyment in reading it.

MOTOR RACING
AUTOSPORT
SPORTS CAR
AND LOTUS OWNER
UP AND COMING DRIVERS
ROAD & TRACK
MINTEX
LOTUS-ELITE
AVON
TBY 484
DUNLOP
LUCAS
MOTOR SPORT
MOTOR RACING and MOTOR RALLY
SUNBEAM ALPINE
Pep, Power Performance
sporting motorist
HOW DUNLOP GO RACING
small car
STIRLING'S RACING ELAN
TESTING
FORD-LOTUS INDY CAR

CHAPTER 1

1	Trials car	1948
2	Trials car	1949
3	750 Formula car	1951
4	Trials car	1952
6	Sports racer	1952
7	Seven	1957
8	Sports racer	1954
9	Sports racer	1955
10	Sports racer	1955
11	Eleven	1956
12	Formula 2	1957
14	Elite	1957
15	Sports racer	1958
16	Formula 1	1958
17	Sports racer	1959

1948-1959

MARK 1&2

Trials Cars 1948 & 1950

which he dubbed the Mark I. The facilities in the lock-up were poor, but for Chapman the process of building these early cars was an important learning curve, applying newly acquired theories to the job in hand and filling any gaps in his knowledge with his usual inspired innovation and creativity. In the end, the four Marks produced just five completed cars (not all of which have survived) but nonetheless between them generated a surprising amount of memorabilia. No scale models of the cars

They were curious looking machines, function having clearly triumphed over form in the lock-up behind the future Mrs Chapman's parental home. But each of those early Lotus designs – three trials cars and one 750 circuit racer – was nevertheless effective in its own way and they also represented a considerable achievement for Colin Chapman. Still a student when, as a novice car dealer, he realised that changes to the basic petrol ration in 1947 had left him with a stock which was now virtually worthless. Spurred into action he set to work on one car in particular, a sad-looking 1930 fabric-bodied Austin Seven, the idea being to modify it for his own use – initially as a tourer, but in the end as a trials car

10

Trials Car 1950 & 750 Car 1951

were ever produced commercially, but some hand-built special orders have been commissioned including these scratch-built 1/43rd scale resin models of the Mark 1, 2, 3 and 3B by Mike Serrifier from South Africa in thre mid 1990's. Each has been painted to match the actual cars – and are so perfectly detailed as to include things such as the power bulge on the bonnet of the 3B supplied to Adam Currie back in 1952. Shown too is the tankard awarded to Chapman on May 7, 1950 for his successful drive in the Mark 2 at the Gravesend Speed Trial that year, and a press-cutting and advertisement from Motor Sport dated November 1950. In September of that year the same magazine also carried an advertisement for the sale of the Mark 2, and two years later one of the first advertisements for Lotus Engineering. The same car starred in the film 'Brothers in Law', a role commemorated on the cover of Sports Car & Lotus Owner in June 1957. Memories of the Mark 4 have also survived in the personal photograph album of Hazel Chapman, press cuttings and photographs detailing it's successful trials career such as Mike Lawson's drive in the Roy Feddham Trophy race in November 1954, and in an article by Chapman himself which appeared in the magazine Motor Racing the following month.

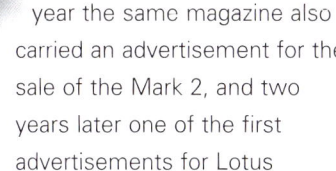

PICTURE DETAILS

Mark1 model, Mike Serrifier-S.Africa, resin, 1/43rd, 1997

Mark 2 model, Mike Serrifier-S.Africa, resin, 1/43rd, 1997

Mark 3 model, Mike Serrifier-S.Africa, resin, 1/43rd, 1998

Mark 3B model, Mike Serrifier-S.Africa, resin, 1/43rd, 1998

Mark 1 advert, Motor Sport, Nov. 1950

Mark 1 press cutting, Wrotham Cup trial, Motor Sport, Nov.1950

Sports Car & Lotus Owner, June 1957

Mark 2 for sale advert, Motor Sport, Sept. 1950

Tankard awarded to Colin Chapman in Mark 2, Gravesend Speed Trial, 7th May 1950

Mark 2, photograph album of Hazel Chapman.

Mark 4 (Mike Lawson), photograph album of Hazel Chapman.

Mark 4 Press cutting, Roy Feddham Trophy, Nov. 1954

Lotus 50th Anniversary poster, USA, 1998

Lotus Eng. Co. advert, Motor Sport, 1952

The Lotus Story, Motor Racing, Dec. 1954

Mark 3 greetings card.

MARK 3 & 4

MARK 6

Sports Car 1952

Colin Chapman's first series-production car – with approximately 110 produced in just four years from 1952 – the distinctive and purposeful Mark 6 was conceived in response to important changes in the 750 Motor Club regulations which allowed the use of a specially modified chassis designs.

Chapman chose a spaceframe, thereby becoming for the first time a real car manufacturer, and after driving the finished result, Autocar reported that, 'few if any cars are quicker through the S-bends'. In the hands of Chapman and others, the Mark 6 – supplied in kit form, it was fitted with engines from MG, Ford, Coventry-Climax, BMW and other manufacturers – was soon a familiar sight on Britain's motor racing circuits. Several of its many early successes are today commemorated by a number of tankards, such as that awarded to A.C.B. Chapman (2nd place, at an average speed of 67.49mph) in the Sports Car Race at Silverstone on September 6, 1953, another 2nd on the same circuit the same year, a 3rd at Goodwood on July 25th, and for an outright victory in the Ford Ten Race at Silverstone on 6th September 1953 at

PICTURE DETAILS

Model, Mike Serrifier, S.Africa, resin, 1/43rd, 1998

Tankard awarded to ACB Chapman, 2nd place Sports Car Race, Silverstone, 6th Sept. 1953

Tankard awarded to ACB Chapman, winner Ford Ten Race, Silverstone, 6th Sept. 1953

Tankard awarded to ACB Chapman, 3rd place, Goodwood, 25th July 1953

Tankard awarded to ACB Chapman, 2nd place, 5 Lap Scratch race, 4th St. J. Horsfall Memorial Meeting, Silverstone 1953

Model Mark 6 chassis, D.Abbott, GB.

The first Lotus Cars brochure, late 1953

Letter, price lists & stop press sheet, Lotus Engineering, 1954

Marks 6 & 9 advertisement, Autosport, 1955

Mark 6 advert, Motor Racing magazine, late 1953

Esso Petroleum advert, Autosport, early 1955

12

Sports Car 1952

an average speed of 65.01mph. The car was also pictured in the very first brochure produced for a Lotus car (four pages, in late 1953) and a full-page advertisement which appeared in Autosport in 1955 showing this car and the later Mark 9. Similar advertisements for the Mark 6 appeared in Motor Racing magazine in late 1953, and early 1954. When Peter Gammon's MG-powered car (UPE 9) scored a notable second place at Silverstone directly behind Chapman driving the new Mark 8, Esso produced an advertisement congratulating him on his performance. Once again, the car was never made into a commercially widely available scale model, although more recently Joker in Japan have produced a 1/24th scale resin kit. South African Mike Serrifier's special 1/43rd resin model is shown here, along with a model of Chapman's pioneering lightweight steel-tube chassis by Dave Abbott in the UK which were originally fabricated by the Progress Chassis Company. The most personal memento of the Mark 6, however, is almost certainly the original letter, price list and stop-press sheet sent to a prospective customer of Lotus Engineering in 1954 and signed by Hazel Chapman since the end of 1952 one of the company's directors.

MARK 6

SEVEN

Sports Car 1957-1968

The car which more than any other set Lotus on the path to success (and a machine whose incredible longevity belies Colin Chapman's throwaway comment that his latest creation was merely 'the sort of thing you could dash off in a weekend'). The Seven may have been a road car first and foremost but it clearly benefited from the experiences garnered from designing and building racing machines like the Mark 6 and in time became a successful club racer in its own right. Launched by the company in October 1957 alongside the more civilised Type 14 Elite, sales literature produced at the time shows that at £536 in kit form the Seven was expensive even allowing for the fact that every single component was supplied brand new. This actually made it something of a rarity in this sector, but the resulting quality shone through and by 1970 more than 2,300 had been sold – enough of them early on to bring in the funds Chapman needed to get the gorgeous Elite into full production. Thriving sales also helped make it the first Lotus to attract the attention of the model-makers, not just in the UK but as far afield as China. There

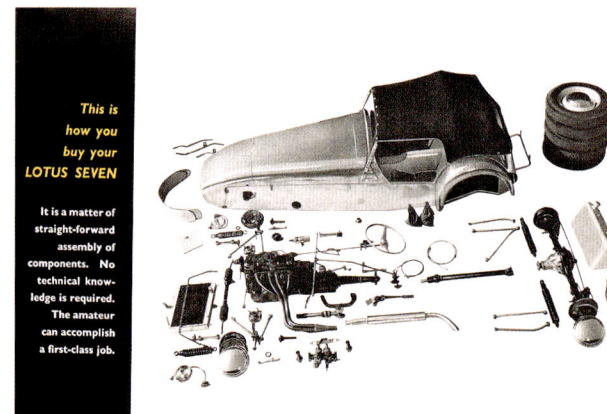

Sports Car 1957–1968

the aptly-named Vitesse Group produced a die-cast 1/43rd scale model of the Series 2, a car also modelled by Auto Kits in Great Britain which produced the box artwork shown here for its larger, white-metal 1/24th scale model.

China was also the country of origin for the Matchbox Collectibles die-cast version, and the newer 1/43rd scale Seven produced by Kyosho. Being a true series-production car, the Seven also required a greater marketing effort on the part of the company than any of its predecessors, with several different brochures being produced over the years which have now become highly collectible. Those shown include what was possibly the first for the Seven, a four-page item with a red cover for the Series 1 which was printed in Bournemouth at Richmond Hill Printing Works in late

PICTURE DETAILS

Box of Seven s2 model Auto Kits GB, white metal. 1/24th

Seven s2 model, Vitesse group., China, die cast 1/43rd scale, 1999

Sales letter, Lotus Engineering, Dec. 1955

Rear cover, 8 page s1 brochure in yellow and black, late 1959

Lotus 7 adverts, Sports Car & Lotus Owner, Nov. '57, Mar '58, Sept. '58

Advert, 'build your own Seven in 7 easy stages' Autosport, Dec. 1969

4 page, s3 brochure, Holland 1969

Super Seven 1500 specification sheet, 1962

Seven s3 brochure and price list, Caterham Car Sales, 1968

Seven s1, full page advert, 1958

Cover, SEVEN Club magazine, Jan. 1974

Sports Car 1957-1968

1957 or early 1958. Others rare survivors from the period include a sales brochure produced in Holland in 1969 for the Series 3, a couple of six and eight page versions for the Series 1 printed in Leicester by A.G. Wood Ltd in 1958 and '59 and featuring two cars UOW 429 and 7 TMT, a bright orange Series 2 brochure from 1960 with 12 pages and featuring 8843 AR by Derick Birdsoll, and another 12-pager in purple for the Super Seven 109E which, in a similar four-page format, was also used as a magazine insert with a mailing section. Magazine advertisements were also created by the company at this time, like the three shown here from 1957 and '58 which appeared on the back cover of Sports Car & Lotus Owner as well as in other publications.

By the late 1960s the company was employing quite sophisticated advertisements, such as the detailed one also booked into Autosport in 1969 showing readers how to build their own cars in seven easy stages. By then of course Autosport readers would have been more

Sports Car 1957-1968

PICTURE DETAILS

Seven model, Kyosho, China, red Zamac (die cast).

Orange and blue square magazine insert.

Orange 12 page s2 brochure, Derek Birdsall design, 1960

6 page s1 brochure [UOW 429] printed by AG Wood Ltd, Leicester 1958

12 page, purple Super Seven brochure.

Red cover, 4 page s1 brochure, printed by Richmond Hill Printing Works, Bournemouth, '57-'58

than familiar with the Seven, thanks not only to its winning performance but also to advertisements like the one shown here with artwork by the cartoonist 'Coles'. Autosport was also the natural place for Surrey-based Caterham Cars to advertise, both before and after Graham Nearn's thriving company became the Seven's sole distributor when Lotus moved out to Hethel. Much of the material shown here was generated by Caterham during this period, including a brochure and price list for the Series 3 in 1968, an advertisement which appeared

Sports Car 1957-1968

in Autosport in 1964, and one dated January 1969 for the Super Seven Series 3 and a number of other secondhand cars. The Super Seven Series 3 poster is also one of Caterham's, and dating from 1973/4 is the first produced by the company after they had taken over the production of the evergreen Seven from Lotus as the energetic Chapman pursued his relentless drive upmarket.

Clubmans Car 1965

PICTURE DETAILS

Mark 7 model, Matchbox Collectables, China, red Zamac (die cast) 1/43rd

Cover, 8 page 7 s1 brochure in yellow and black, late 1959

Super 7 s3 folding brochure/poster, Caterham Cars, 1973/4

Advert for s3 etc. Caterham Cars, Jan. 1969

Advert, Caterham Car Sales, Autosport 1965

Advert for s1 with cartoon by Coles, Autosport April 1964

Team Lotus spec sheet for 3-7, 1965

Lotus Components spec sheet/brochure for 3-7, 1970

A truly great concept but one which never quite made it through to production, the idea of a racing Lotus Seven with independent rear suspension had been kicking around the factory for some years before the one and only car built to this specification - correctly referred to as the Three-7 - was finally put into commission by one of the sales team, more or less in his own spare time. In this form, the unique and in its day highly competitive car survives, its detail specification shown here alongside a surprisingly professional sales sheet with a photograph of its rescuer/creator John Berry, the company's erstwhile Home Sales Manager.

TYPE 3-7

MARK 8

Sports Racer 1954

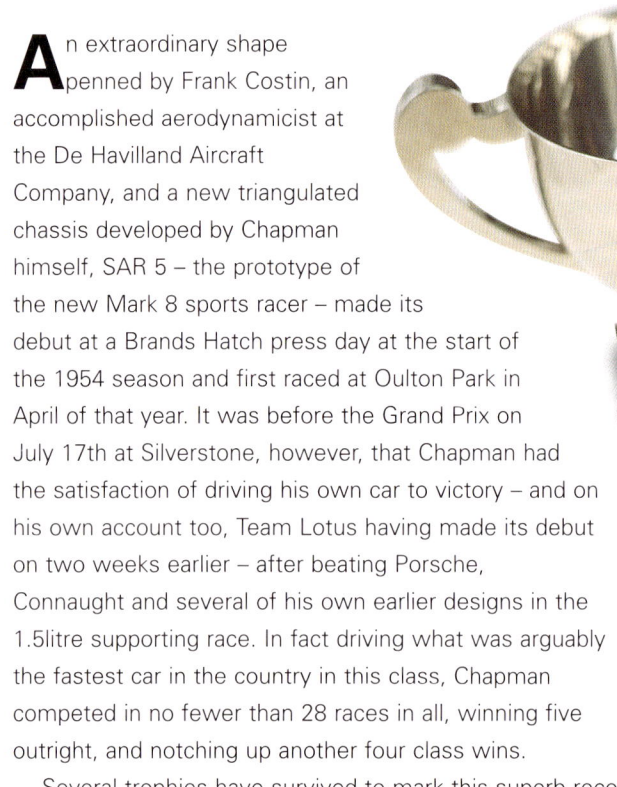

An extraordinary shape penned by Frank Costin, an accomplished aerodynamicist at the De Havilland Aircraft Company, and a new triangulated chassis developed by Chapman himself, SAR 5 – the prototype of the new Mark 8 sports racer – made its debut at a Brands Hatch press day at the start of the 1954 season and first raced at Oulton Park in April of that year. It was before the Grand Prix on July 17th at Silverstone, however, that Chapman had the satisfaction of driving his own car to victory – and on his own account too, Team Lotus having made its debut on two weeks earlier – after beating Porsche, Connaught and several of his own earlier designs in the 1.5litre supporting race. In fact driving what was arguably the fastest car in the country in this class, Chapman competed in no fewer than 28 races in all, winning five outright, and notching up another four class wins.

Several trophies have survived to mark this superb record, including those awarded for victory in the aforementioned International Daily Express Sports Car race at Silverstone, but also in Germany at the Nurburgring 17th International ADAC Eifelrennen meeting and at Crystal Palace in September of the same year where Chapman took the chequered flag in the Annerley Trophy Race. Other important memorabilia for this singularly effective sports-racer include an original photograph from Hazel Chapman's own album, an advertisement from Motor Racing trumpeting its successes, and an official reprint of an article ordered by the company after the car appeared in Autosport in November 1954.

Sports Racer 1955

So enthusiastic was Chapman about the prospects for a larger-engined Mark 8 (after enquiries by Mike Anthony and others) to compete in the 2 litre series that the Mark 10 – as the new car came to be called – actually predates the Mark 9.

Its engine, well-proven already by Brian Lister, Johns Cooper and John Tojeiro, was the Bristol-built version of BMW's pre-war OHV six, its weight and height requiring the fuel tank to be a repositioned and a distinctive bonnet bulge to be fitted. Shown here is a page from Chapman's own notebook marking some suspension modifications, as well as a price list for the Mark 9 and its similarly aerodynamic sister cars. The most enduring mementoes of this car, however, depend more on its screen rather than circuit appearances: namely, in an ITV production with June Whitfield behind the wheel, and in the movie 'Checkpoint' which starring Anthony Steel at the wheel of a 10 and in the company of James Robertson Justice and Stanley Baker. James Dean ordered a Mark 10 too, but unfortunately he never managed to take delivery before his untimely death.

PICTURE DETAILS

Mark 8 model, Wolfgang Reichert, Germany, white metal, 1/43rd, 1998

Trophy won at Nurburgring 17th Int. ADAC Eifelrennen meeting, 23rd May 1954

B&W photograph, personal photo album, H.Chapman.

Trophy won by ACBC, 1st place BRSCC Annerley Trophy Race, Crystal Palace 18th Sept. 1954

International Daily Express Sports Car Race, up to 1 1/2 litre team award, Silverstone Grand Prix meeting 17.7.54

Lotus Engineering, Marks 6 & 8 advert, Motor Racing, Oct. 1954

Mark 10 model, Wolfgang Reichert, Germany, white metal, 1/43rd scale, 1998

Lotus Engineering, Mark 8 reprinted article from Autosport, Nov. 1954

Drawings for Mark 10 from Colin Chapmans notebook, 1955

Lotus Engineering, Marks 8, 9, 10 (for cars with aero-dynamic bodies) price list, April 1955

Cover Motor Racing magazine, 1955

Advert, Valspar.

MARK 10

MARK 9

Sports Racer 1955

Continuing where the Mark 8 left off, the svelte, evolutionary Mark 9 is another crucial landmark car for Lotus. Accepted for Le Mans in 1955, and with Chapman now a full-time manufacturer having quit his job with British Aluminium, the car also appeared on the company's first ever stand at the Earls Court Motor Show. Smaller than its predecessor, more than 200lbs lighter and with even better aerodynamics, it was to score some notable victories for Team Lotus and for the privateers who bought some of the two dozen built. At Brands Hatch in September 1955, for example, Chapman came in ahead of Ivor Bueb's rival Cooper (and was awarded the Lex Trophy shown here) while Peter Lumsden won the BARC Brooklands Trophy the following year. Victory in the big endurance races was not to be, however, well not yet. Chapman was black-flagged at Le Mans for a minor infringement, and an illegal push-start ruled another, class-leading Mark 9 out at Sebring, but Climax-engined cars were soon branded 'Le Mans' anyway and sold at a premium over the Ford side-valve 'Club'. Whilst no privateers could beat the Team Lotus cars, their business was vital to the fledgling company which tempted them with detailed price lists of engine options for the car. Autosport's John Bolster tested two of them – MG and Climax-engined – identifying in both 'phenomenally high cornering power' and impressive overall

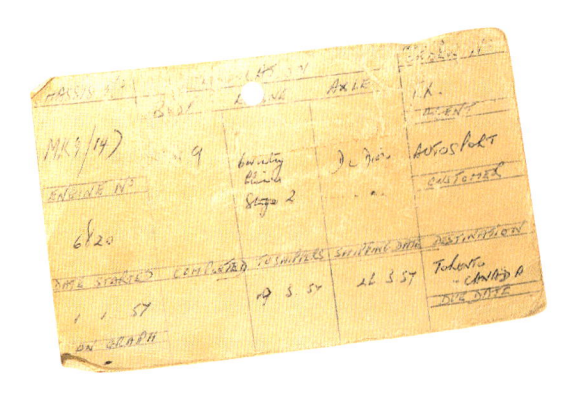

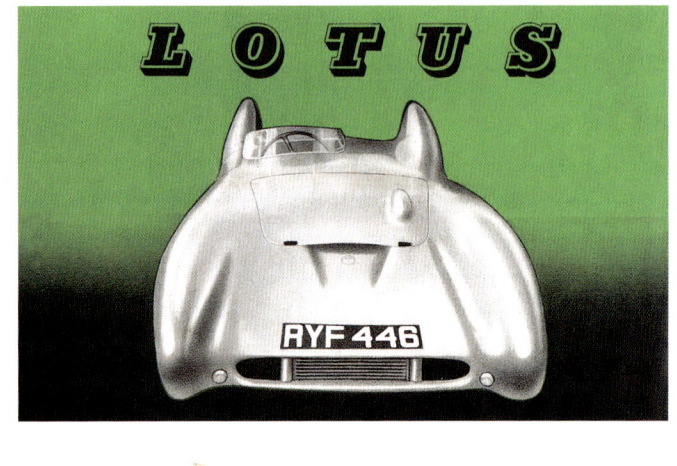

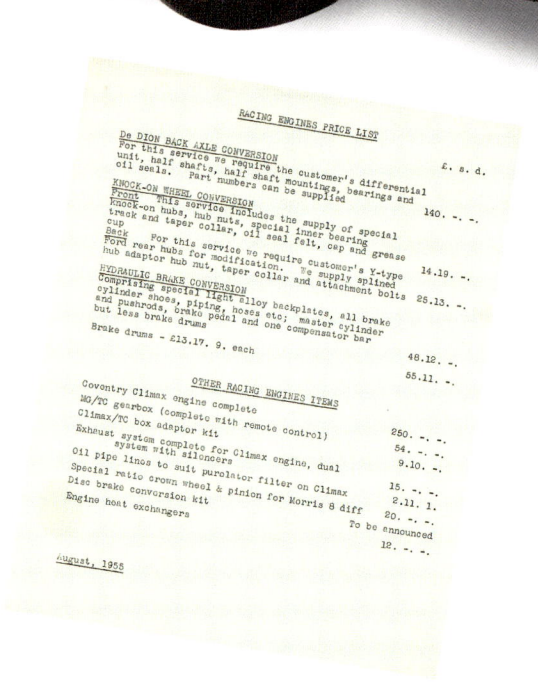

Sports Racer 1955

MARK 9

PICTURE DETAILS

Model, Midlantic, GB, resin, 1/43rd

The Lex Trophy awarded to C. Chapman, Brands Hatch, 1955

Cover, Sports Car & Lotus Owner, Feb. & May 1957

Lotus Engineering, Mark 9 reprinted article from Autosport March 1955

Team Lotus build card for Mark 9 chassis 14

Lotus Engineering, 8 page Mark 9 brochure, 1955/56

Lotus Engineering, Mark 9 price list, Aug. 1955

performance. The latter achieved a top speed of 128mph and a 0-60mph time of just 7.8 seconds. Once again to support sales Lotus Engineering ordered magazine reprints and one of these, from Autosport dated March 1955, is shown here along with two covers from Sports Car & Lotus Owner from early 1957, and a technical build card from the Team Lotus archive for the 14th car to be constructed. Two versions of the official Mark 9 brochure featuring RYF 446 are also included, showing the tempting sign-off back page asking, 'Can I build a Lotus?' Finally, the 1/43rd scale model (shown from two angles) was made more recently in resin by British company Midlantic.

ELEVEN

Sports Racer 1956

Dropping the word 'Mark' and using the word Eleven instead of numerals to avoid confusion with his second trials car, this was Chapman's most aerodynamic car yet. To cope with demand – it was to sell no fewer than 270 units – production was rationalised to just one chassis. Even so, a wide variation in detail specification meant the Eleven was available in three distinct versions: Le Mans; the Club, for less committed sportsmen; and the Sports, intended chiefly for road use and substituting a Ford sidevalve for the expensive Climax engine. In 1100cc form, the Le Mans had only one true rival – the rear-engined Cooper – and it soon notched up some phenomenal successes many of which are commemorated by items illustrated here. The 1/43rd scale resin model of the record attempt car, for example, was made in France by Provence Moulage after Stirling Moss achieved 135.5mph at Monza in 1956. Similarly the cut glass vase, one of two, marks Kieth Hall and Cliff Allison's class win and victory in the Index of Performance at Le Mans the following year. After 24 hours, with only 744cc, they came 14th overall – an extraordinary achievement. Closer to home the trophy is for the team award in the 1500cc Sports Car Race at the 9th International Daily Express Trophy meeting at Silverstone on 14 September 1957. This particular car, a derivative of the Le Mans variant, was still powered by a Coventry Climax unit but the larger 1,460cc FWB developing up to 100bhp at 6,200rpm. Significantly the Eleven was probably also the first factory vehicle to be widely available as a model, the die-cast silver Lotus Eleven Club No. 7 shown here having been manufactured in the UK by Corgi. No. 13, also 1/43rd scale and its accompanying Transporter although much later, are also British-made, of white metal and painted appropriately in British Racing Green. Still competitive in 1958, the car's most successful performance in a world championship race was actually not at Le Mans but at Sebring where no fewer than three of them finished in the first ten. The highest-placed was that driven by Weiss and Tallaksen which finished in fourth place behind a brace of Ferraris and a Porsche. That said, the most unusual memento of the car's competition record refers back to

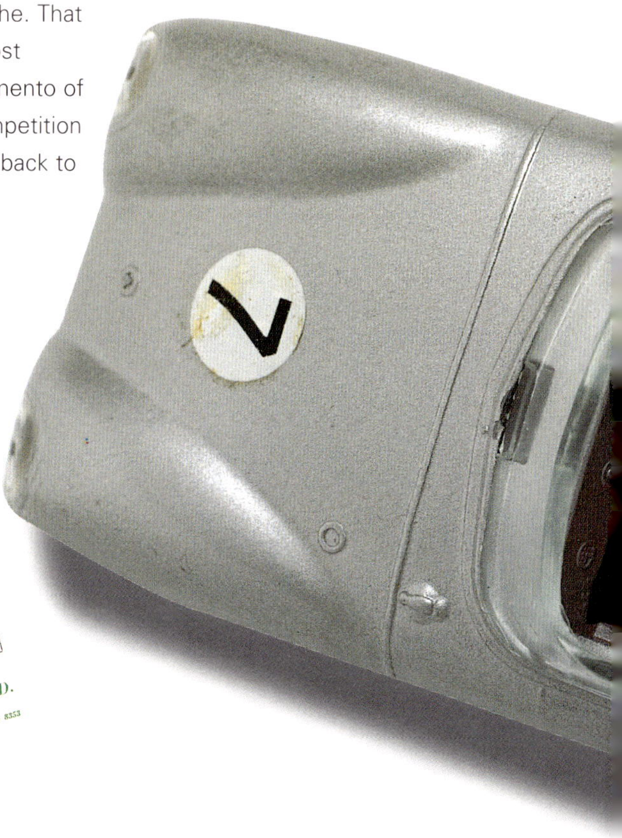

Sports Racer 1956

PICTURE DETAILS

Team award, 1500cc Sports Car Race, 9th International Daily Express Trophy meeting, Silverstone Sept. 14th 1957

Cut glass vase for 1st Index of Performance, Le Mans 24hour race 1957, Allison & Hall.

Adverts from Sports Car & Lotus Owner, 1958-59

Jigsaw puzzle box, France, circa. 1960

Lotus Eleven Club, Corgi GB, 1/43rd scale, die cast.

ELEVEN

ELEVEN

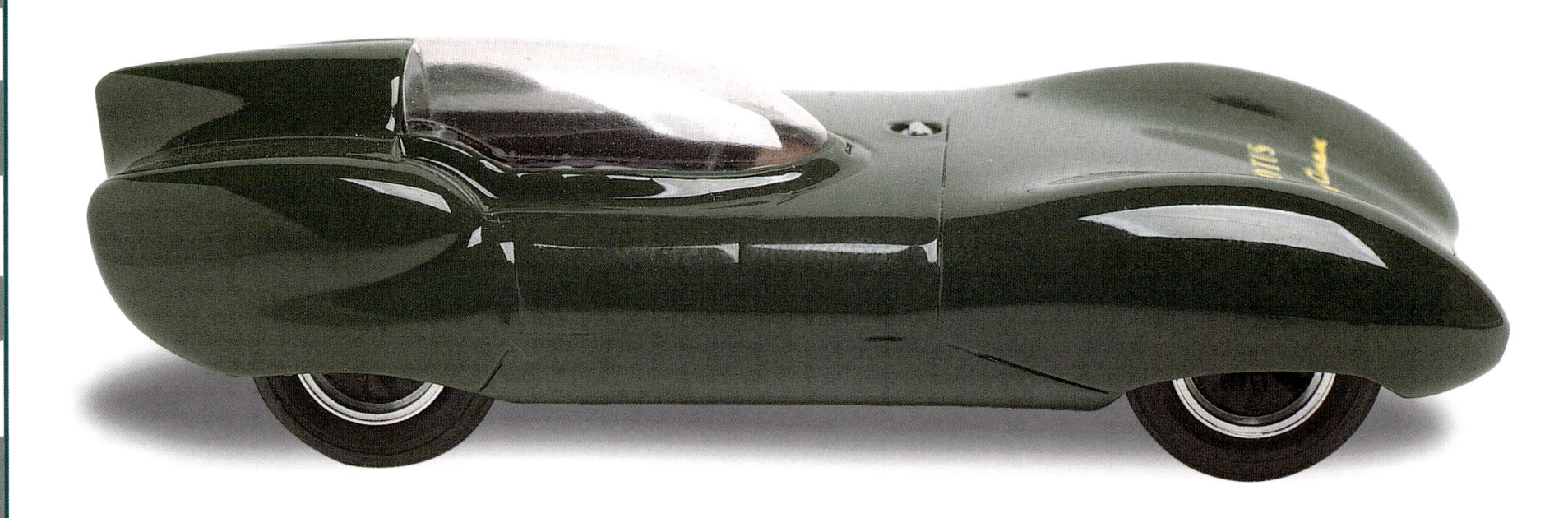

Sports Racer 1956

Le Mans, and is the jigsaw puzzle made in France around 1960. Still in its original box, this depicts in fine style an event where in 1957 no fewer than five cars made the start, the best coming ninth overall and winning its class. No less interesting is the Eleven's depiction in the box artwork for the maroon No.8, a 1/24th scale plastic kit produced by Otaki in Japan the car actually looks surprisingly like a Ferrari! Far more accurate however are the model Elevens made by a company named Graphic Designers in the UK. From 1956 onward, the company owned by brothers Bill & Ted Friend, produced these highly detailed 1/24th scale kits (scaled from original Lotus drawings supplied by Colin Chapman) which were the first ever models to be made of white metal.

A completed model is shown here with it's original packaging and full instructions. Given the relatively high production figures for the car, it is perhaps unsurprising that so much paperwork was generated and that so much of it has survived. Shown here, along with an original specification sheet for the Le Mans model, are two 6-page brochures, one each for Series 1 and 2. The former, with a green cover, features photographs courteousy of The Motor magazine and was printed by Norman Bros of London in 1955 or '56. Confusingly, that produced for the Series 2 actually shows a

Sports Racer 1956

PICTURE DETAILS

Model, original pack, Otaki, Japan, plastic, 1/24th

Adverts from Sports Car & Lotus Owner, 1958-59

Eleven and transporter model, Kenna, GB, 1/43rd, white metal.

Lotus Cars, Eleven 'Le Mans' spec sheet.

Model, Monza speed record attempt, Provence Moulage, France, resin, 1/43rd

Brochure for Eleven, Jay Chamberlain, USA, 1958

Green cover, 6 page brochure for s1, printed by Norman Bros. London, 1955/6

Model, Graphic Designers GB, white metal, 1/24th, 1956

Yellow cover s2 brochure, printed by Richmond Hill Ltd. Bournemouth, Aug/Sept 1957

car with Series 1 bodywork on the front cover. It was printed by Richmond Hill Printing Works Ltd. of Bournemouth in August or September 1957. A third brochure is also shown from the following year, produced for the American market by main agent Jay Chamberlain, and various contemporary full-page advertisements featuring the Eleven, promoting Lotus Engineering Limited and appearing primarily in Sports Car & Lotus Owner magazine in 1958-9.

ELEVEN

TYPE 12

Formula 2 & 1 1957

The company's first single-seater, unveiled at the 1956 Earls Court Motor Show, the Type 12 was created to compete in the new Formula 2 series but was subsequently modified to compete in Grand Prix events when it became apparent that the Type 16 would not be ready in time. In the event, with its Costin bodywork and trademark magnesium alloy 'wobbly-web' wheels, the car was not particularly successful in either formula, with only one outright win to its credit in the hands of Ivor Bueb at Crystal Palace in 1958. That said, Cliff Allison came sixth at Monaco and his car might actually have won the Spa GP in 1958 had the race been one lap longer since, after he had finished fourth and as is well documented, the three cars ahead of him all coasted to a halt on the slowing-down lap.

It was an important car nonetheless for Lotus, and is commemorated by a superb Theo Page cutaway illustration reproduced here from Autosport in December 1956. It was also modelled nicely if rather inaccurately in wood – at 1/43rd scale by R.D. Marmande of France, as shown here – and a more accurate white metal version (shown in it's parts and built up) in 1/43rd scale is the Circuit Series No.28 in 1/43rd scale manufactured around 1980. Years later Camel Team Lotus also recognised the car's pioneering role in the company's long and successful single-seater campaign by reproducing the original Type 12 press release shown here for one of its own high profile media events.

28

Elite 1957

TYPE 14

With no Type 13 for obvious reasons, Chapman's next real triumph was the beautiful road-going Type 14 Elite. This was surprising, given that it was common knowledge that, like Enzo Ferrari, his interest in non-competition cars was at best only marginal. In the search for a good power-to-weight ratio, Chapman persuaded Leonard Lee to create a larger version of his Coventry Climax FWA engine which came to be known as the FWE. But in other respects he realised that his road-going car could not be produced using the same design principles as his circuit racers. His solution was inspired – the world's first workable glassfibre monocoque, highly experimental but simple, elegant and perfectly in tune with the times. And with its final shape penned by a Lotus owner and accountant named Peter Kirwan-Taylor,

PICTURE DETAILS

Type 12 model, RD Marmande, France, wood, 1/43rd, 1978

Cut-away drawing, Theo Page, Autosport, Dec. 1956

Type 12 reproduction press release, Camel Team Lotus, 1987

Model & kit form, Equipe circuit series no. 28, white metal, 1/43rd, 1975.

Elite Super 95 sales sheet.

Elite model, RD Marmande, France, wood, 1/43rd, 1977

TYPE 14

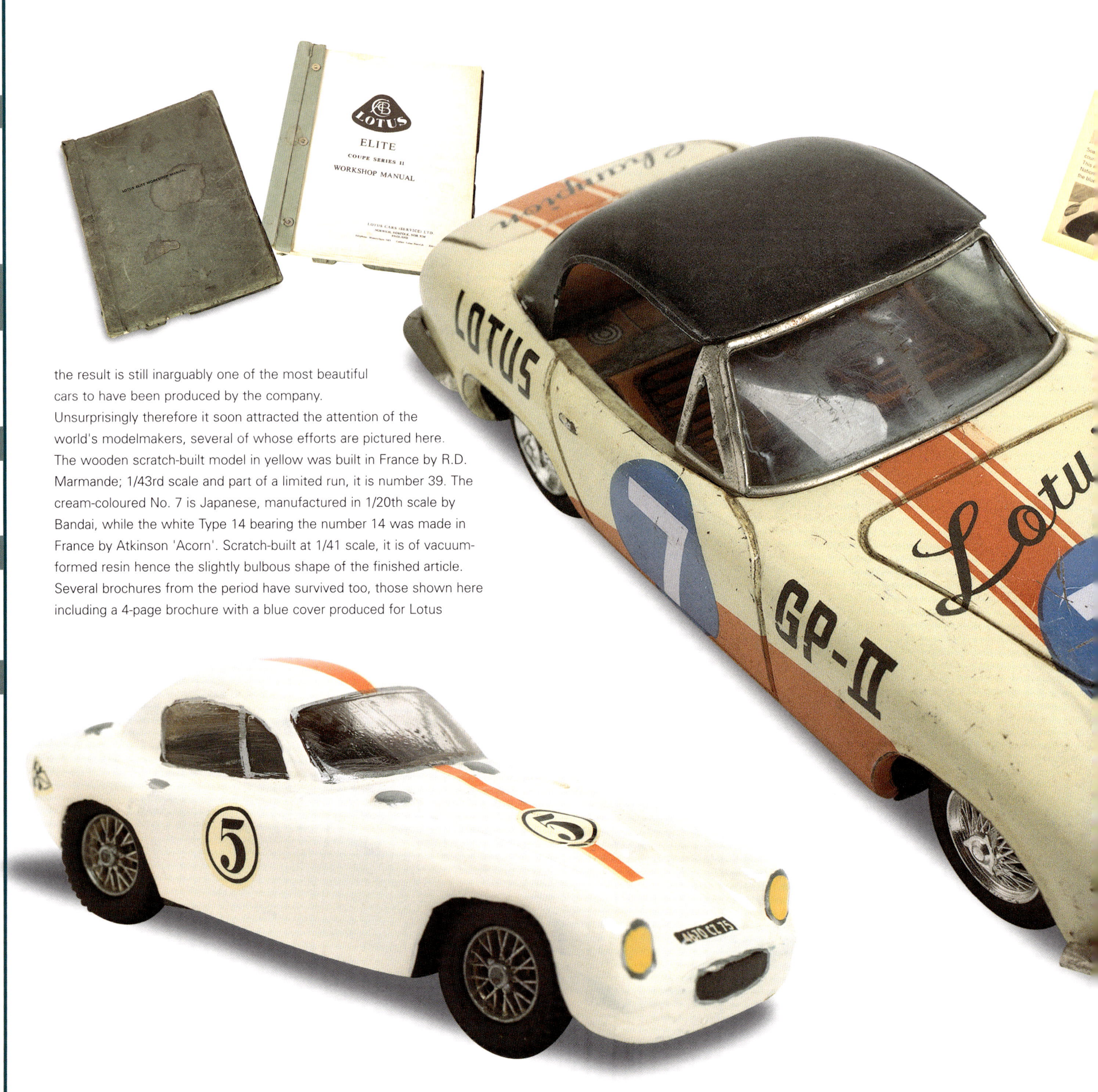

Elite 1957

the result is still inarguably one of the most beautiful cars to have been produced by the company. Unsurprisingly therefore it soon attracted the attention of the world's modelmakers, several of whose efforts are pictured here. The wooden scratch-built model in yellow was built in France by R.D. Marmande; 1/43rd scale and part of a limited run, it is number 39. The cream-coloured No. 7 is Japanese, manufactured in 1/20th scale by Bandai, while the white Type 14 bearing the number 14 was made in France by Atkinson 'Acorn'. Scratch-built at 1/41 scale, it is of vacuum-formed resin hence the slightly bulbous shape of the finished article. Several brochures from the period have survived too, those shown here including a 4-page brochure with a blue cover produced for Lotus

Elite 1957

Engineering Co. Ltd of Tottenham Lane London N8 and printed by Richard Hill Printing Works Ltd, Bournemouth around 1957/58. Two 6-page items are also shown, one for Lotus Engineering Co, printed by A G Wood Ltd of Leicester circa 1958/59, and another for Lotus Cars Ltd of Delamare Road, Cheshunt, Hertfordshire, with the front cover showing a woman resting her hand on car in front of house.

This is believed to date from 1959 or 1960, but the printer is unknown. A particularly well-known Type 14, registration DAD10, was featured along with 713 HJH in a 12 page brochure with an orange cover designed by Derek Birdsall/BDMW Associates. This was printed by Balding and Mansell in late 1961, around the time the company announced that it would be selling the car in kit form. A magazine insert from this period advertised 'no purchase tax' and a price of £1, 299.

Another 12-pager for the Series 2 with a grey cover opens to show a woman shutting the Elite's notably large doors, and another well-known car, WUU 2, shown on the back. Again designed by Derek Birdsall, this too was printed by Balding and Mansell around July 1960. Before being superseded by the Elan (whose separate chassis enabled the

PICTURE DETAILS

Model, Bandai, Japan, tin, 1/20th

Elite work shop manual 1959

Model, Atkinson "Acorn", France, vacuum formed resin, 1/41

Advert, National Petrol.

12 page brochure, orange cover, Layout Derek Birdsall/BDMW Associates, Oct 1961

Ticket, Team Elite, Le Mans, 1960

Advert, Smiths Industries.

Lotus cars Ltd. Delamare Road, 6 page brochure, 2 versions, Circa 1959/60

TYPE 14

TYPE 14

Elite 1957

company to curtail the Type 14's spiralling production costs) the Elite was to sell extremely well, some 1050 examples in all. Promotion came in many forms, typical of the advertising material produced at the time being the full-page advertisement from Motor Sport (July 1960) showing the Elite and the Seven along with the current racing Types 15, 17, and 18. Other advertisements appeared in Practical Motorist (October 1963), on the back cover of Sports Car & Lotus Owner of course, and more unusually in Autosport in 1960 one for Bristol Plastics the Elite bodybuilding company. The company's agent in California, Bob Challman, also generated his own advertisements, one example of which is shown here – portraying the Elite as a member of the Lotus Race Team, complete with Seven, 22 and 23 – whilst Castrol Oils chipped in with a recommended grades data sheet for the different Elite models. Finally, there is an original and well-used Elite workshop manual, along with an Elite Super 95 sales sheet, and three illustrations showing tickets used by Team Elite at Le Mans in 1960. The irony of the latter being that this car – created for the road and so merely to produce the financial wherewithal

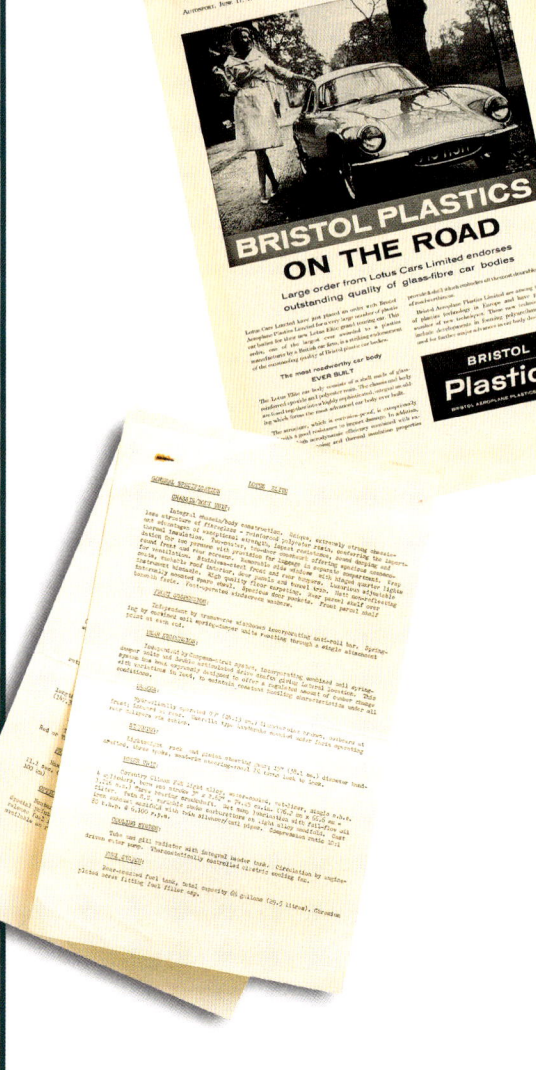

Elite 1957

PICTURE DETAILS

Lotus Engineering Co. Ltd, Tottenham Lane, 4 page brochure, blue cover, printed by Richard Hill Printing Works Ltd, Bournemouth, circa 1957/58.

6 six page brochure, Lotus Engineering Co. Printed by A G Wood Ltd Leicester circa 1958/59.

Series Two 12 page brochure, grey cover, Layout by Derek Birdsall, printed by Balding and Mansell, July 1960

Advert Elite, 7, 15, 17, & 18, Motor Sport, July 1960

Lotus Cars, 2 page specification sheet circa. 1958

Castrol Oils, data sheet, Elite models.

Advert, Bob Challman, California USA.circa.1962

Advert, Bristol Plastics, Autosport, 1960

Cover, The Elite Register.

for the company to carrying on racing – eventually took to the circuits itself. And once there, it too scored some notable successes for the company. One privately entered car, for example, was eighth overall and first in class (1500cc) at Le Mans in 1959. The following year, hot on the heels of some significant rule changes, no fewer than four cars were entered, two of them finishing first and second in the 1300cc class and also first and second in the Thermal Efficiency Index. Indeed for the next four years Colin Chapman's Elites were consistently to be found at the head of their class at Le Mans, whilst also scoring numerousother victories in literally dozens of other international events.

TYPE 14

TYPE 15

Sports Racer 1958

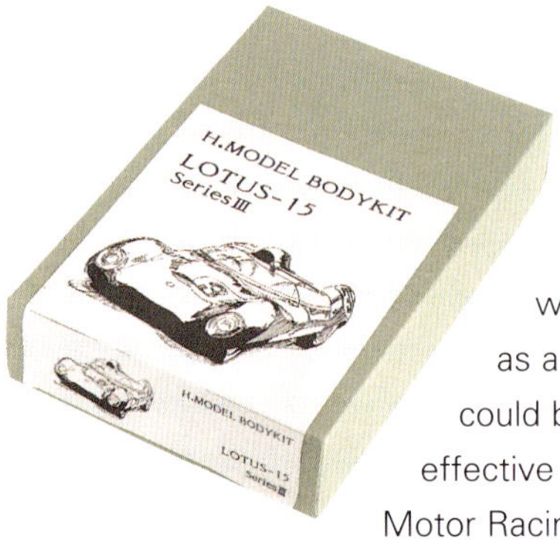

Clearly based on the successful Eleven though never intended as its replacement, the Type 15 was announced in early 1958 as a sports racer although cars could be, and were, modified for effective road use. Prescient as ever, Motor Racing magazine quickly declared that lightweight Climax-engined machine would 'probably cause acute embarrassment to the manufacturers of larger and more powerful cars' – and before long a Type 15 driven by Graham Hill did just that. Posting the fifth-fastest laptime in practice at Le Mans, it crossed the line well ahead of at least one 3.litre Ferrari. The race itself, however, from which Colin Chapman's original Team Lotus grandstand pass has survived, proved disappointing with both cars retiring early. But elsewhere the car met with some success, Roy Salvadori taking the John Coombs 2 litre car to second place at Silverstone before the British Grand Prix, and as late as 1962 test pilot 'Dizzy' Addicot fitting his car with a 3.5litre Buick V8 and to great effect. In addition the trophy shown here marks the performance of the Type 15s of the Gran Turismo team and was awarded by the British Racing Drivers Club at the 11th Annual International Trophy meeting in 1959. The svelte Type 15 was also modelled by various companies, including this 1/24th-scale resin rendering of a Series III variant which was made by H. Model in Japan. The lovely tin-plate model is also Japanese,

Sports Racer 1958

made by Yonezawa and fitted with a friction motor. A full nine inches long and painted bright yellow, it wasn't actually sold as a Lotus Type 15 but given its date couldn't really be anything else. Also shown are the front, back and inside spreads from an extravagant 1959 Lotus 15 Series 2 brochure (six pages in all and printed by AG Wood Ltd of Leicester), an advertisement for the Climax-engined 2 litre Type 15, and several Team Lotus competitor passes for the British Empire Meeting at Oulton Park in 1958. In 1980 Camel Team Lotus also paid homage to the car, producing a facsimile of the company's original Type 15 press release, which is shown here.

PICTURE DETAILS

Model Box s3, H. Model, Japan, resin, 1/24th

BRDC Gran Turismo team trophy, 11th International Trophy meeting 1959

Model, Yonezawa, Japan, tin plate, friction motor, 9" long.

Model, unknown, plastic, 1/24th

6 page s2 brochure, printed by AG Wood Ltd, Leicester, 1959

Team Lotus grandstand pass, Colin Chapman, Le Mans 1958

Advert, 2 litre Type 15, Sports Car & Lotus Owner, 1959

Team Lotus competitor passes, British Empire Trophy Meeting, Oulton Park 1958

Reproduction press release, Camel Team Lotus, 1987

TYPE 15

Formula 1 & 2 1958

TYPE 16

Bowing out as a would-be Grand Prix driver after an incident involving his Vanwall and Mike Hawthorn's at Rheims in 1956, it was perhaps to be expected that when Chapman's thoughts returned to developing his own car for the formula he should seek to replicate much of what he and Frank Costin had achieved for Tony Vandervell. In fact, one of the most sought-after of Lotus single-seaters (at the time of writing an ex-Innes Ireland 16 made £130, 200 at auction), the car looks not unlike a miniature Vanwall, albeit one based around Chapman's own choice of components – like the Climax FPF – and with its own definite Lotus style. Aerodynamically it was extremely advanced, although in Formula One at least it was never placed higher than sixth. That was Graham Hill's drive in Italy, and Cliff Allison almost finished second in Germany. But the car is also notable as the one in which Jim Clark took his first ever drive in a Lotus, and as one of the prettiest of the era it has also lent itself to some distinctive modelling. The 1/10th scale friction-motor model with its original box was made by Lincoln International in Hong Kong. The red plastic No.3 is also from the former colony, made by Roxy in 1/24th scale and also fitted with a friction motor, while the BRG white-metal No.6 model was made by MAE on the Chinese mainland. Unusually the yellow plastic toy also made by Lincoln

Formula 1 & 2 1958

under the brand name 'Empire' was supplied with inflatable tyres and its own air pump. Other memorabilia from the period includes a competitors armband from the 1959 Aintree 200 meeting, a pair of scrutineering cards for Team Lotus at the US Grand Prix at Sebring the same year, and a selection of passes and tickets issued to Team Lotus at Monza the previous September. The car was also shown alongside its stablemates in a 1958 advertisement which appeared in Sports Car & Lotus Owner Dec. 1958, and years later the John Player Team Lotus reproduced the original Type 16 press release as part of its own promotional campaign.

PICTURE DETAILS

Model & box, Lincoln International, H.Kong, plastic, friction motor, 1/10th, 1960's

Scrutineering cards, Team Lotus, US GP Sebring, 1959

Model, Lincoln International "Empire", H.Kong, plastic, inflatable tyres.

Passes, Team Lotus, Italian GP Monza, 13th Sept 1959

Model, Roxy, Hong Kong, plastic, friction motor, 1/24th

Lotus Engineering advert Types 14, 15 &16, Sports Car & Lotus Owner Dec. 1958

Model, MAE Models, China, white metal, 1/43rd

Competitors arm band, Aintree '200' 1959

JPTL reproduction press release.

TYPE 16

TYPE 17

Sports Racer 1959

The Eleven having proved more or less invincible in Britain during the two years after its launch, the appearance of its replacement was keenly awaited. When it appeared with its neat Len Terry bodywork it seemed to promise much: just nine square feet of frontal area, proven allies in the Coventry-Climax FWA and M engines, and a simplified and much lighter suspension set up. But by any reckoning the Type 17 flattered onlookers only to deceive them, and plagued by handling difficulties it rapidly proved to be no match for the rival Lola. Admittedly it looked fantastic, and from every angle, but once they had taken delivery many privateers were disappointed with the car, as indeed was Team Lotus. Driving for Team Alan Stacey had to withdraw from Goodwood on Easter Monday 1959, the car's competition debut, after encountering problems with its handling. And worse was to come for once this was sorted out (in time for Le Mans the same year, a ticket for which is shown here) a plague of minor electrical and overheating gremlins stepped up to do their worst. Eventually most of the problems were resolved (with modifications being retrofitted by Lotus when customers' cars were checked in for servicing) but the damage was done and today one of the most handsome Lotus sports racers has a decidedly ragged reputation. Three decades later echoes of those unhappy handling days include the front cover of Autosport from July 29th 1960 showing one of the nearly two dozen Type 17s being pushed to the limit or beyond at Oulton Park by Rudi de Waldkirch, a spread from Sports Car & Lotus Owner dated April 1959 with a cutaway drawing of the car by James A. Allington, and a rather

38

Sports Racer 1959

minimalist advertisement from the same publication for the entire Lotus range. The model seen here, in parts with its 1/24th scale resin body and original box, was made fairly recently by H. Model in Japan, and the press release is another facsimile from Camel Team Lotus many years later. The cover of a very well used Coventry Climax workshop manual is also shown, along with both sides of a rare engine information sheet for the FWA.

PICTURE DETAILS

Coventry Climax Engine badge

Model & box, H. Model, Japan, resin, 1/24th, 1995

Camel Team Lotus reproduction press release.

Autosport, July 1960

Cut-away drawing, James A. Allington, Sports Car & Lotus Owner, April 1959

Coventry Climax FWA engine information sheet.

Ticket, Le Mans 1959

Lotus Engineering advert, Sports Car & Lotus Owner.

Coventry Climax workshop manual.

TYPE 17

MOTOR RACING
ROAD & TRACK
MOTOR SPORT
LOTUS
Autocar
THE LOTUS PROJECT
AUTOSPORT
LOTUS NEWS
Motor
WIN A CAR
THE LOTUS STORY
WORLDBEATERS FOR 1973?
SEVEN
Stress Cracks
classic cars
Autosport
SLIPSTREAM
On Four Wheels
Formula 1
CAR GRAPHIC
auto
STRESS CRACKS
WIN THIS LOTUS TURBO!
THE MARQUE
THE CAR
Special
chicane
John Player Special
Lotus 91 unveiled
Lotus: 30 years on
Monte Carlo drama
CLASSIC

CHAPTER 2

18	Formula Junior	1960
18	Formula 1	1960
19	Sports racer	1960
19B	Sports racer	1963
20	Formula Junior	1961
21	Formula 1	1961
22	Formula Junior	1962
23	Sports racer	1962
24	Formula 1	1962
25	Formula 1	1962
26	Elan S1,S2	1962
26R	Elan race car	1962
27	Formula Junior	1963
28	Lotus Cortina	1963
29	Indy car	1963
30	Group 7 sports	1964
31	Formula 3	1964
32	Formula 2	1964
32B	Tasman Formula	1964
33	Formula 1	1964
34	Indy car	1964
35	Formula 2	1965
35	Formula 3	1965
36	Elan fhc S3,S4	1965
3-7	Clubmans car	1965
38	Indy car	1965
39	Tasman Formula	1965
40	Group 7 sports	1965
41	Formula 3	1966
41B	Formula 2	1967
42	Indy Car	1966
42F	Indy car	1967
43	Formula 1	1966
44	Formula 2	1966
45	Elan dhc S3,S4	1966
46	Europa	1966
47	Group 4 sports	1966
47D	GKN Europa	1968
48	Formula 2	1967
49	Formula 1	1967
50	Elan +2	1967
51	Formula Ford	1967
54	Europa S2	1968
55	Formula 3 prototype	1968
56	Indy car	1968
56B	Formula 1	1971
57	Formula 1	1968
58	Formula 2	1968
59	Formula 3	1969
59B	Formula 2	1969
59F	Formula Ford	1969
60	Seven S4	1969
61	Formula Ford	1969
62	Group 6 prototype	1969
63	Formula 1	1969
64	Indy car	1969
65	Europa federal spec	1969

1960-1969

TYPE 18

Formula 1 & Junior 1960

Combining John Cooper's well-proven rear-engined layout and Colin Chapman's inspired ideas, the Lotus 18 was, according to its creator, the first true Formula 1 car to have been built by Lotus. Its front-engined predecessors Chapman felt were just the results of some dabbling, but the new car with its low centre of gravity and minimal frontal area was the real thing. Intended all along to be simple and easily maintained – not just because the previous season's race results had been disappointing, but also because life at the works was complicated enough. The car, which made its debut on Boxing Day 1959, was a multi-purpose machine. Initially it competed in Formula Junior, but was of course designed to compete in Formulas One and Two as well, during the following year. Taken from drawing board stage to compete at Brands Hatch in just five weeks, it was not without its problems. Not for the first first time Lotus had produced a car which was too light initially and which had to be toughened up as time progressed by replacing broken components with stronger ones until the optimal set-up eventually emerged. It was, nonetheless, the car which more than any other established the company as a serious presence in the front-rank of motorsport with more than 150 put into production over a two-year period and some outstanding track performances along the way.

This included the company's first Grand Prix-class win at Goodwood at Easter, and the marque's first championship Grand Prix victory at Monaco a few weeks later. That day the car was driven by Stirling Moss

42

Formula 1 & Junior 1960

(beaten into second place in his Cooper at Goodwood, Rob Walker had immediately ordered him a Type 18 of his own) and the highly-detailed model shown here in blue commemorates a winning partnership of great car and great driver. It was made by John Day in Great Britain and its white metal body painted with the number 28 to represent the same type 18 driven to victory by Sir Stirling – agian at Monaco in the following year, – by which time he had chalked up a another win in the US GP. With a detachable body it is possible to see all the chassis and engine details, and the small figurine made to scale (1/43rd) of Stirling Moss himself. Other contemporary models of the Type 18 shown here include a British-made slot car with packaging made by VIP Club Special, a 1/32rd scale plastic car painted British racing Green with the number 4, and a wooden 1/43rd scale model

TYPE 18

PICTURE DETAILS

Model slot car & box, VIP 'Club Special", GB, plastic, 1/32nd

John Davy Trophy, J. Clark, 1st Formula Junior race, 1960

Team Lotus passes, USGP 1960

Team Lotus Scrutineering cards, USGP 1960

Beer mat, The Donington Grand Prix Collection.

Lotus Group of Companies calendar 1962

First day cover stamps Monaco 1987

1996 calendar Michael Turner artwork.

Post card Donington Grand Prix Collection.

43

TYPE 18

Formula 1 & Junior 1960

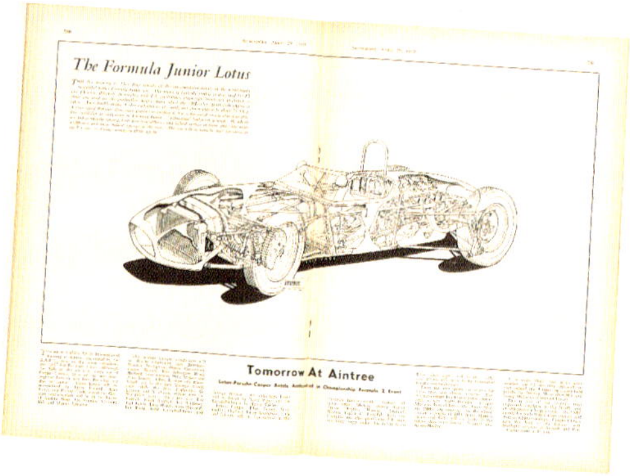

scratch-built by RD Marmande in France. The Type 18's Monaco wins were also marked in the mid 1960's by special edition first day cover presentation sets of Monaco stamps, two of which are shown here depicting the cars on the circuit. Some even rarer mementoes of the Type 18 in America have also survived the years, including various mechanics' pit passes and the personal pass No. 0783 of Team Lotus manager Stan Chapman (actually Colin's father) and the scrutineering record cards for the three Team Lotus entries. Of the two trophies shown, one (the John Davy Trophy) was awarded to Jim Clark for a Formula Junior race win in 1960, whilst the other is the Lanson Bi-Centenary Trophy for a Formula Junior race. It was awarded at the Twelfth International Trophy meeting at Silverstone 1960. An elegant and inspired design, the Type 18 was, not unnaturally, made the subject of a number of attractive magazine features. These include a double-page spread from Autosport in 1960 showing a Theo Page cutaway, and an excellent set of illustrations with accompanying history of the car which was produced by The Motor to be given away with the magazine as part of a series. Also shown is the front cover of the presentation folder which accompanied the series when it went on sale in the USA through Autobooks of California, and two advertisements showing the car which appeared in Sports Car & Lotus Owner. Finally in 1962 and again in 1996 the car was depicted by Michael Turner and used for the Lotus Group of Companies calendar. The car also appeared on a beer mat, one of a series for Tom Wheatcroft's Donington Grand Prix Collection, they also produced the postcard shown here.

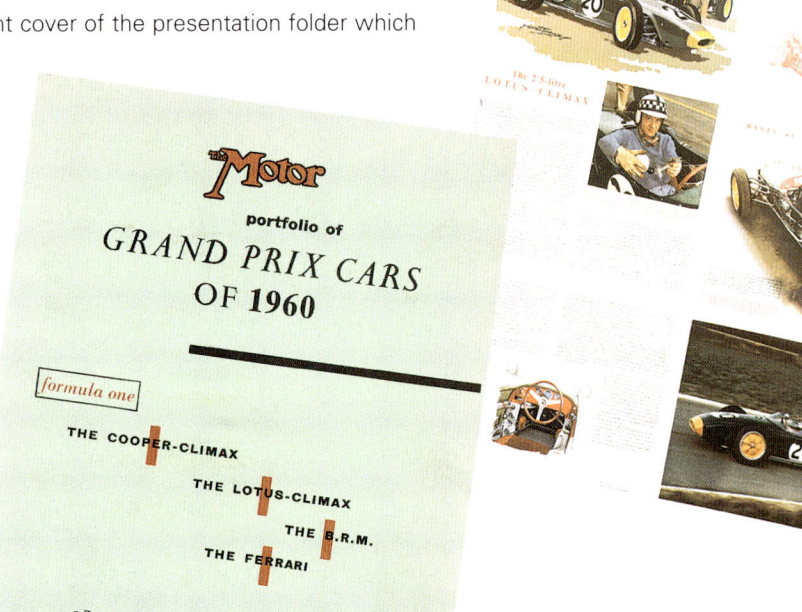

Formula 1 & Junior 1960

PICTURE DETAILS

Model, John Day 'Museum', GB, white metal, 1/43rd

Lanson Bi-Centenary Trophy, Formula Junior, Twelfth International Trophy meeting, Silverstone 1960

Model, RD Marmande, France, wood, 1/43rd

JPTL reproduction press release.

Cutaway drawing, Theo Page, Autosport, 1960

Cover & illustration sheet, 'The Motor' USA by Autobooks of California, 1960

Advert, race results, Sports Car & Lotus Owner, July 1960

Advert, specifications, Sports Car & Lotus Owner, 1960

TYPE 18

TYPE 19

Sports Racer 1960

So close was it in appearance to the Cooper Monaco that the Type 19 was quickly nicknamed the Lotus Monte Carlo – and even described as such on the box of a 1960s model produced by Imai in Japan and pictured here. Then as now its full-width bodywork belied the fact that it was closely based on the winning configuration of the Type 18, but there was never any disguising its potential. Indeed, when Stirling Moss, in his first drive since his F1 crash at Spa, took one out for testing at Silverstone he was soon smashing the circuit record for a sports car of this class. Not long afterwards he raced the car too – at Karlskoga in Sweden, where he won easily – after which it was lent to Jo Bonnier who for his own part broke the Swedish record for the flying kilometre at 157.5mph.

Many of the car's most impressive performances, however, were in the USA, where, re-engined using American powerplants, the Type 19 of Dan Gurney proved uncatchable through the corners. Racing for the Arciero Brothers' team, his car is commemorated here by the red model No.96 made in resin by Provence Moulage in France in 1/43rd scale. The 1960s Strombecker slot-car model shown with its packaging is also American in origin, a plastic kit in 1/24th scale. The silver model,

Sports Racer 1960

however, is British and by GP Models. Showing the Type 19 prototype, its 1/43rd scale white metal body is painted silver to represent the bare aluminium of the first car as production subsequently switched to glass fibre. The car was also depicted on the front cover of Sports Car & Lotus Owner in October 1960 (with Colin Chapman testing his new creation) whilst the survival of the Team Lotus build cards for chassis numbers 952, 953, 954, 955 and 966 provides valuable clues as to the original buyers and their precise specifications. Finally the cheap plastic model of Type 19 shown here actually post-dates the car itself, having been made in Hong Kong around 1964, some two years after the factory ceased production.

PICTURE DETAILS

Model, GP Models, GB, white metal, 1/43rd

Model, Provence Moulage, France, resin, 1/43rd

Slot car model, Strombecker, USA, plastic kit, 1/24th

Model box, Imai, Japan, plastic kit, 1/32nd

Sports Car & Lotus Owner, October 1960

Team Lotus build cards.

Model, H.Kong, plastic, 1/24, mid 1960's

TYPE 19

TYPE 20

Formula Junior 1961

The Type 18 having dominated Formula Junior for much of its life, Chapman was naturally keen to maintain his lead with the Type 20. No longer adaptable to other formulae as its predecessor had been, the Type 20 nevertheless packed similar componentry into an even smaller shape and still managed to achieve even greater aerodynamic efficiency. Despite its sleek appearance, however, it seems not to have attracted the serious modelmakers. Thus, the curious maroon model shown here could actually be a Type 20 or even an 18– it's that hard to tell. The second offering is a fairly standard British-made Scalextric model of 1964 although it was made in four different specifications, with minor changes in things such as fixings, guide mountings and wheels, as well as in four colours, blue, red, green and yellow. Ford, however, recognised its worth, using the car to promote the Lotus Ford Cortina and in advertisements for its 'sister' car, the Anglia, which of course used a similar engine. In 1961 Autosport ran a James A. Allington cutaway drawing, and painted by Michael Turner the Type 20 was also used to promote a 1964 meeting at Crystal Palace in south-east London. The most unusual memento, however, must be the cartoon by artist JAK showing J. Paul Getty driving his Type 20 receiving pit signals in the form of on-going share prices.

THE 1961 FORMULA JUNIOR LOTUS

NEED WE SAY MORE !

The Lotus Twenty

48

Formula Junior 1962

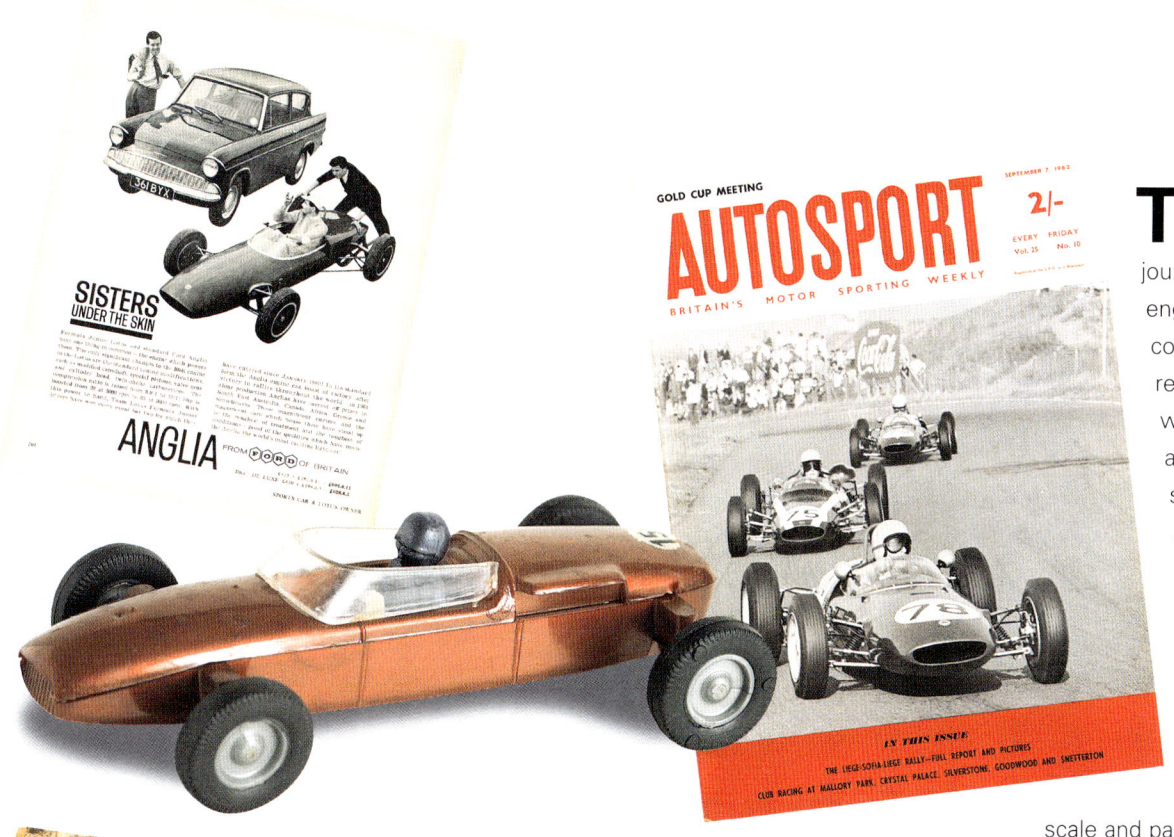

The subject of a celebrated £1,000 wager between Colin Chapman and a German journalist who couldn't believe such a small engine could produce such fast lap times – it could and did, he lost – the Type 22 was the recipient of some valuable free publicity when Peter Arundell averaged 117.169mph around Monza and the car was promptly sold to a delighted Italian. Closer to home, Autosport featured the Team Lotus driver and his car on its cover in June 1962, and it was also modelled by Meccano in 1/43rd scale under their brand name Dinky in the UK during the 60's, . The other model shown here is a scratchbuilt wooden rendering by RD Marmande in France, also in 1/43rd scale and painted yellow with the No.53.

More significantly perhaps, Arundell scored 18 wins out of 25 starts in the 1962 season – a record which still stands and is unique for any FIA sanctioned international race series.

TYPE 22

PICTURE DETAILS

Model, Ingap, India, plastic, 1/32rd

Slot car, Scalextric, GB, plastic, 1/32nd, 1964

Lotus Ford Cortina brochure.

Cut-away drawing, James A Allington, Autosport 1961

Poster, Crystal Palace Race Circuit, London County Council Supplies Dept. printed by Fosh & Cross Ltd, 1964

Advert, Ford Anglia & Type20, SC&LO.

Advert, 'Need we say more', SC&LO.

Cartoon by JAK.

Model, RD Marmande, France, wood, 1/43rd

Model, Meccano Ltd (Dinky), UK, metal, 1/43rd

Autosport June 1962

TYPE 21

Formula 1 1961

Visibly very similar to the Ford 105E-powered Type 20, but intended to use the by now ageing Coventry-Climax FPF engine to comply with the new 1.5 litre Formula One regulations, the Type 21 was another phenomenally rapid car in terms of product development: six weeks from planning to prototype, although it went on to win just one Grand Prix race during the 1961 season.

The original press photograph reproduced here shows Moss behind the wheel, but the victory was actually Innes Ireland's drive at Watkins Glen. Regardless the American win was enough to hand Lotus the runner's up position behind Ferrari with its more powerful and technically superior V6, but not to secure the Scotsman his place in the team and he left at the end of the season. Second place in the Championship was still a particularly impressive effort, especially in the absence of Coventry-Climax's own FMWV V8 engine, and certainly it proved sufficient to persuade the engine supplier to use images of the car to promote sales of its forklift trucks and fire-pumps. Earlier in the year the Type 21 had also been the subject of a James Allington cutaway which appeared in Autosport in May 1961 and a feature in The Autocar the following July describing Innes Ireland's performance in the German Solitude GP as 'probably his finest race victory'. The car was also modelled by various makers, including this finely detailed 1/28th scale blue No. 3 slot car from Stabo in Germany which even has a tiny Lotus badge imprinted on the nose of car. The second blue car, No.12, was made in France by RD Marmande around 1978 from wood and in 1/43rd scale depicts the Rob Walker team's type 18/21 – the car driven by Moss as already mentioned.

50

Formula 1 1961

The Scalextric car (no. 6) is a rare French made variant only produced for two years, rather surprisingly given this it can also be found in red, yellow and green.

A year earlier the official calendar produced for the Lotus Group of Companies also featured the car, showing Jim Clark in a Type 21 and, close behind, England's Stirling Moss in the Rob Walker 18/21.

TYPE 21

PICTURE DETAILS

Slot car model, Stabo, Germany, plastic, 1/28t

Model, RD Marmande, France, wood, 1/43rd

Press photo, Rob Walker, 1961

Model, Scalextric, France type 21 from 1963

Cut-away drawing, James Allington, Autosport, May 1961

Coventry Climax brochure.

Lotus Group of Companies calendar, 1962

The Autocar, Solitude GP, July 1961

TYPE 23

Sports Racer 1962

The last small-capacity pure sports racer designed by Colin Chapman (the later Types being instead modified road cars), a ridiculous debacle over the number of wheel-fixing studs ensured that the Type 23 was also the last car Chapman ever took to Le Mans. Hot property from the start (and assisted by a great victory at Montlhery and an opening price of just £1,495), it sold well – 111 in less than two years – and unsurprisingly attracted plenty of attention from the world's model-makers particularly in the US. Bearing the number 16, the white-painted car shown here, for example, was made as recently as the 1990s in the US by MA Scale Models and shows the famous Type 23B car which, fitted with a Porsche engine went on to race in the domestic USRRC series. A similar car was modelled in 1/24th scale grey plastic by Atlas in the USA and is shown here. The Revell 23 is also American, another 1/24th scale kit in plastic and styrene, as is the 1/32nd scale Strombecker slot-car, another kit and most definitely of a Type 23 despite the description on the box which refers to the 2.5 litre Type 19. Also shown is the box from a model made by Imai in Japan (numbered 13, a 1/32nd scale plastic kit car fitted with a motor) and that from a 1/24th scale Mitsuwa-built plastic kit bearing the number 5. The other two boxes depicting

Sports Racer 1962

Type 23s, however, are American again: two plastic Russkit models in 1/24th scale and 1/32nd respectively. Number 47, the British Racing Green car, is another scratch-built model made of wood by France's RD Marmande, and No.2 reproduces the white-painted Type 23B in which Peter Warr drove to victory in the Japanese Grand Prix at Suzuka. Made in Japan, it is a white metal kit and to 1/43rd scale. The final appearance of Team Lotus at Le Mans in 1962 is represented here by one of the official team armbands, also shown is an original, if rather tatty Type 23 specification sheet printed for Lotus Components quoting a price of £1650 for the car in component form and £1725 assembled for export only.

PICTURE DETAILS

Model box, Imai, Japan, plastic kit, motor, 1/32nd

Model Type 23b, MA Scale Models, USA, resin, 1/43rd.

Model, Revell, USA, plastic kit or bodyshell, 1/24th

Model box, Mitsuwa, Japan, plastic kit, 1/24th

Model box, Type 19 or 23?, Strombecker, plastic kit, USA 1/32

2 model boxes, Russkit, USA, plastic kit, 1/24th & 1/32nd

Model, Atlas, USA, plastic, 1/24th

Model, RD Marmande, France, wood, 1/43rd

Model, Tandhaus, Japan, white metal, 1/43rd

Team Lotus armband, Le Mans 24, 1962

Team Lotus specification sheet.

TYPE 23

53

TYPE 24

Formula 1 1962

Resembling the 21 but sharing none of its components, the Type 24 raced with various different engines but was actually designed around the long-awaited Coventry Climax FWMV V8 engine. It made its debut on April Fool's Day 1962, although it had to wait another fortnight before notching up its first win – at Snetterton in the hands of Jim Clark. It was undoubtedly going to be a good year for Lotus but in the final analysis the fate of the Type 24 was a curious one, for whilst not unsuccessful – Team Lotus, Scuderia Filipinetti, Jack Brabham's team and UDT-Laystall all campaigned cars to good effect – it was destined almost from the start to be completely overshadowed by the arrival just a few months later of the truly revolutionary monocoque Lotus Type 25. Nonetheless, various Autosport magazine front covers from 1963 depicted the successful Team Lotus Type 24s as well as Innes Ireland who drove a Type 24 for the UDT-Laystall team. The car also appeared on the cover of the well produced but short-lived Historic Racing magazine of 1992, shown here with Trevor Taylor driving. Taylor, would be responsible for what was perhaps the car's most outstanding

54

Formula 1 1962

result, namely second place behind Graham Hill at Zandvoort on the very day the Type 25 took its first bow. Workshop build cards for various customer cars have also survived in the Team Lotus archive, including those for chassis numbers 940, 947 and 950 delivered to Rob Walker, Jack Brabham and Scuderia Fillipinetti respectively. It was they that had the most to lose by the appearance of the Type 25, which went on to completely dominate the sport for the whole of the coming season. Whilst undoubtedly lacking the simple elegance of the 25, the 24 was nevertheless made the subject of various excellent models both at home and abroad including this blue number 18 made by MAE Models in Britain, a highly detailed 1/43rd scale white metal rendition. Also shown is another scratch-built RD Marmande model from France to 1/43rd scale, and nicely proportioned in wood to represent the No.2 Team car.

PICTURE DETAILS

Model, MAE Models, GB, white metal, 1/43rd

Model, RD Marmande, France, wood, 1/43rd

Team Lotus build cards

Historic Racing magazine, February 1995.

Autosport magazines April, December 1962, May 1963.

TYPE 24

TYPE 25

Formula 1 1962

Unwilling to be silenced, Colin Chapman's carping critics may continue to insist that machines of the type had existed before, or even that the Type 25 was in reality no more than a double tubed structure. But for once it is no exaggeration to say that even given his own impressive record for inspired innovation, the Lotus founder's pioneering 1962 single-seater was a truly radical design which genuinely revolutionised Formula One racing. Abandoning the traditional tubular spaceframe in favour of a stressed-skin aircraft-style monocoque, and sketching out his ideas on a paper napkin over lunch with Mike Costin, Chapman's concept represented nothing less than a complete departure from conventional thinking and its ramifications are with us still nearly 40 years on. Slim, spare, elegant and tailored tightly around the almost horizontal form of the young Jim Clark, the car itself was actually created in secret by a small handpicked team working away from the rest of the team in Cheshunt. It made its debut at Zandvoort, the first event of the new World Championship series and its performance there was unimpressive – a Fifeshire farmer's son, Clark managed only ninth place – but a victory of another sort

56

Formula 1 1962

had been achieved simply by getting such a radical proposal accepted by the sport's scrutineers. In any event, even coming ninth, it was clear that the new Type 25 – and for that matter Clark himself – was more than competitive and that before long Chapman's latest creation would more than prove its credentials as the fastest car of its day in Formula One. In its first season, and mostly in Clark's hands, it won World Championship events in Belgium, Britain, the US, Mexico and South Africa.

TYPE 25

PICTURE DETAILS

- Model, Roadace "Major", GB, resin, 1/43rd
- Model box, Lincoln International, H.Kong, plastic, 1/12th
- Advert, Girling brakes.
- Postcard, Donington Grand Prix collection.
- Model box, Renwal, USA, Plastic kit, 1/48th
- Trophy, winning entrant, News of the World 200 mile race, Goodwood 1964
- Team Lotus Ltd calendar, 1964
- Programme, Monaco GP, 1963
- Model box, Russkit, USA, plastic kit, 1/24th

TYPE 25

Formula 1 1962

Mechanical failures denied the team victory in several other rounds, however, as well as robbing it of the Constructors' title (by just one point) and leaving Clark to come in second behind Hill in the Drivers' Championship. The following season though the Scotsman hit an all-time high, with seven undisputed wins in the one year, so that by the close his domination and that of the Type 25 had guaranteed the World Constructors' Championship for Team Lotus and the World Drivers' Championship for himself. Both, incidentally, with the maximum 54 points. Various trophies associated with both car and driver are shown here including the Barnes Trophy awarded to Clark at the Grand Prix of South Africa on Christmas Day 1963, another trophy awarded for the News of the World's 200 Mile International Race at Goodwood the following year, and a third for the 54th French Grand Prix de I.A.C.F. Other mementoes from the period include the cover of the programme for the 1963 Monaco GP and an original team member's armband from the same event; also the official Team Lotus Limited calendar for the following year which features a wonderful photograph of Jim Clark in his Type 25. Not unnaturally various suppliers to the team also got in on the act, three advertisements here using the Type 25s success to promote their own images to the trade. And of course, as the original Team Lotus press release for the Type 25 shows, Lotus was not quick to promote it's newest star either. By the same token it is also unsurprising that the car proved extremely popular with model-makers. From these, several

58

Formula 1 1962

PICTURE DETAILS

Model box, Revell, USA, plastic 1/24th

The Barnes Trophy, Jim Clark, 1st South Africa GP, 25th December 1963

Trophy, 54th Grand Prix de I.A.C.F. (French GP)

Team Lotus press, 1962

Advert, Champion spark plugs 1963

Advert, Vandervell bearings.

Team Lotus armband, Monaco GP, 1963

Team Lotus Christmas card 1963.

Model box, MSK tm, Japan, plastic slot car, 1/24th.

interesting boxes have survived including three American items: one from Revell (for a plastic 1/24th scale plastic model made in the USA), another for a scatchbuilt 1/24th scale Russkit Type 25, and third for a Type 25 Lotus Ford Grand Prix model made by Renwal to 1/48th scale. The fourth box shown here is from Lincoln International whose 1/12th scale plastic BRG-painted kit was made in Hong Kong and carries the number 1.

Only one model is shown here, however, a Roadace 'Major', scratch-built in Britain to 1/43rd scale in resin, but the Type 25 was also made the subject of two highly collectable cards, one depicting the car owned by Tom Wheatcroft and on display at the Donington Grand Prix collection, and another the official Team Lotus Christmas card from 1963 which featured a characteristically detailed illustration by Michael Turner. By the time these were mailed the car had more than made its mark on the world, demonstrating beyond doubt the arrival of Team Lotus as a consistent winner in Formula One and of Colin Chapman as one of motorsport's most impressive innovators.

TYPE 25

TYPE 26
Elan S1 & S2 1962

Technically advanced, superb to drive and beautiful to look at the ambitious Type 14 Lotus Elite was a success in so many ways but the company lost money on every one of the 1050 it built and sold, a situation Chapman was desperate to rectify with its replacement, the 1962 Type 26.

Using a simple deep backbone chassis and clothing it in a tightly-drawn glassfibre body designed by Ron Hickman, the all-new car also employed a brand new twin-cam Lotus engine designed by Harry Mundy of The Autocar. Formerly employed by both BRM and Coventry Climax, he had based his new design initially on Ford's 109E block until the new 5-bearing 116E became available. Thereafter it quickly progressed from 1,499cc to the familiar 1,558cc by the time the 23rd car rolled off the line.

Although build-quality difficulties were never satisfactorily resolved, the resulting combination of new car and new engine – called the Elan – quickly gained a reputation as an ultra-responsive, well-balanced and quick little sports car. With sales in excess of 2,000 in the first three years it also did much to save Lotus from an untimely demise, whilst attracting the attention of modelmakers almost as quickly as it did that of enthusiasts who fancied building the full-size kit themselves with its starting price of just £1095. The boxes shown here are from Japan and are for two plastic Elan kits, one made by Sharp in Japan to 1/32 scale and the other for a Series 2 model made by Yamada in 1/24th scale. A development of the original introduced by the factory in November 1964, the Series 2 Elan benefited from numerous detail improvements including larger front calipers, a polished veneer dash with lockable glovebox, and new rear lights. Another model of the Elan Series 2 is also shown here with its box, made by Telsalda in Hong Kong to 1/32nd scale. Corgi also modelled the car in 1/43rd scale of die cast metal painted metallic blue, and produced a commemorative box set for The Avengers television

60

Elan S1 & S2 1962

PICTURE DETAILS

Model box, Sharp, Japan, plastic kit, 1/32

S2 Model & box, Telsalda, H.Kong, plastic kit, 1/32nd

S2 Model box, Yamada, Japan, plastic kit, 1/24th

Advert, Lotus Cars.

12 page Elan 1500 brochure 1962

12 page Elan brochure 1962

12 page Elan S2 brochure 1963

Lotus group of companies, calendar, 1964

Advert, Lotus Cars 'How to build your Elan in a weekend' 1968-1970

Advert Elan S1, 'the good life' American dealers

Advert, Lotus Cars, 'The Elan exposed'.

Lotus Cars, Elan 6 page fold out brochure, German.

Lotus Cars, Elan S2 6 page fold out brochure, German.

Elan Handbook French edition.

Advert, 'new Elan 1600', Autocar, 1963

TYPE 26

TYPE 26

Elan S1 & S2 1962

series showing John Steed in his Bentley and Diana Rigg as Mrs Peel in her famous white Series 2 Lotus Elan. The other white car is a Series 1 with a hardtop kit, incidentally, made by Kogure in 1/20th scale in 1964. An original Elan workshop manual is shown here too, along with a French-language handbook, and a Lotus Cars plastic wallet containing a personal letter to the new owner, his handbook and the roadworthiness test certificate for the car. Also several brochures issued at the time, including three versions of the same brochure with, originally, the Elan 1500 on the cover, then the 1,558cc car and finally the S2. That with a blue cover showing a white S2 folds out to eight pages, and the two similar style black and white brochures for the Elan and Elan S2 are both German versions of original English edition ones. Of the imaginative advertising material produced, one of the most distinctive was that for a fast BRM conversion produced by Mike Spence's company, the former Lotus GP driver. Jim Clark also put in an appearance, wearing a kilt for the 1964 official Lotus Group of Companies calendar, a picture which also surfaced in several advertisements for Lotus Cars Ltd and its dealers. Another popular advertisement showed how to build your own Elan in a weekend and was placed in many different publications around 1968-70. For their part, the company's US dealers devised their own advertisement for the S1 under an easily understood 'Good Life' banner.

62

Elan S1 & S2 1962

The other advertisements shown here appeared in Autocar in 1963 (for the new Elan 1600) and in Motor in November 1965 highlighting the car's durability, reliability and dependability. Another, showing the Elan's distinctive backbone chassis, carried the provocative headline 'The Elan Exposed'.

Finally a full-page magazine advertisement for the entire UK Lotus dealer network is reproduced here, as well as an original Lotus Elan Special Equipment specifications sheet: 115bhp engine, close-ratio gearbox, and servo-assisted brakes.

PICTURE DETAILS

S2 model, Corgi, GB. die cast, 1/43rd, 1964

Elan workshop manual, 1965

Advert, Elan 'BRM', Mike Spence ltd.

Model S1 with hard top, Kogure, Japan, plastic, 1/20, 1964.

Model box set 'The Avengers', Corgi Toys, GB, die cast.

8 page fold out brochure, Elan S2.

Advert, Lotus Cars Ltd & dealers 'Jim Clark'.

Lotus Cars handbook, letter & test certificate.

Advert, Lotus Cars, 'durability, reliability and dependability', Motor, Nov 1965

TYPE 26

TYPE 26R

Competition Elan 1964

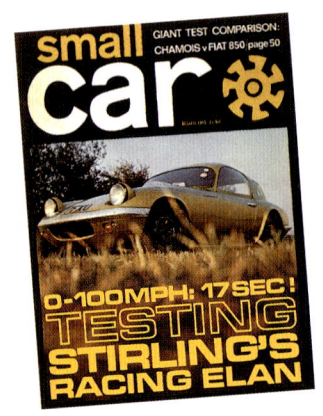

What Jackie Stewart insisted was 'a difficult little sod of a car', the Elan nevertheless underwent the expected transformation into a circuit racer and to good effect. That was after considerable development not by Chapman himself (who was too busy with other things) but by racing team boss Ian Walker and his distinctive 'Gold Bugs' and Graham Warner of London's Chequered Flag with a car registered, famously, LOV 1. Thereafter, and observing the privateers' successes, Chapman not unnaturally incorporated several of their modifications into his own works racer – the Type 26R – which went on sale in component form for £1995. In club events it quickly proved a useful tool and many private teams took to the circuits with cars of their own, including the Stirling Moss Automotive Racing Team which is represented here by an unusually styled 'SMART' white metal Elan, in Stirling's favourite green, made by Marsh Models in Great Britain to 1/43rd scale. (This car was also pictured on the cover of the now defunct Small Car magazine.) Team Willment campaigned the racing Elan too, fitting it with a BRM Phase 2 Lotus engine and giving John Miles what he needed to win the 1966 Autosport Championship. The most distinctive cars, however, were the 20 or so Shapecraft fastbacks built between 1963 and 1964. Peter Sellers bought one such car, and shown here is the cover and interior of an extremely rare brochure produced for another, the so-called Surbiton Motors Elan GT. The other models shown are of a more conventional Elan hardtop made by ATC in Japan, red and black-painted tin to a 1/20th scale, a diecast Lotus racing team set made by Corgi in Great Britain, and a Japanese Asahi-made 1/20th tin-plate model Elan with friction motor.

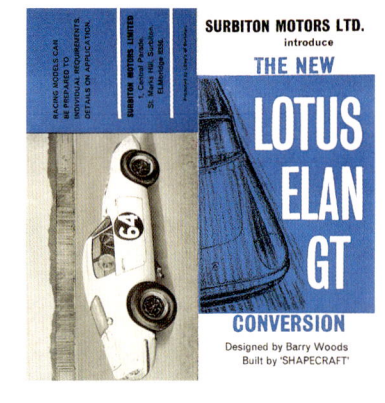

64

Formula Junior 1963

The first monocoque for Formula Junior, the Type 27 was a direct development of the Type 25 and (as this wooden scratch-built 1/43rd scale model by RD Marmande of France testifies) one of the most striking-looking machines of its era. Team Lotus build cards for all 35 cars built are shown here but, underdeveloped due to poor winter weather, the 27 had a shakey start until aluminium replaced the original glassfibre monocoque when the car came into its own. As the works Ron Harris-Team Lotus leaflet pictured bears witness, it scored some notable successes in the 1963 British Formula Junior Championships, winning 8 races driven by Peter Arundell and a couple of second places by Mike Spence & John Fening.

PICTURE DETAILS

Model, 'Smart Elan' Marsh Models, GB, white metal, 1/43rd

Model box, ATC, Japan, tin plate, 1/20th

Lotus racing team, Corgi, GB, die cast, 1/43rd

Model 26R Asahi, Japan, tin plate, friction motor, 1/20th

Small Car magazine March 1965.

Brochure, Surbiton Motors Elan GT

Model type 27, RD Marmande, France. wood, 1/43rd

Leaflet, Ron Harris Team Lotus, 1963

Team Lotus build cards Type 27

TYPE 27

TYPE 28

Lotus Cortina 1962

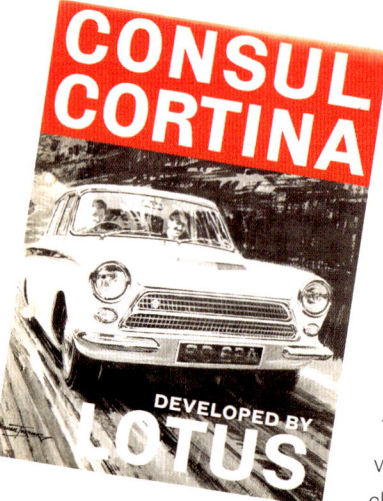

When the top brass at a company as big and as powerful as Ford decide they want to go racing, it is perhaps not that surprising that eventually they end up winning. Certainly not when you calculate the amount of money Ford must have spent from the early 1960s onwards, and certainly not when you look at the sheer variety of classes and different formulae which they set out to contest.

The results are well known now – the Blue Oval successfully dominated virtually an entire motorsport generation – but what is less well appreciated is that the forerunner to all of this, to everything from the BDA Escort to the Le Mans GT40 and MkIV, owes more than a little to the first true homologation special, a car enthusiast could actually go out and buy. Officially the Lotus Type 28, though known the world over as the Lotus-Cortina (except at Ford where they insisted it be called the Cortina-Lotus), the car had its origins in the Cortina GT, a machine that had already enjoyed some success in both rallies and circuit racing. It was the product of a scheme whereby Lotus – strapped for cash, and with capacity to spare – would assemble on Ford's behalf 1000 cars homologated for Group 2 racing. These used a new 1,558cc version of the already proven Twin Cam Ford engine which had been developed for competition by Mike Costin and Keith Duckworth of Cosworth and the same close ratio 'box as the Elan. With around 150bhp (instead of 105) and lightweight alloys skins for the doors, boot and bonnet competition versions quickly attracted all the right names: Graham Hill, Jim Clark and Jackie Stewart, and a host of other competitive club racers. Ordinary folk could buy them too, the basic price being some £910 and the vast majority of the nearly 2,900 built being ordered in white with a trademark Sherwood Green flash. A few white-only cars

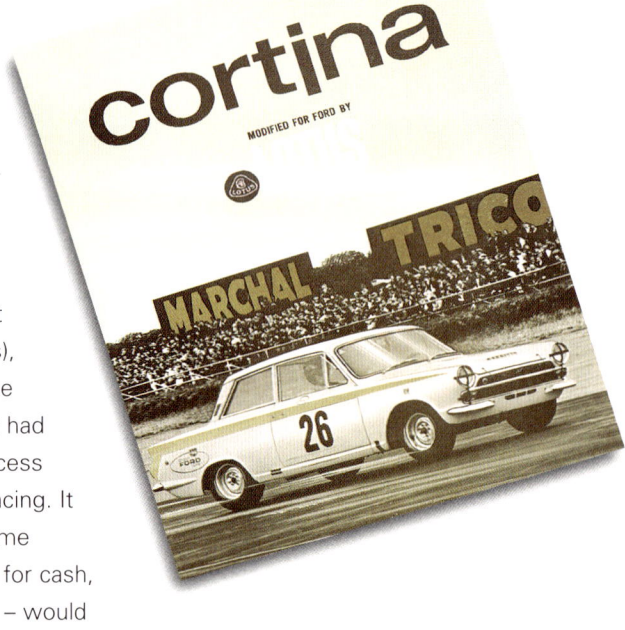

Lotus Cortina 1962

went to the West Sussex Constabulary. Later an SE model became available, it had 10 bhp more and such extras as seatbelts ! Advertisements issued at the time included several from suppliers jumping on the Lotus-Cortina bandwagon like this one produced by Britax safety belts congratulating Sir John Whitmore on winning the 1965 European touring car championships, and another which appeared on the back of Autosport in June 1963 promoting AP Borg & Beck. For their part the car's makers produced several of their own, including one shown here placed in The Motor in 1963 and two others showing the Lotus-Cortina. Inevitably given the early cars' successes on road and track, the modelmakers were not far behind the factory either and produced their own versions. Of the many scale models available at the time this white Cortina Mark 1 was made by Classic Car Kits in Great

PICTURE DETAILS

Slot car, Airfix, UK, 1/32nd

Owners handbook & service book, 1966

Consul Cortina fact sheet, Ford Cars, 1962

Advert, Britax safety belts, 1965

Advert, Lotus Cars, 'This is the Lotus developed Cortina', 1963

TYPE 28

TYPE 28

Lotus Cortina 1962

Britain to 1/43rd scale in white metal, and the slot-car version of the Mark 1 was made by Airfix in the UK. A second version of the real car followed too, still in white and green, still with a proliferation of Lotus badges, although as these cars were assembled by Ford using parts supplied by Lotus they are more correctly known only as Twin Cam Cortinas. Eventually eclipsed by the all-conquering Twin Cam Escort – but not before they had racked up an impressive race record of their own – these so-called MkIIs have never quite matched the appeal of the original Lotus Cortina, or the value. Value? Well yes, you can forget jokes about old Cortinas because in 1995 one 30 year-old car with a racing history – and Sir John Whitmore's personal provenance – sold for a staggering £34,642. Once of course millions of company cars were Cortinas, but there was never one like this.

Several other equally rare mementos from the period have survived intact too and are pictured here, including an original owners handbook and service book for the Mark 1 Lotus Cortina, and the cover and inside of a Consul Cortina fact sheet produced by Ford with detailed specifications on the reverse. The other original owner handbook shown is for the later Mark 2 Cortina Lotus. And finally two brochures have survived the ravages of time, both for the Mark 1 Cortina.

Lotus Cortina 1962

PICTURE DETAILS

Model, Classic Car kits, white metal, GB, 1/43rd

Advert, Lotus Factory Sales dept, The Motor 1963

Advert, AP Borg & Beck, Autosport, June 1963

Owners handbook for Mark 2 Cortina Lotus.

Advert, Lotus Cars, 'Hurry'.

Advert, Ford Cars, 'A brilliant blend'.

Brochure, Ford Cars, 'Cortina Lotus'.

TYPE 28

69

TYPE 29

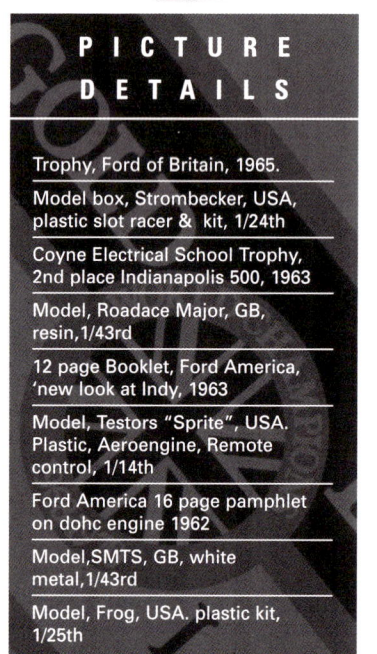

Indianapolis Car 1963

Impressed after watching a Type 25 in action it was a Porsche-racing American who most encouraged Colin Chapman to contest the celebrated Indianapolis 500 in 1963, and indeed it is Dan Gurney's own Type 29 which appears on the box for the American Strombecker 1/24th scale slot racer kit shown here. Gurney felt the sophisticated mid-engined Lotus would do well against the native front-engined behemoths, and doubtless spurred on by his words – not to mention a crowd of 300,000 and what is believed to have been the world's richest purse – Chapman responded with the new Type 29. Longer, wider and higher – it had to be to accommodate Ford of America's hefty 253 cubic inch dry sump V8 and Gurney himself who was a taller man than Clark – it offset the engine and Colotti gearbox by nearly three inches to counteract the centrifugal effect of the fast banked oval. After testing at Snetterton two more cars were built, one each for Clark and Gurney, and in the event itself they came second and seventh respectively.

Clark's achievement is marked here by the idiosyncratically-named Coyne Electrical School Trophy. Also shown is a very special trophy-model of the Type 29 presented to Chapman by Ford of Britain to commorate his record-breaking Indy win two years later. Revell produced a model of the Lotus Ford Type 29 Indy car too, confusingly describing it as a Grand Prix car, and in Britain a Roadace

PICTURE DETAILS

Trophy, Ford of Britain, 1965.

Model box, Strombecker, USA, plastic slot racer & kit, 1/24th

Coyne Electrical School Trophy, 2nd place Indianapolis 500, 1963

Model, Roadace Major, GB, resin, 1/43rd

12 page Booklet, Ford America, 'new look at Indy, 1963

Model, Testors "Sprite", USA. Plastic, Aeroengine, Remote control, 1/14th

Ford America 16 page pamphlet on dohc engine 1962

Model, SMTS, GB, white metal, 1/43rd

Model, Frog, USA. plastic kit, 1/25th

70

Indianapolis Car 1963

Major version was scratch-built to 1/43rd scale in white-painted resin bearing the number 93. The white No. 22 model was made by Testors in the USA to 1/14th scale and with a remote control 'Aeroengine', and the BRG No.92 is a 1.43rd scale white metal model by SMTS in Great Britain. Jim Clark's own car was modelled by Frog in the USA as a 1/25th scale plastic kit car, and 'The New look at Indy' is a 12 page booklet produced by Ford America for the 1963 event.

TYPE 29

TYPE 30

Group 7 Sports Racer 1964

Purposeful-looking but certainly one of the most disappointing machines ever built by Lotus, the company's 'big banger' – the Type 30 with its Ford 289 engine – was never really a match for its more accomplished McLaren and Lola rivals. Depending on large capacity American V8s (it was indeed very much a US-inspired formula) Group 7 racing understandably enjoyed considerable popularity in Britain in the 1960s but was never to prove a particularly happy milieu for Lotus, although the company did build some 33 examples of this car in all. The Type 30's appeal clearly crossed continents, however, for several models were produced, the boxes for which are shown here and include two for American Hawk 1/32nd scale plastic kits, a rare unopened one made by Otaki in Japan (also for a 1/32 scale plastic kit, bearing the No.5), an American-made Strombecker plastic kit for a 1/24th scale slot racer, a 1/32nd slot racer made by Toyko Plamo in Japan and painted blue with the number 97, and finally another for an American model made by MDC with a vacuum foam packed body. Closer to home John Shelford produced an attractive scratch-built wooden model to 1/43rd scale and painted British Racing Green with the number 17, and the car was also featured in Motor magazine which reproduced this double-page spread of the car from Road & Track in April 1964. The original Team Lotus build cards for a Type 30, chassis number 30/L/20, and its replacement have also survived, the first car having been written off in an accident. It was by no means the Type 30's only expensive misfortune, and in 1965 Chapman called a halt to production.

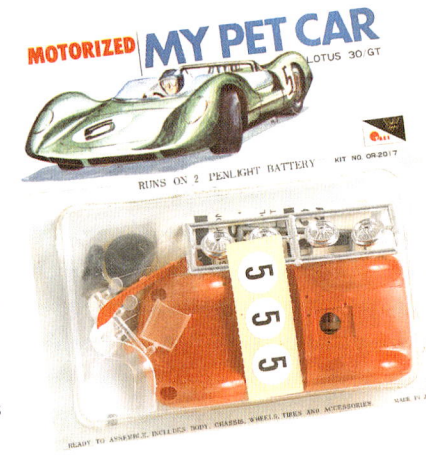

Formula 3 1964

Representing a reduction in power even compared to Formula Junior, Chapman's uncharacteristic response to the new Formula 3 category was to look backwards rather than forwards. As rivals pursued more advanced construction methods, the monocoque's innovator returned to tubular steel construction, merely updating his Type 22. The Type 31 was as a result uncompetitive against Tyrrell's Cooper-BMCs, but found a niche as a racing school trainer at Brands Hatch and Snetterton. Build cards for the initial batch of 12 survive, however, also a rare article on the car from Motor Racing Magazine. The model was scratch-built by RD Marmande in France, during the late 1970's.

PICTURE DETAILS

Model alternative boxes, Hawk, USA, plastic kit, 1/32

Model box, Otaki, Japan. plastic kit, 1/32

Model, John Shelford, GB, wood, 1/43rd

Model box, Strombecker, USA, slot car kit, 1/24th

Model box, Toyko Plamo, Japan. plastic slot racer & kit, 1/32

Model box, MDC, USA, vacuum formed body, 1/24th

Team Lotus build card Type 30

Article, Road & Track, USA, April 1964

Model, RD Marmamde, France, wood, 1/43rd

Article, Motor Racing magazine featuring the type 31

Team Lotus build cards for all 12 type 31's

TYPE 31

TYPE 32

Formula 2 & Tasman car 1964

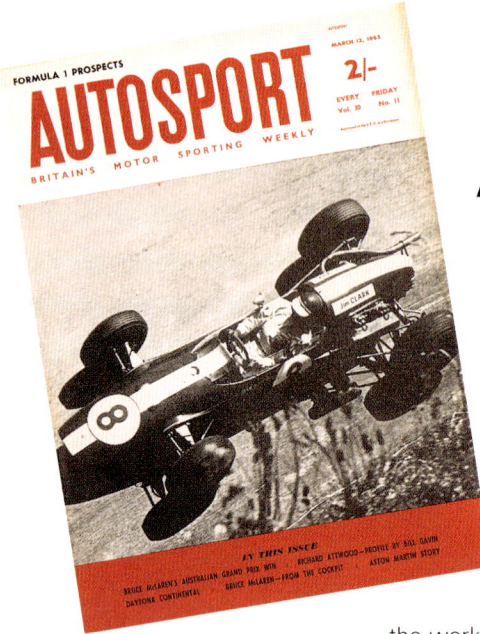

A skillful and intelligent development of the Type 27 for Formula 2, Chapman's larger Type 32 saw a return to monocoque construction and to his previous winning form and that in spite of the fact that his lead drivers – Jim Clark and Mike Spence – were often engaged elsewhere leaving stand-ins to do much of the work. One of these, the young Jackie Stewart, won at Snetterton and finished second in France. And elsewhere some of the dozen Type 32s built over a two-year period performed extremely impressively. Wins recorded by the car included the Pau GP, the Guards' Trophy at Brands Hatch, the F1 Aintree '200', and the Eifelrennen in Germany. In fact, all told, Lotus took the flag in no fewer than seven of the 18 major races of 1964. Perhaps the most outstanding of the cars, however, was the one-off Type 32B built for the Tasman series in Australia and New Zealand. Powered by a Coventry-Climax FPF in place of the usual 998cc Cosworth-Ford SCA, it is depicted here in a poster celebrating its victory in the Tasman Championship and produced by Classic Team Lotus in 1996 in a limited edition of 500. In this form the car also made the cover of Autosport in March 1965 and was the subject of a major technical article, reproduced here, which was written for a Japanese magazine. Fitting the 2.5 litre Climax unit in place of the much smaller Cosworth (itself based on the Ford Anglia 105E block) required considerable reworking of the forward monocoque to combine it with a modified tubular rear subframe. RD Marmande in France once again produced a wooden scratch-built 1/43 scale model showing this modification and painted British Racing Green bearing the number 9. And finally a charming children's pedal-version of the Type 32 was also produced at some point in the late 1960s. The 32B itself, which remained a one-off, was later the subject of numerous modifications but has since been returned to its original specification by Lotus collector John Dawson Damer based in New South Wales, Australia. and is now owned and campaigned by Classic Team Lotus.

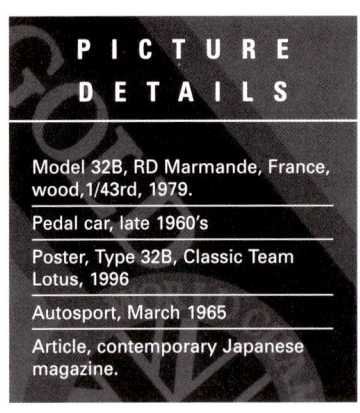

PICTURE DETAILS

Model 32B, RD Marmande, France, wood, 1/43rd, 1979.

Pedal car, late 1960's

Poster, Type 32B, Classic Team Lotus, 1996

Autosport, March 1965

Article, contemporary Japanese magazine.

74

Formula 2 & Tasman car 1964

TYPE 32

TYPE 33

Formula 1 1964

The final iteration of the Type 25, the 1964 Type 33 looked almost identical although no parts were interchangeable between the two cars and the latter design was in fact easier to build and even stronger. Once initial suspension glitches had been ironed out and leaving aside a major collision during its debut race, the car also proved to be extremely competitive and enabled Jim Clark to dominate F1 for much of the 1965 season. Scoring six clear victories, five of them with the 33, he went to to win the Championship as is shown in the accompanying postcard. He actually destroyed his car at the non-championship Brands Hatch Race of Champions, but even here the Type 33 was victorious – this time driven by Mike Spence. The trophy shown here is from this period, being the 1965 F.I.A Coupe des Constructeurs Formule 1 awarded to Lotus. A rule-change the following year – allowing engines up to 3.0 litres – meant it was outclassed by Brabham

76

Formula 1 1964

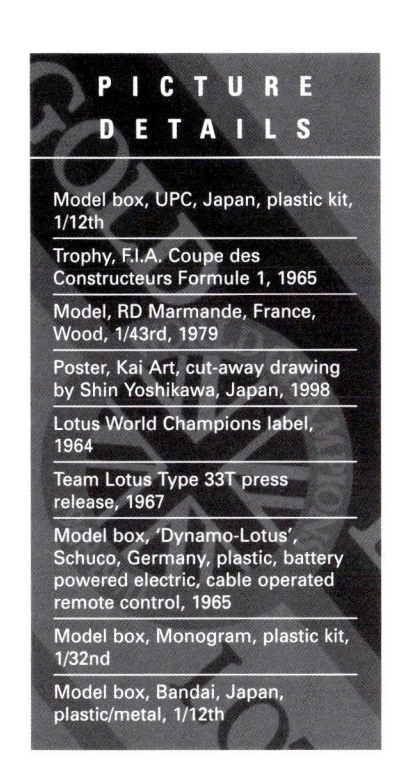

PICTURE DETAILS

Model box, UPC, Japan, plastic kit, 1/12th

Trophy, F.I.A. Coupe des Constructeurs Formule 1, 1965

Model, RD Marmande, France, Wood, 1/43rd, 1979

Poster, Kai Art, cut-away drawing by Shin Yoshikawa, Japan, 1998

Lotus World Champions label, 1964

Team Lotus Type 33T press release, 1967

Model box, 'Dynamo-Lotus', Schuco, Germany, plastic, battery powered electric, cable operated remote control, 1965

Model box, Monogram, plastic kit, 1/32nd

Model box, Bandai, Japan, plastic/metal, 1/12th

LOTUS 33 F1

TYPE 33

and Ferrari although it still took two third places, one fourth, and a first and third in the South African Grand Prix. Thereafter the car was modified again, becoming the 33T for Tasman – another series Clark dominated with five wins in 1967 and three second places – before the car was finally superseded by the new Type 49. This particular car is represented here by an original 1967 Team Lotus press release but the poster is for the standard Type 33, a 1998 cut-away drawing by Shin Yoshikawa which was produced by Kai Art in Japan. Also shown is a wooden scratch-built car, No.1, by RD Marmande in France, a motorised 1/12th scale toy from Bandai in Japan and a 1/32 scale hobby kit, made by Monogram. The box is from another Japanese kit, made by UPC to 1/12 in plastic, and the final example uses a battery powered motor with cable operated remote control. Called Dynamo-Lotus, it was made around 1965 by Schuco in Germany.

TYPE 34

Indianapolis Car 1964

Having come so close to victory in '63, Lotus had high hopes for its 1964 Indianapolis 500 contender, a development of the Type 29. Fitted with Ford of America's fuel-injected new quad-cam, quad-valve V8 – the original FoMoCo development notes for which are shown here – this Type 34 was to be driven by Clark and Gurney, with A.J. Foyt denied the chance to join them (Ford's wish) as Chapman wished to keep the final car in reserve. Despite tyre problems in early testing – Chapman having selected Dunlop over Firestone – Clark took pole position ahead of Bobby Marshman in a modified Type 29 in second place and Gurney in the other Type 34 in 6th. After a massive shunt and restart, Clark led for several laps but crashed after the suspension collapsed as a result of the tyres shedding tread. Gurney sensibly retired and Foyt, ironically, went on to win the 500 for another team. A year later they tried again, this time with Foyt and Jones driving the cars, but another suspension failure put paid to any victory and prompted the USAC Safety Committee to ground not just these cars but also the replacement Type 38. The car was modelled by AK in 1/16th scale, two versions of which are shown here in British racing green and white. Bandai in Japan also produced a version, to 1/12th scale in tin and painted with the number 27, and some years later the car was again commemorated by a Camel Team Lotus reprint of the original Type 34 information sheet.

78

Formula 2 & 3 1965

A logical evolution of the Types 27 and 32, the Type 35 was the realisation of Chapman's plan to build a car capable of taking a choice of seven different power units to compete in various different formulae. Peter Sellers bought one, probably to be driven by Brian Hart in its early races, but it was Jim Clark who made the car a star – winning at Pau, Crystal Palace, Rouen, Brands and Albi, and being placed on three other occasions. The model shown is by RD Marmande in France, a wooden, scratch-built car made to 1/43rd scale with rather 'chunky' tyres, whilst the surviving paperwork from the period includes a membership card, details and official letterhead for the Lotus Junior Club – honourary president: Jim Clark – for younger Lotus enthusiasts. Camel Team Lotus also re-issued the original press release for the Type 35, a copy of which is reproduced alongside.

PICTURE DETAILS

Model, AK, Japan, plastic, 1/16th, green.

Model, AK, Japan, plastic, 1/16th, white.

Reproduction press release, Camel Team Lotus 1987

Model, Bandai, Japan, tin, 1/12th

Notes, Ford Motor, Co, USA, DOHC

Model, RD Marmande, France, Wood, 1/43rd

Membership card & letterhead, Lotus Junior Club, 1965

Camel Team Lotus reproduction press release, 1987

TYPE 35

TYPE 36

Elan Fixed Head Coupé S3 & S4 1965

A driver's car beyond compare – and that in spite of some justifiable criticism about its specification – the fact that the next development of the brilliant Elan warranted a new Type number speaks volumes for the way the factory viewed the car. The demise of its expensively-made Elite left Lotus with no closed GT, a shortcoming which the new S3 (which was made initially only in fixed-head form) would put right at a stroke. It was also hoped in this way to introduce the brand to a whole new market of potential buyers. Its intended new appeal was thus further underlined by such refinements as chrome bumpers, (which subsequently only ever appeared on the press car), a better interior with electric windows and new seats, even a new axle ratio for more relaxed high speed driving. It was also hoped that no less than three-quarters of the cars built would go for export. Approximately 3,000 Type 36s were built between its launch in 1965 and 1973, including the fixed-head S4 which retained the Type 36 designation at the factory. And in both guises it was modelled by several companies including DM Modeles in France whose 1/43rd scale resin model is shown here painted dark blue. The white metal model painted light blue

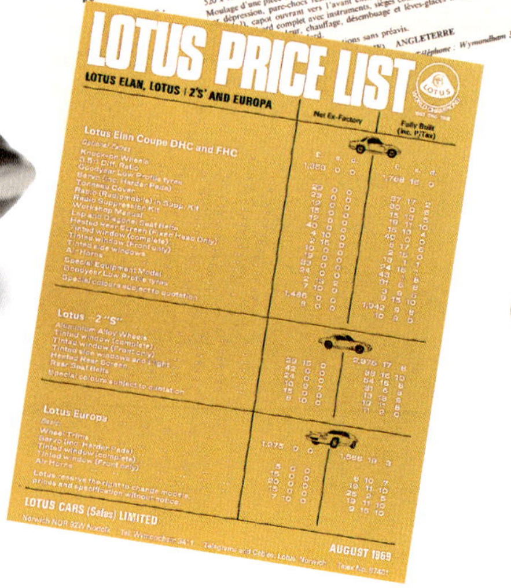

80

Elan Fixed Head Coupé S3 & S4 1965

PICTURE DETAILS

Model, DM Modeles, France, resin, 1/43rd

Model, Elan Sprint, GP models, GB. White metal, 1/43rd

Lotus Cars, 4 page brochure, 1967

Elan Coupe handbook, 1966

Lotus Cars price list, 1967

Lotus Cars, Elan coupe specification sheet, 1965

Lotus Cars, Elan coupe specification sheet, 1966

Advert, Springal steering wheels, Autosport April 1968

Advert, Lotus Cars, Motor Racing, Nov. 1965.

over white is by Britain's GP Models.. An Elan FHC 4-page brochure from 1967 is also reproduced here showing in a series of black and white photographs the official press car in front of a lake, which had also appeared in the previous year's largely similar brochure, this time with Graham Arnold's famous swans instead of ducks! Also shown is an original Elan Coupe owner's handbook from 1966 and a price list from the following year. Finally, the two different specification sheets are similar in design, one being in colour and one in black & white, also refer to the fixed-head coupé while the advertisements are for Springal steering wheels, showing one of its products fitted to an Elan, and the new 'Luxury Coupe' from Lotus which appeared in Motor Racing in November 1965.

TYPE 36

TYPE 38
Indianapolis Car 1965

Despite its understandably frosty relationship with the chairman, Ford stayed with Lotus for the 1965 assault on the Brickyard, Len Terry stepping up to the challenge of designing a new car as Chapman was busy with the Tasman Championship. His car, the Type 38, was the stiffest Lotus single-seater yet, longer and smoother than the earlier Indy cars and using a new 500bhp alcohol-fuelled derivative of the Ford V8. Chapman was very much back on board for the race itself, however, Team Lotus actually skipping the Monaco GP in order to concentrate on the Indianapolis '500'. The commitment paid off too, with Lotus cars completely dominating the event, taking the first five places in qualifying and Clark himself winning the race whilst averaging a blistering – and record-breaking – 150.686mph. A valuable signed photograph of him taken at the time is shown here. The following year Clark came in second – Graham Hill's Lola had somehow passed him during an early spin – and in 1967, whilst the car was no longer competitive, its influence was there for all to see with so many rival manufacturers having adopted the 38's construction principles that the field resembled nothing less than a host of Lotus clones. A winner, a record-breaker, and even now an influential design, the Type 38 not unnaturally proved the inspiration of

82

Indianapolis Car 1965

numerous models, several of which are shown here. These include two cars (one showing the underneath) made by Russkit in the USA, unusual twin motor slot cars built to 1/24th scale and painted British racing green with the number 82. That painted red with the number 19 is a white-metal 1/43rd scale model by SMTS in Great Britain, and the two Scalextric plastic slot cars are also British and to 1/24th & 1/32nd scale respectively. The plastic kit box art showing car number 19 clearly illustrates its offset suspension and was made by Imai in Japan to 1/16th scale. Two other boxes are for different 1/24th scale plastic kits of the Type 38 made by IMC in the USA. The tiny 1/40th scale red tin car was made by Schackman in Japan, while the box and 12-inch long No.19 car are also Japanese being made in 1966 by Diamond-X in tin.

Among the other

PICTURE DETAILS

Model, SMTS, GB. white metal, 1/43rd

Scalextric plastic slot car, GB, 1/24th, 1968

Scalextric plastic slot car, GB, 1/32nd, 1969

Model boxes, IMC, USA, plastic kit, 1/24th

Signed Jim Clark photo, Indy, 1965

Trophy awarded at Indy 500 festival 1965

Model, Ford V8 engine to commemorate Indy win 1965, unknown

Team Lotus press photo, prototype 38, 1964

Model box, AutoKit, USA, white metal, 1/43rd

Model, unknown, white metal, 1/43rd

TYPE 38

83

TYPE 38

Indianapolis Car 1965

models and boxes shown is an American Autokit box for a Type 38 1/24th scale white metal kit car.

Also shown are two of many advertisements from various motor manufacturers which appeared after the Lotus success at the Brickyard in 1965, also an original official Team Lotus press release with a press photo of the Type 38 itself. Another press photo shows the early prototype 38 out testing. The trophy was awarded to Colin Chapman at the Indy 500 Festival in '65, recognising his outstanding achievement and important contribution to auto-racing at Indianapolis, and the lovely model of the Ford V8 engine was produced to commemorate the 1965 Indianapolis winner 'powered by Ford.'

Tasman Car 1965

PICTURE DETAILS

Two models, Russkit, USA. twin motor slot cars, 1/24th

Model box, Imai, Japan, plastic kit, 1/16th

Model, Schackman, Japan, tin plate, 1/40th

Model & box, Diamond-X, Japan. Tin plate 12" long, 1966

Team Lotus press release and press photo, 1965

Advert Smiths Instruments, Autocar June 1965

Advert, Girling brakes, 1965.

Poster, Type 39, Brian Baldersmith, Australia, 1998

Article, Type 39, recent Japanese magazine.

A one-off monocoque built to house an engine from Coventry Climax that materialised, the Type 39 found life 'down under' after being hastily converted from a would-be F1 car into a viable Tasman contender, which, Graham Hill admitted was a 'bloody quick old bastard' after it beat him in qualifying at Sandown Park. The poster shown on the right, by Australian Brian Baldersmith, celebrates the Geoghegan brothers, one of whom, Leo, acquired the car from Team Lotus and became the leading owner-driver in Australian racing for much of the 1960s. More recently a Japanese magazine detailed the chequered history of this rare car, one page of which is reproduced here.

TYPE 39

TYPE 40

Sports Racer 1965

Understandably keen to eradicate distasteful memories of two lack-lustre seasons for the Type 30, Chapman and John Joyce conceived the Type 40 to take its place in 'big banger' Group 7 racing.

Rushed development, however, meant the careers of the three built were scarcely more glorious. 'Hard work,' Jack Sear's called it, 'a highly-strung and twitchy car', and Jim Clark was no more complimentary although he at least took second place in the US at Riverside – albeit it more than nine seconds behind Hap Sharp's Chaparral. Undeterred, Fleischmann Auto-Rallye produced two plastic slot-car versions of the Rallye Monte Carlo Ford-Lotus Type 40s in 1/32 scale (the blue car is particularly rare). While the box and number 7 car are from Cox in the US, a 1/24th scale plastic kit for slot-car racing. The other box is for a Japanese Tamiya 1/24th racer, number 17, and the number 12 car is a German die cast model made by Gama to 1/40th scale. Also shown is a booklet of press releases, detail specifications, and the results for the famous Pink Stamps Special-sponsored Lotus Type 40.

86

Formula 3 & 2 1966

TYPE 41

High production and repair costs for the Types 27, the 32 and the 35 prompted Colin Chapman to forgo his precious monocoque for the junior formulae in favour of the tried and tested steel spaceframe. The result, the Type 41, was a clean sheet design from John Joyce and in the hands of the late Piers Courage it won its debut race on Boxing Day 1965. Thereafter another 60 cars were built but the results overall suggest that, while a useful tool when correctly prepared and set up, most of the time it was out-performed by the easier-to-master Brabham BT18. That said, the car was still winning races as late as 1968 – albeit with its new wedge profile and dubbed Type 41X, intended as testbed the forthcoming Type 55 F3 car – and by which time the evocative new Gold Leaf colours shown here had made their official debut.

The four prints - one featuring the 41X - shown are by Michael Turner, and the car is also the subject of these original press releases, as the original Type 41 issued by Team Lotus in 1966 and then as 41X issued by Gold Leaf Team Lotus in 1967 (In March 1968 the 41 driven by Mo Nunn made the cover of Autosport.) The model, a resin 1/43rd scale Type 41, was made by Tenariv in France.to represent one of the Ron Harris Team Lotus cars.

PICTURE DETAILS

Slot car models, Fleischmann Auto-Rallye, Germany, plastic, 1/32nd

Model & box, Cox, USA. plastic slot car kit, 1/24th

Model box, Tamiya, Japan. plastic slot car kit, 1/24th

Model, Gama, Germany. die cast, 1/40th

Booklet of press releases, specifications and results, Pink Stamps Special, 1965

Model, Tenariv, France, resin, 1/43rd

Autosport March 1968

Team Lotus press release, type 41, 1966

Gold Leaf Team Lotus press release & photo, type 41, 1967

Set of 4 prints, Michael Turner, GOLD LEAF cars types 41, 47, 48 & 49

87

TYPE 42 & 43
Indianapolis Car & Formula 1 1966

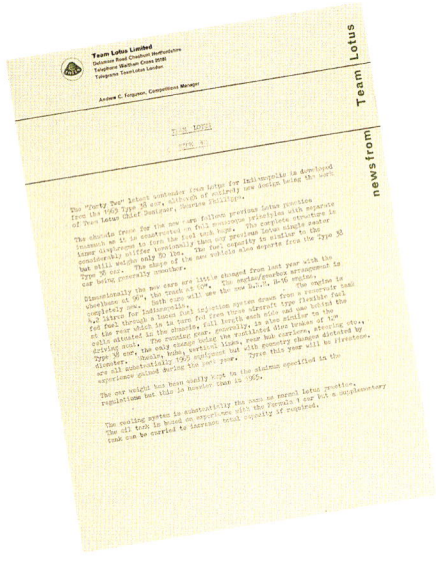

Intended as a contender for the 1968 Indianapolis 500, and once more powered by the 4.2 litre Ford V8, the Type 42 had actually been conceived to run with the complex BRM H16 and indeed in prototype form completed a few laps with this engine at Snetterton before it became apparent the engine was underdeveloped. However even when rejigged to accept the Ford V8 – what even Chapman admitted was 'a real old cobble up' – the rechristen Type 42F was still no match for the opposition and in the race itself Graham Hill was placed only 38th after retiring with a failed piston.

This short, unsuccessful career is mirrored by a total absence of memorabilia – an original Team Lotus press release is shown here – but as a learning exercise the Type 42 had something to recommend it as it encouraged Lotus designers to experiment with longer wheelbases instead of always striving for the shortest measure possible. The Type 42F probably produced some collectable items in the USA but surprisingly no models have been made, considering the interest in Indianapolis cars.

Another switch in F1 regulations, returning the size limit to 3 litres, meant Lotus had at first to defend its title with a 2 litre Type 33 whilst work continued on its Type 43 replacement. Designed around the BRM H16 – compact but complex and relatively heavy – the car arrived in July for Reims but retired with gear-selection problems. In fact, reliability problems continued to dog the car and although it won a single unexpected victory at Watkins Glen – which made the cover of Motor Sport – few were surprised when both cars were sold and refitted with Ford V8s, for the new Formula500 series. The car shown here wearing the number 1 is by Britain's Scale Racing Cars, a white metal 1/43rd scale model. Also one by Penny of Italy, in unusual but rather cute 1/63rd scale, and still unassembled a white metal 1/43rd scale Equipe kit. The original Team Lotus press release is also reproduced here with the photograph which was issued at the same time.

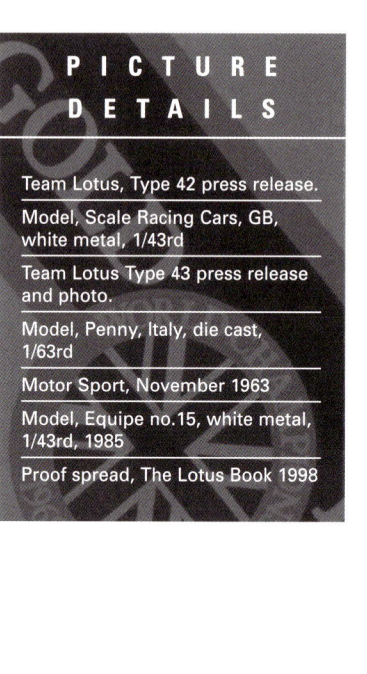

PICTURE DETAILS

Team Lotus, Type 42 press release.
Model, Scale Racing Cars, GB, white metal, 1/43rd
Team Lotus Type 43 press release and photo.
Model, Penny, Italy, die cast, 1/63rd
Motor Sport, November 1963
Model, Equipe no.15, white metal, 1/43rd, 1985
Proof spread, The Lotus Book 1998

Formula 2 1966

TYPE 44

Depicting the Type 44, one of the most graceful and elegant Lotus single-seater designs, a signed limited edition proof spread from The Lotus Book (Coterie Press, 1998) provides a useful reminder of Colin Chapman's undeniably impressive record during the three years of one-litre Formula 2 racing. Until the formula switched to 1,600cc, Lotus stuck with the venerable Cosworth SCA engine and it served them reasonably well, eventually developing 138bhp from only 997cc at a screaming 11,000rpm and notching up 12 wins in 48 races. Lotus finished well ahead of Lola, Cooper and Matra – and only slightly behind the powerful Honda-powered Brabhams.

TYPE 45

Elan Drop Head S3 & S4 1966

LOTUS ELAN S.4

Essentially the drophead version of the Type 36 or Elan S3, the Type 45 designation was retained when the car was developed into the S4. Launched in March 1968, these later cars can be identified by the flared, squared off wheel arches (made necessary by the adoption of wider, lower profile tyres) and by their purposeful twin exhausts. In both guises its detailed development mirrored almost exactly that of the hardtopped Type 36, with the car becoming gradually more refined and with enhanced levels of equipment being added to the range as time progressed. Approximately 4,000 were produced between 1966 and 1973 – interpretation of Lotus road-car production figures over this period is a notoriously difficult and innaccurate science – a total which includes between 900 and 1,353 Elan Sprints with their characteristic Tony Rudd-developed 'big valve' heads and strengthened drivelines. For the first time an estate version of a Lotus was also offered, though not by the factory. Nicknamed the 'Elanbulance' – and the reason is obvious – just two estates were produced by Hexagon in Highgate, north-west London. They are notable for their professional execution and elegant

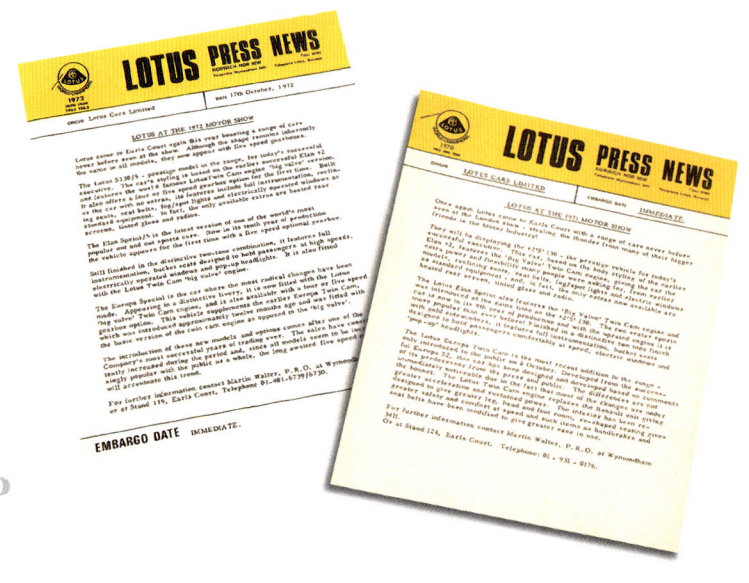

Elan Drop Head S3 & S4 1966

PICTURE DETAILS

Lotus Cars, 4 page S4 brochure, 1968

Model, Kyosho, China, die cast, 1/43rd

Specification sheet, Elan Sprint, 1970

Lotus Press News, Motor Show, 1971

Lotus Press News, Motor Show, 1972

Advert, Lotus Dealers, Motor, 1967

Advert, Cheshunt Lotus Centre, Autosport, October 1967

Lotus Press news, 5,000th Elan, October 1967

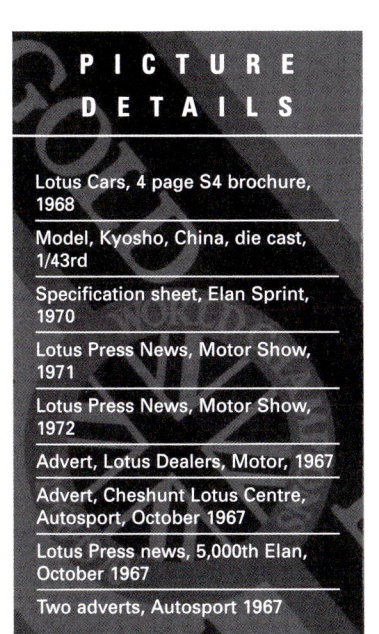

Two adverts, Autosport 1967

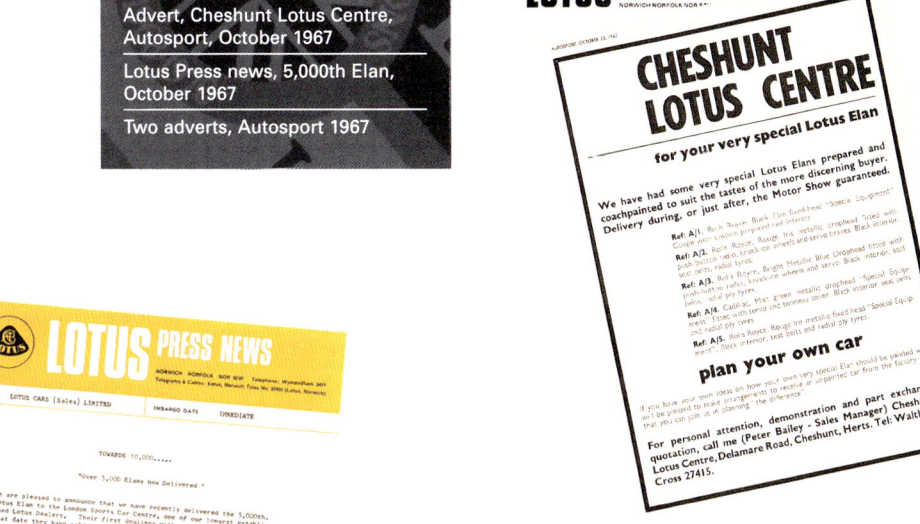

lines, however, and their distinctive style has since been copied by a number of private conversions, though to varying quality. A few later cars, probably no more than a handful, were also fitted with a +2 five-speed transmission, derived from the Austin Maxi gearbox, and although this was never more than an unofficial factory exercise it certainly improved the car's performance on the growing network of British motorways. A top speed of 130mph was deemed possible, the extra gear making cruising far more comfortable.

As befits a Lotus produced in such large numbers, a considerable amount of paperwork from the time has survived including price lists from August 1969 and May 1968, various official publications such as 'Lotus Press News' from the 1971 Motor Show announcing the new Elan +2 'S' and another for the following year, and a large-size 4-page Elan S4 brochure from 1968. Far rarer, however, is the Elan Sprint specification sheet pictured here and describing a distinctively painted car which was for a time driven by Lotus Grand Prix driver Jochen Rindt; also another for an Elan SE – denoting Special Equipment – this time in French. From 1967 have survived three different Elan advertisements from Autosport

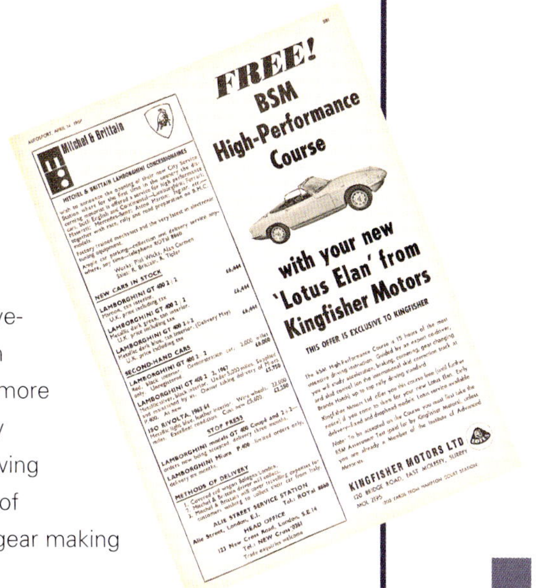

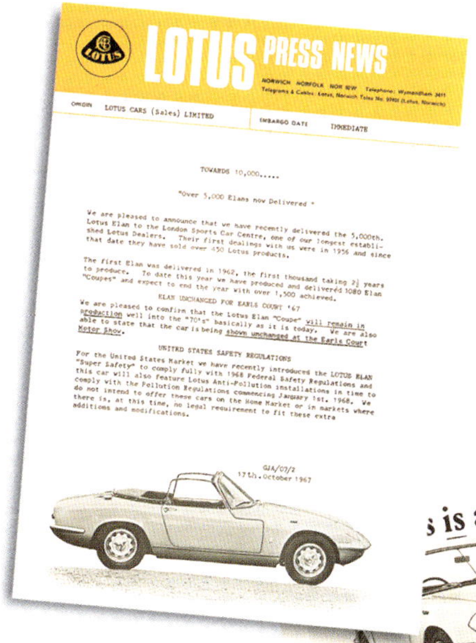

TYPE 45

TYPE 45

Elan Drop Head S3 & S4 1966

magazine, also another Lotus Press News announcing the completion of the 5,000th Elan 'towards 10,000' in October of the same year, and two more advertisements, one for the Cheshunt Lotus Centre (from Autosport, October 1967) and another which appeared in Motor listing a number of Lotus dealers. The S4 also appeared in this advertisement entitled 'Who's just arrived', precisely the same image being used for the cover of Autosport's 'Special Lotus Supplement'. Autosport is also the source of the advertisement shown here for the Elan Sprint, entitled for obvious reasons 'The Yardstick'. Particularly in Sprint form – outputting a respectable 126bhp at 6,500rpm, and sold in kit form only initially for £1,686 – the big Elan S4 is still, after nearly 35 years, one of the most sought-after Lotus road cars. Supplied as standard with an instantly recognisable duo-tone paintscheme including elaborate Elan Sprint striping and knock-on, black-painted steel wheels, it gained even greater distinction when it inherited the by then well established Gold Leaf livery of gold, red and white, with gold wheels and gold bumpers

92

Elan Drop Head S3 & S4 1966

PICTURE DETAILS

Model, Kyosho, China, die cast, 1/43rd

Advert, Elan Sprint, Autosport 'The Yardstick'.

'Special Lotus Supplement', Autosport.

Advert, Lotus Cars, new Elan S4 "Who's just arrived?".

Lotus Cars, Elan SE specification sheet, France.

Lotus Cars, price list, August 1969

Lotus Cars, price list, May 1968

Detail, Elan brochure.

Model box, Gunze Sangyo, Japan, plastic, 1/24th, 1994.

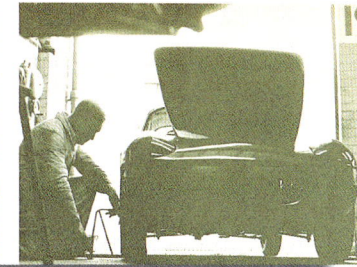

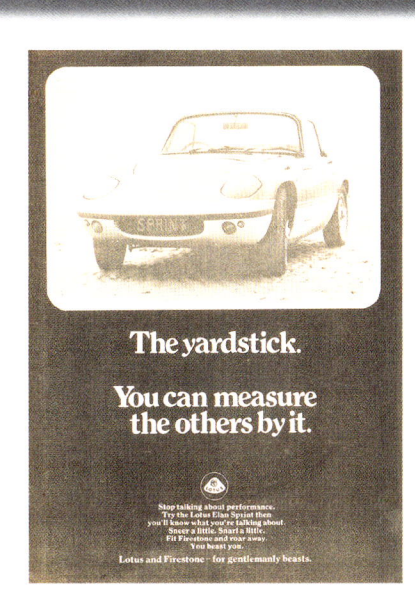

to commemorate the factory team's triumphant record in Formula One.

As familiar in its time as the John Player Special car's black-and-gold livery was to become a generation later, the Gold Leaf Elan Sprint is inarguably one of the definitive sports car of its era. Nonetheless, the only assembled model shown here of the many produced is painted, unusually, in leaf green rather than the more traditional British racing green and is of an Elan S3 drophead coupe. It was made by Kyosho in China to 1/43rd scale. The model box shown, is by Gunze Sangyo in Japan also an S3 this time in 1/24th scale.

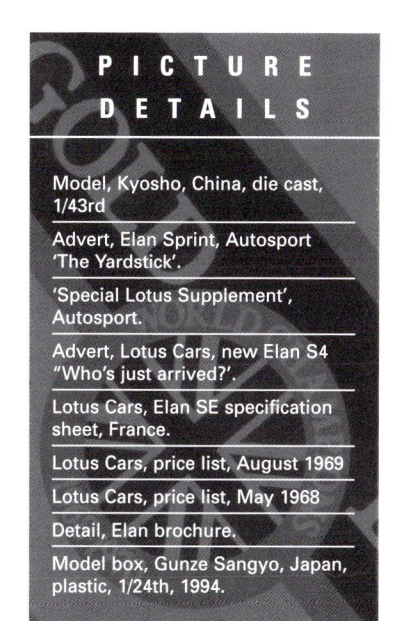

TYPE 45

TYPE 46

Europa S1 1966

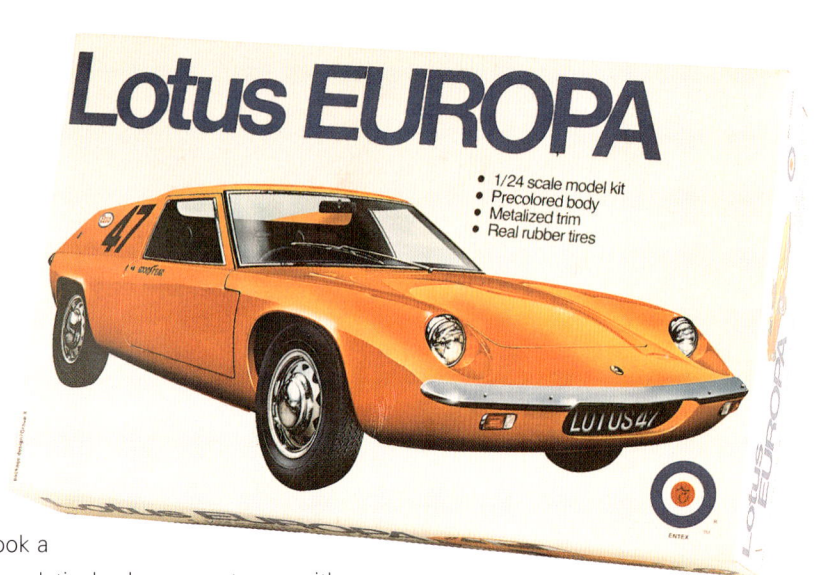

With mid-engined designs now dominant in racing it was presumably only a matter of time before the same configuration jumped the divide and became acceptable for specialised road cars too.

Credit for the first goes to Frenchman René Bonnet in 1961, but Colin Chapman was only a few years behind and when the Type 46 took a bow in 1966, it promised enthusiasts a relatively cheap sports car with the handling characteristics and finesse of a genuine Grand Prix racer. Codenamed the P5 during its hush-hush two-year development, but always known as the Europa, Chapman's much-vaunted 'Lotus for Europe' used an adaptation of the Elan's Y-fork chassis and a modified version Renault's 1.5 litre 'four' and associated gearbox mounted amidships and turned around to drive the rear wheels. 'For Europe' meant the car would not be available in the UK for a while, and indeed an edition of Lotus Press News from October 1967 (entitled 'Progress of the Europa' and reproduced here) admitted the car would not be available on the home market for at least two years.

Unsurprisingly this did not prevent the company from using a photograph of its striking new creation in the Lotus Cars calendar for the year, but they company were

94

Europa S1 1966

TYPE 46

PICTURE DETAILS

Model box, Entex, Japan, 1/24th

Model, Hong Kong, plastic, 1/16th, cable operated from Shell petrol pump.

Model, Politoys, Italy, metal, 1/42nd

Lotus Cars, Calendar, 1967

Model, Dinky, England, die cast, 1/43rd

Renault news, December 1966.

First Lotus Europe S1 brochure, French, published by Temple Press of London 1966

Cut away drawing, Hatton, French brochure.

---

quick to announce that the first 500 cars would be earmarked for French dealers and priced at FFr 20, 000. Such a price undercut the Elan, but in truth these early Europas which actually carried the badge 'Europe' never matched the latter's broad appeal. Accordingly, the early brochure shown here (published by Temple Press of London in 1966) uses only French text, as does the 4-page specification sheet for the car featuring a cutaway drawing by Hatton. This was actually produced a year later by France's official Lotus importer, Roal Elysees of Paris. The first model shown is French too, a 1/43rd scale resin Europa made by DM Modeles in France and painted British racing green. Another 1/43rd scale model, this time in

TYPE 46

Europa S1 1966

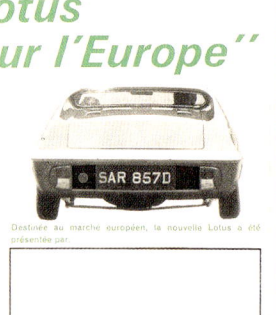

metal, was produced by Politoys in Italy, and the approximately 1/16th scale cable-operated plastic toy shown here was made in Hong Kong, concealing its battery within a replica Shell petrol pump. Finally the box of a model kit Lotus by Entex in 1/24th scale is also for a Type 46 Europa despite mistakenly carrying a Type 47 number plate. In the UK, press reports about the car were enthusiastic from the start – though not blind to its shortcomings, which included appalling rearward visibility – but to no avail. By the time the 644th and last car had been produced and sold, would-be British drivers were still waiting and indeed had to wait still longer until the arrival of the Type 54, the much improved Europa S2.

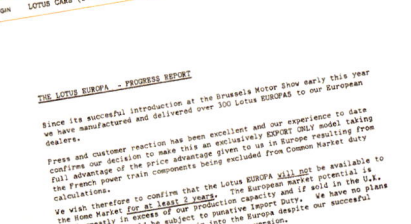

96

Racing Europa 1966

A road-going car based on racing car design principles, it didn't take anyone at Lotus Components long to realise that in the Type 46 Europa S1 the company might have the makings of a first rate circuit racer. The Renault 16 engine had to go of course, replaced by a dry-sump 1,594cc twin cam Lotus-Cosworth 13C, and the lightened chassis gained a host of modifications to the suspension, driveshafts and brake assemblies. Thereafter fuel injection boosted the power output to around 165bhp and a Hewland FT200 five speed gearbox replaced the Renault 'four'.

Externally, however, the most visible difference was the new, lighter bodyshell with wider, fatter arches and – in time – NACA ducts slotted in behind the rear doors. John Miles drove the car in its first official outing, taking first place at Brands Hatch on Boxing Day 1966 and subsequently going on to win his class in the following year's World Championship Brands Hatch 500 race with team mate Jackie Oliver. Thereafter the car became established as a fast and reliable competitor and,

PICTURE DETAILS

Model, DM Modeles, France, resin, 1/43rd

Lotus Cars, press news, 'Progress of the Europa', Oct 1967

Brochure, 4 page, France, 1967.

Model, SMTS, GB, white metal, 1/43rd

Model & box, Bandai, Japan, plastic Mabuchi motor, 1/20th

Model, Japan, tin.

Press release & photo for GKN 47.

Advert, Lotus Racing Sales, race programme.

TYPE 47

TYPE 47

Racing Europa 1966

after setting 10 new circuit lap records in 1968, became a favourite amongst modellers both in the UK and abroad. Of those shown here the white number 115 car is painted white metal by SMTS in Great Britain, and the box is for a motorised plastic kit of a Lotus 47GT made by Crown Model in Japan to 1/24th scale. Also shown is box artwork depicting the rear view of the Type 47, made by Nitto Kagaku in Japan to 1/24th scale. (The tin model of the high-wing variant is also Japanese.) Car number 29 was made by DM Modeles in France and represents the one-off Lotus Components works Type 47 with its distinctive twin snorkel air intakes, and the other model shown with its box is a Japanese Bandai Lotus 47GT in 1/20th scale with

PICTURE DETAILS

Black & white brochure, with notes by Andrew Ferguson.

Model box, Crown Model, Japan, motorised plastic kit, 1/24th

Model box, Nitto Kagaku, Japan, plastic kit, 1/24th

Model, DM Modeles, France, resin, 1/43rd

GLTL, press release and results with postcard, 1968

Advert, Lotus Racing Sales, Autocar September 1968

Cover and reverse, specification brochure, GKN 47D.

Print, Michael Turner.

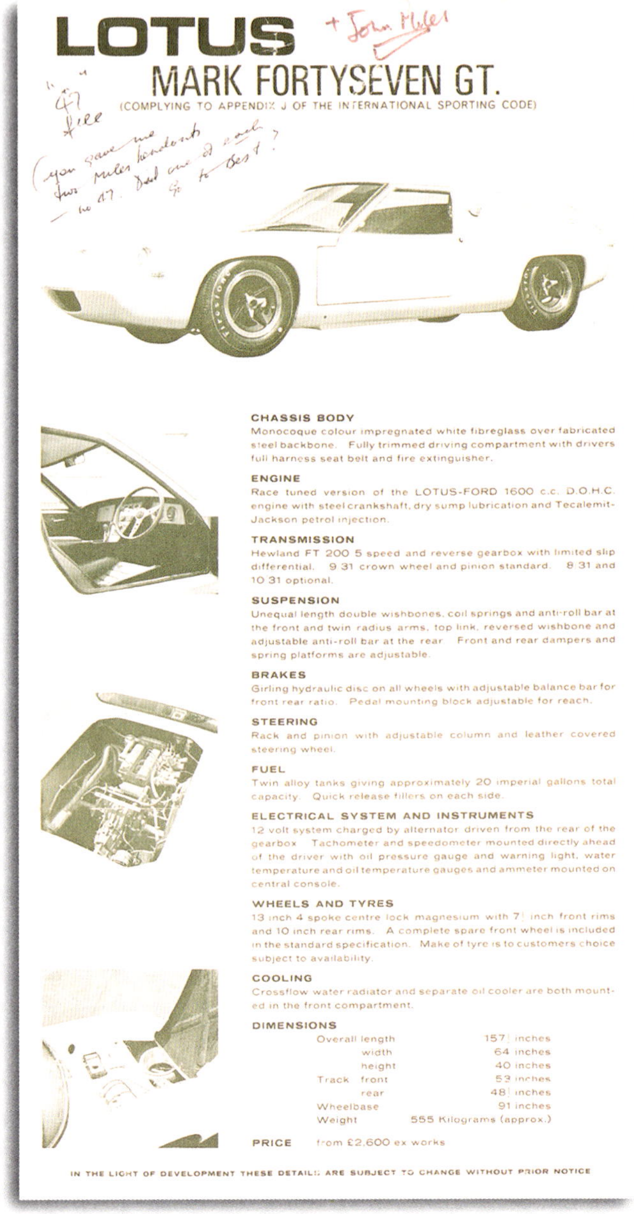

98

Racing Europa 1966

a Mabuchi motor. An advertisement placed by Lotus Racing Sales in Autocar in September 1968 offered a Type 47 for sale at just £3180; another was placed on the rear cover of a race-meeting programme and shows several cars for sale including a Type 47a. The press release and photograph for the GKN Type 47 are accompanied by a cover and reverse of a rare specification brochure for same; the other press release is one issued by Gold Leaf Team Lotus and includes the results for the Type 47 with postcard showing the car. The Type 47 was also painted by Michael Turner, a print of it (one of a set of four) being reproduced here, and finally this very rare type 47GT black & white brochure from the Team Lotus files includes handwritten notes on the copy by Andrew Ferguson.

TYPE 47

TYPE 48

Formula 2 1967

To meet the new Formula 2 regulations, which raised the permitted capacity limit to 1,600cc, Lotus employed the twin-camshaft Cosworth-Ford FVA – essentially a multivalve head fitted to a Cortina block – and a new but largely conventional chassis of the sort already seen in the Types 42 and 43. Announced in the usual fashion – see the Lotus Press news announcement below, and the two black and white press photographs and postcard issued with it at the time – the car made its debut in the Tasman championship and, closer to home, at the International Spring Club charity race at Oulton Park with Graham Hill at the wheel. In the by-now familiar Gold Leaf Team Lotus livery – officially announced in the press release also reproduced here – Hill's car didn't actually win on that occasion, but incredibly its best lap time of one minute 33.4 seconds succeeded in equalling the new Formula One record. Even so, by the end of the 1967 season Type 48s had won five races out of 25 compared to the rival Brabham cars' total of eleven. It wasn't a bad tally by any standards, but after three decades the ill-fated car is best remembered not for its performance but for the tragic accident at Hockenheim in April which claimed the life of Jim Clark OBE. He was just 32. The Type 48 also formed the subject of another print in the series by artist Michael Turner, and has been modelled

Formula 2 1967

TYPE 48

on several occasions. The box illustrated here is from an example made by UPC in Hong Kong to 1/32nd scale, a plastic kit car painted in the colours of Gold Leaf Team Lotus number 7. The number 12 car, a 1/43rd scale resin model also in the colours of Gold Leaf Team Lotus, was made by Tenariv in France.

PICTURE DETAILS

Model box, UPC, H.Kong, plastic kit, 1/32nd

Model, Tenariv, France, resin, 1/43rd

Team Lotus, black and white press photo, 1967

Gold Leaf Team Lotus, black and white press photo, 1968

Print, Micheal Turner.

Team Lotus Press news & postcard, 1967

Gold Leaf Team Lotus press release, 1968

Team Lotus, Pit boards, 1967

TYPE 49

Formula 1 1967

No fewer than a dozen stunning Grand Prix victories and a second Driver's World Championship for Graham Hill, a clutch of other equally impressive drivers, an all-new, all-conquering Ford Cosworth V8, and a really stunning looking design from any angle – that the 1967 Type 49 Lotus is still celebrated as one of the greatest single-seaters ever to have left the factory is perhaps hardly surprising. This was, after all, the first car to use the new 3 litre Ford Cosworth DFV or Double Four Valve, an engine which (for once, without a word of exaggeration) was to completely dominate Formula One for the whole of the coming decade. Just what Chapman needed given the unsatisfactory performance of the BRM H16 in 1966, it was developed with the technical assistance of Ford of Britain's Harry Copp, not to mention his considerable investment by the standards of the time of around £100, 000. Significantly Colin Chapman's close relationship with the DFV's creators Mike Costin and Keith Duckworth (who had met at Lotus in the 1950s) also meant the new car was able to actually evolve alongside the new power unit. The happy result being

Formula 1 1967

TYPE 49

of course that in the Type 49 one finds a purposeful design in which the engine, gearbox and chassis are all completely integrated in a way which had never previously been the case. With the 90-degree V8's stressed crankcase functioning as another chassis member, the car's monocoque was in effect little more than a simple nacelle containing the driver. Seating the driver as low as possible to make the most of the engine's superbly low and narrow profile, the whole ensemble was also incredibly light – reports at the time quoted 400bhp from 9,000rpm, and in something which weighed no more than a roadgoing Mini – thanks in part to new rocker arms, cast magnesium suspension uprights and new super lightweight wide-section wheels. It was left to Graham Hill and Jim Clark to prove the design's worth, however, and in June 1967

PICTURE DETAILS

Model, Merikits, Italy, white metal, 1/43rd

Model 49B, Merikits, Italy, white metal, 1/43rd

Rear wing, Gold Leaf Team Lotus, 1970

Autosport October 1969

Group Lotus Calendar 1970

Print, Michael Turner.

Model, unknown, Japan, tin, 9"

Advert, Autolite, Autosport, April 1968

Advert, Rob Walker, Autosport, March 1968.

Calender, Group Lotus, 1970

TYPE 49

Formula 1 1967

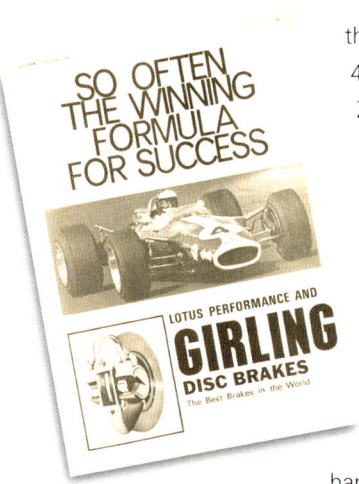

they took the first two of the 12 Type 49s built between '67 and '69 to Zandvoort for the Dutch Grand Prix. The results were far from disappointing, the former rocketing away from pole position although he was soon foced to retire, and the latter assuming the lead, setting a devastating pace (and new lap record) and handing the new car the first of five victories in a season in which Type 49s also took pole position in 12 succesive events. The following season Clark did it again – what was to prove his last victory, in the South African Grand Prix, bringing his total to 25 – before his place was assumed by Jackie Oliver. For the remainder of the year he partnered Hill, who showed where he was heading with a very quick win at Jarama. By the season's end, however, the Type 49 story was far from concluded and in the new 49B – distinguished by a more wedge-shaped profile, a slightly longer wheelbase and adjustable front and rear wings – Hill won again at Monaco, a victory commemorated by the Trophy shown here which was awarded to him on May 26, 1968. An original rear wing of the same type is pictured here too, incidentally, though from a later 1970 car, and also shown in action on the cover of an issue of Autocar magazine dated October 1969. Unsurprisingly the car and its victories (Hill won again at Monaco the following year, as shown in the accompanying Michael Turner painting) was to form the basis of numerous advertisements. Those shown include four produced by Team Lotus suppliers celebrating the car's successes, and another for Rob Walker's Corsley Garage which appeared in Autosport magazine in March 1968. The victorious Type 49s also appeared in the official 1968, 1969 and 1970 Gold Leaf Team Lotus calendars shown here, and in a saucier fold-out calendar which was issued by Motor Racing Magazine in 1969. Elsewhere it was depicted on a beer mat produced for Tom Wheatcroft's Donington Grand Prix Collection, and on the cover of the official programme produced for the Grand Prix

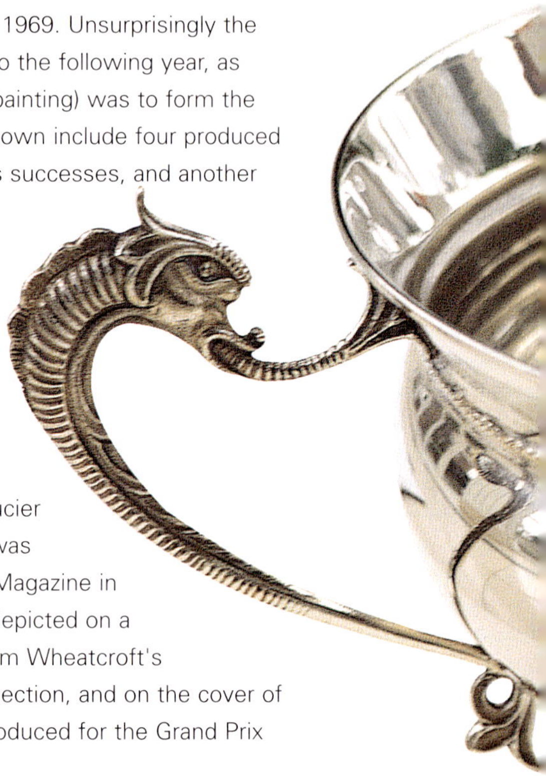

104

Formula 1 1967

PICTURE DETAILS

Model & box, Daishin, Japan, tin, 1/10th

Trophy, 26th Monaco Grand prix, 26th May 1968.

Beer mat, Donington Grand Prix Collection.

Model kit, Dinky, UK, white metal.

Advert, Girling, Autocar, Sept 1968

Model, Grand Prix Classics, China, plastic, 1/18th, 1998

TYPE 49

TYPE 49

Formula 1 1967

of the United States in 1968, a race which was won by Jochen Rindt driving another Type 49. Rindt's winning form was to last: whilst waiting for the new Type 72, he and John Miles competed in the 1970 season in a pair of Type 49Cs – characterised by their revised steering assemblies, 13" wheels and new uprights – Rindt winning yet another Monaco race for the 49 before it was finally pensioned off. The car's striking and distinctive shape, with and without the vast, pedal-operated rear wing of the sort which was very much in vogue in 1968, was also modelled by several companies around the world. The number 27 car shown here, for example, is a large (1/10th scale) model made by Tada in Japan and painted British racing green. Also shown is a rear view of a model Type 49, No.9, made by Meri kits in India, of white metal and painted with the colours of Gold Leaf Team Lotus. No.4 is another model by Merikits built to1/43rd scale and also painted British racing green, while the No.47 car and its accompanying box were made by Daishin in Japan, a rare 1/10th scale tin red-painted model. The other box depicted here, showing a drawing of a Type 49 carrying the number 1, is for a car made by Heller in France, the model inside being a 1/24th scale plastic kit car painted with the vibrant colours of the Gold Leaf Team Lotus cars. Also shown is another large tin-plate model, also in

PICTURE DETAILS

Model, Tada, Japan, plastic, 1/10th
Model box, Heller, France, plastic, 1/24th
Whiskey Decanter, REM, India, china, 1/12th
Calender, Team Lotus, 1968
Calender, Gold Leaf Team Lotus, 1969
Calendar, Motor Racing Magazine, 1969
Programme, USGP, October 1968
Advert, Autolite, Autocar, Sept 1968
Advert, Armstong, Autocar, Sept 1968

106

Formula 1 1967

Gold Leaf livery, a bizzare REM original made in India to 1/12th scale which is actually a Whisky decanter painted with the number 2, and a lovely 23-piece Dinky Action model kit of a Type 49 which very unusually is still in its original packaging. Finally the two shots showing the excellent detailing of a 1/18th scale Type 49 are of a Grand Prix Classics model made in China in 1998 – proof, were it needed, that the quality of the Type 49 with its superb Ford Cosworth engine has endured for more than 30 years and still attracts the collector's eye.

TYPE 49

TYPE 50

Elan +2 1967

Squeezing in an extra pair of seats for the children, the 1967 Elan +2 represented a radical departure for a company which (Ford-inspired Lotus Cortina aside) had hitherto restricted its road-going designs to fast, purposeful two-seaters. Not that there was any lack of purpose in the Elan +2, and with up to 126bhp from the by-now standard 1, 558cc Lotus-Ford Twin Cam it was certainly fast, but at the same time it was clearly a car which had evolved with its creator, and as Colin Chapman grew older he presumably began to give some thought to the plight of the motoring enthusiast who was nevertheless also by now a dad. Lengthening the chassis by just a foot, and the bodyshell by almost twice as much, but without uprating the engine to match meant the +2's performance was never going to eclipse that of a conventional Elan. But that said, improved aerodynamics – the new car was beautifully tapered, front and rear – meant the differential was less than one might have expected so that the new car could still achieve a credible 120mph and hit 60mph from standstill in around eight seconds.

It also had a better ride, thanks to the longer wheelbase, and later cars were quicker too, once they gained the new 'Big Valve' engine developed for the Elan Sprint. Styled by Ron Hickman, and based on the earlier 'Metier' prototype built at Cheshunt, the new car offered a good deal more space and refinement than the standard Elan, and a larger, more practical boot. What's more, offered only as a hardtop coupé (although some cars were later converted privately), it was also very well priced at £1, 672 in component form and £1, 923 for a factory built car.

Its more practical aspects were more than adequately summed up in the +2 brochure shown here, with illustrations of a family and a large amount of luggage which was supposedly able to fit into the boot. The other promotional material shown here includes an advertisement for

108

Elan +2 1967

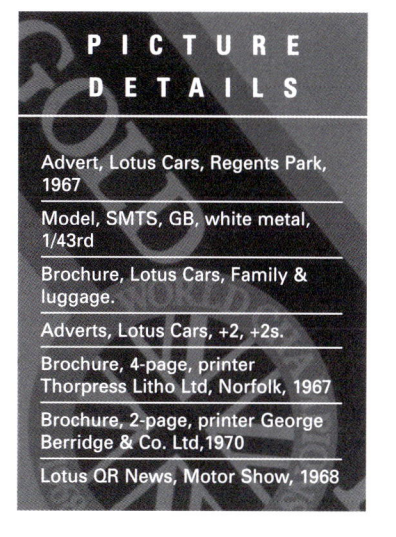

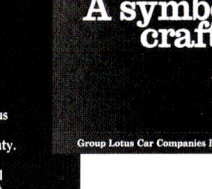

PICTURE DETAILS

Advert, Lotus Cars, Regents Park, 1967

Model, SMTS, GB, white metal, 1/43rd

Brochure, Lotus Cars, Family & luggage.

Adverts, Lotus Cars, +2, +2s.

Brochure, 4-page, printer Thorpress Litho Ltd, Norfolk, 1967

Brochure, 2-page, printer George Berridge & Co. Ltd, 1970

Lotus QR News, Motor Show, 1968

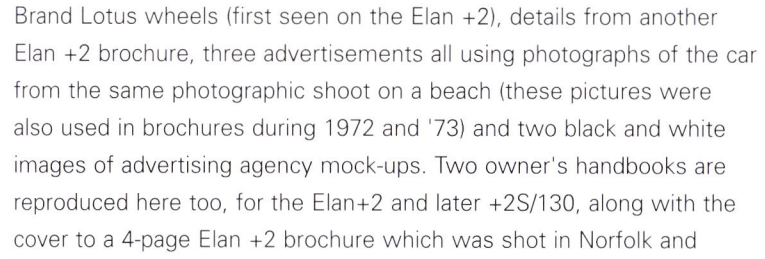

Brand Lotus wheels (first seen on the Elan +2), details from another Elan +2 brochure, three advertisements all using photographs of the car from the same photographic shoot on a beach (these pictures were also used in brochures during 1972 and '73) and two black and white images of advertising agency mock-ups. Two owner's handbooks are reproduced here too, for the Elan+2 and later +2S/130, along with the cover to a 4-page Elan +2 brochure which was shot in Norfolk and

TYPE 50

TYPE 50

Elan +2 1967

printed by Thorpress Litho Ltd of Norfolk in 1967. The advertisement in Dutch was produced for the grand opening of Lotus Holland, and the two variations of the later +2S/130 brochure were printed by George Berridge & Co. Ltd in 1970 and '71 to take account of the company's recent World Championship-winning performance.

Photographed parked outside the gates of London's Regent's Park, the Type 50 also put in an appearance on the cover of the Group Lotus Annual Report and Accounts for 1968 as well as in several brochures; the same year an edition of Lotus News published to coincide with the London Motor Show concentrated on Lotus 'QR' – for quality and reliability, clearly two key requirements needed to sell the idea of this new 'family' Lotus. In October 1968 the +2 was joined by another variant, the +2S, the 'S' standing for Special Equipment and whose

Lotus +2 'S' ... for the discerning motorist who requires the renowned Lotus roadholding and performance coupled to an attractive two plus two body. The 'S' combines the handbuilt reliability, safety and comfort of previous Lotus models engineered to an even higher degree of luxury; a luxury which offers forty detail refinements to the mechanical and coachwork specification.

World Champions 1963 · 1965 · 1968

110

Elan +2 1967

new enhanced specification benefitted from the addition of improved interior trim, an alternator and extra kit including front fog lamps. The 'S' – which was actually announced a year previously via the single-sided information sheet reproduced here and the accompanying copy of Lotus Press News dated October 1967 – was also, significantly, the first-ever Lotus road car which could not be ordered in component form. Finally, the model, one of suprisingly few produced of this popular and enduring car which in total sold some 5,200 examples before being retired in 1974, was made by SMTS in Great Britain of white metal painted blue and silver and to 1/43rd scale

PICTURE DETAILS

Annual report, Group Lotus, 1968
Handbooks, Elan+2 & +2s130.
Sales sheet, Brand Lotus wheels, 1968
Advert mock-up, Lotus Cars, +2.
Advert, opening of Lotus Holland.
Brochure, 6-page, printer George Berridge & Co. Ltd, 1971
Information sheet, Elan+2 SE, 1967
Lotus Press news, Oct 1967
Lotus press news, Motor show, 1972

TYPE 50

TYPE 51

Formula Ford 1967

For what was essentially a formula three car with narrower wheels and tyres, and a Ford Cortina GT pushrod engine, Lotus was in a good position to meet the demand when the new Formula Ford single-seater category was launched in 1967, and quickly applied itself to rejigging the old Type 22/31 spaceframe to accept the 1.5 litre Ford block. Mildly tuned to develop between 80 and 90bhp, the Lotus Type 51 clearly hit the spot immediately, so that by the time the first car went racing – at Brands Hatch, in July 1967 – the entry list of 20 included no fewer than 15 Lotus cars, the majority of which were the new Types 51s. A Type 51 took pole too, before spinning off and out, but Ray Allen in another Type 51 led almost unchallenged to take the flag and was followed home by a trio of older Type 31s with two Type 51s coming in fifth and sixth. Sold through Motor Racing Stables at Brands, already a well-established Lotus customer, the car cost just £955 fully-built and was soon joined by several modified versions including, in 1968, a one-off 'flower power' fun-car, the 51R, a less-than-serious attempt to turn it into a road car. Incredibly someone bought it,

Formula Ford 1967

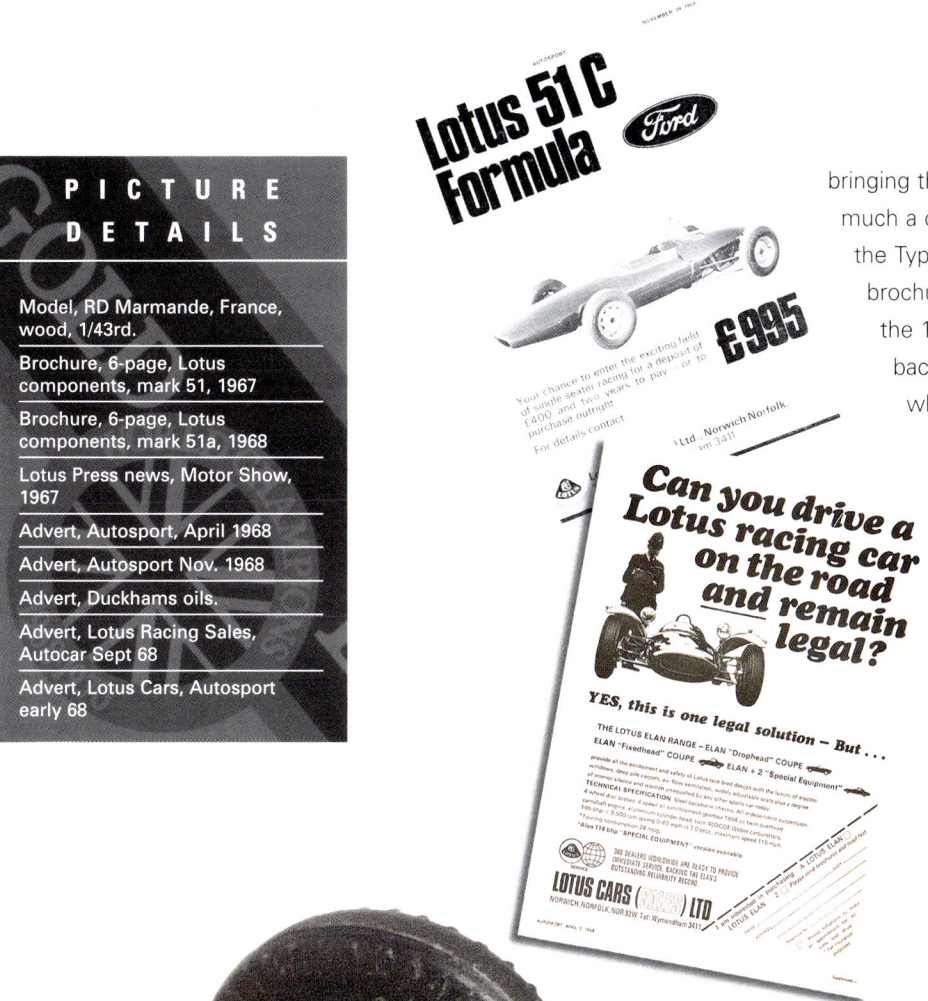

PICTURE DETAILS

Model, RD Marmande, France, wood, 1/43rd.

Brochure, 6-page, Lotus components, mark 51, 1967

Brochure, 6-page, Lotus components, mark 51a, 1968

Lotus Press news, Motor Show, 1967

Advert, Autosport, April 1968

Advert, Autosport Nov. 1968

Advert, Duckhams oils.

Advert, Lotus Racing Sales, Autocar Sept 68

Advert, Lotus Cars, Autosport early 68

bringing the total sold to a healthy (if disputed) 218 all-told. Very much a customer car, a welter of sales material was produced for the Type 51 including two broadly similar versions of the one brochure for the Types 51 & 51A, an advertisement to promote the 1968 Lotus Formula Ford Trophy and which appeared on the back of Autosport early that year, another for the Type 51C which appeared in Autosport in November, and one for Lotus Racing Sales (Autocar, September 1968) promoting the Type 51B. The curious Type 51R (R for road) was featured in the 1967 London Motor Show edition of Lotus Press news, and the same car was featured in an Autosport advertisement in April the following year. Duckhams also used a standard race car in its own advertisements, as seen here. The model is a yellow scratch-built wooden car made by RD Marmande in France, to 1/43rd scale and beautifully detailed.

TYPE 51

TYPE 54

Europa S2 1968

Once again intended – initially at least – only for export, the second-series Europa S2 was visibly not dissimilar to its predecessor although the factory took the opportunity to replace the latter's fiddly, labour-intensive bonded-on fuselage with a detachable body which simply bolted onto the chassis in much the same way as did the Elan's. Crash repairers must have been grateful at the time for the change; later restorers certainly were. Mechanically little changed however with only minor tweaks to the pedal box, wheel bearings and so on. But inside it was a more luxurious and refined machine than its forerunner with fuller instrumentation set into a polished wooden dashboard, opening side windows (made possible by the inclusion of slender quarterlights) and adjustable seats – a long overdue modification. Perhaps even more significant than these changes though was the decision a year later to at last sell the car on the home market, and the first cars went on sale for £1,667 in July 1969. That was for a complete car, home-builders having to wait a little while longer until a purchase tax-avoiding component version went on sale for just £1,275.

Between 1968 and August 1971, by which time Renault had ceased production of the

114

Europa S2 1968

TYPE 54

1,470cc engine, 3,615 S2 Europas had been sold – a superb total for such an uncompromising car, although even this was soon to be comprehensively eclipsed by its replacement, the Europa Twin-Cam Type 74. Of the 3,615 total, no fewer than 865 were actually Federal-specifications cars produced for the North American market and which required so many detail modifications that they were awarded their own type-number: 65.

Changes included a larger 1,565cc (from the Renault 16TS, the modified 1,470cc falling foul of the regulations), a catch tank and charcoal canister to overcome any emissions problems – this in 1969 – and a slightly revised bodyshell with raised front wings and headlamps, new door locks, a different wiring loom able to sustain brake-fail and hazard warning lights. With an SAE-rating of 87.5bhp at 6,000rpm – 80bhp, in other words – the Type 65's performance at least was similar to those Type 54 cars produced for the European and domestic markets. The number and

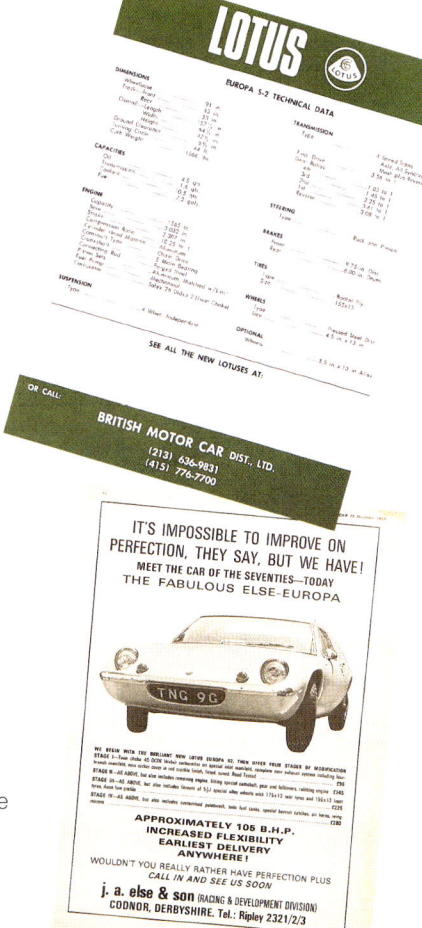

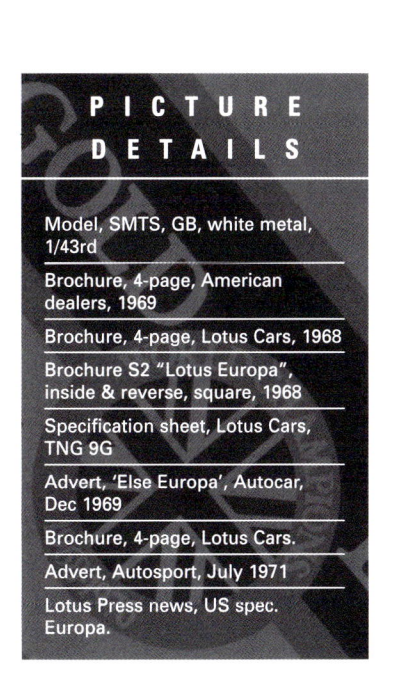

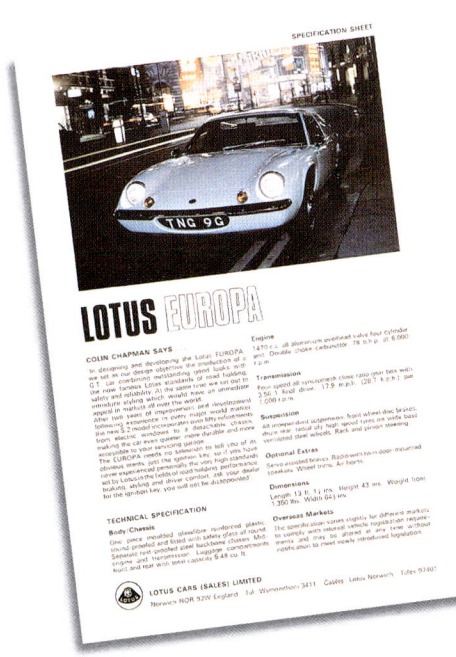

PICTURE DETAILS

Model, SMTS, GB, white metal, 1/43rd

Brochure, 4-page, American dealers, 1969

Brochure, 4-page, Lotus Cars, 1968

Brochure S2 "Lotus Europa", inside & reverse, square, 1968

Specification sheet, Lotus Cars, TNG 9G

Advert, 'Else Europa', Autocar, Dec 1969

Brochure, 4-page, Lotus Cars.

Advert, Autosport, July 1971

Lotus Press news, US spec. Europa.

115

TYPE 54

Europa S2 1968

nature of the changes more than anything underline the fact that the US was at this time clearly a very important market for the company and the 4-page black and white Europa S2 brochure shown here was actually produced for the firm's American dealers in 1969 as part of the extensive promotional push for the new car. The cover and reverse of the Europa S2 technical data sheet is also for the US market car, and Lotus Press News also made mention of the car, a copy of the relevant issue being reproduced here. Clearly Colin Chapman wasn't about to waste all the 'free' publicity garnered by his cars' racing successes Stateside, including of course the Indy victory. The other literature, however, was produced closer to home, the 4-page colour brochure for the car issued for the home market in 1968 including the Type 49 F1 car inside as one of the company's best-ever ambassadors. From the same year is shown the cover, interior and reverse of a square colour brochure with pictures of an S2 (although it is entitled simply 'Lotus Europa'), another Europa S2 brochure, and also two otherwise identical Lotus Europa S2 specification sheets, one featuring the pale blue press car (TNG 9G) and the other showing a later

PICTURE DETAILS

Model, AMR, France, white metal, 1/43rd

Brochure, S2 "Lotus Europa", cover, square, 1968

Lotus Cars, Specification sheet.

Technical data sheet, reverse, US market, BAH 977J

4 page Europa S2 brochure.

Advert, Autosport, December 1970

Advert, July, 1969

Europa S2 1968

TYPE 54

red car. The S2 was also extensively advertised throughout its production life, and shown here are an advertisement from Autocar dated December 1969 for the 'Else Europa', an aftermarket development of the Series 2, and three separate full-page advertisements for ordinary production S2s. Finally, the models shown are a racing Zakspeed Europa, made in France by AMR to 1/43rd scale of white metal painted white with the number 22, and another 1/43rd scale Europa S2 made by SMTS in Great Britain, also of white metal this time painted a vibrant banana yellow.

TYPE 56

Indianapolis Car 1968

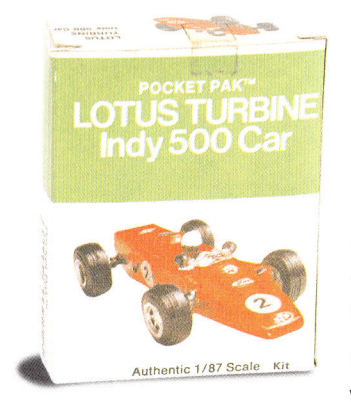

With a distinctive wedge profile, Ferguson Formula four-wheel drive, and a Pratt and Whitney gas turbine engine burning aviation-grade kerosene, somehow the words 'pioneering', 'radical', even 'revolutionary', seem insufficient to fully encompass the technical tour-de-force that was the 1968 Type 56 Lotus Indianapolis car and its kissing cousin in F1, the Type 56B. All-wheel drive wasn't actually new to the Brickyard – the P104 Novi had raced there, albeit without success, as early as 1965 – and neither was the gas turbine, having crossed over from American Speedway racing to come within an ace of winning the 1967 event. But the Type 56 was something else altogether, a genuine hands-across-the-water effort between United Aircraft of Canada, STP-boss Andy Granatelli, and of course Lotus which clearly had the racing skills to make it all happen. The Type 56B version made its debut two years later at Brands Hatch when this press release and dramatic official Gold Leaf Team Lotus photograph were issued to announce the arrival of the new 'Lotus jet car'. In F1 guise it also

118

Formula 1 1971

TYPE 56B

made the cover of Autosport in May 1971, with journalist Simon Taylor – still with the magazine 30 years later – tracktesting the Type 56B version at Silverstone. In the US Road & Track magazine had previously featured the Type 56, giving the 'Lotus Indy Turbine car' a double-page spread with an attractive cutaway and plan view. The clean profile also made it more of a winner for the model-makers than on the circuit, and shown here are three British-made 1/43rd scale cars by SMTS, the box from one by Entex in Japan, a 'Pocket Pak' 1/87th scale plastic kit painted red with the number 2, another box and car, this time made by MPC in the US to 1/25th scale, and a Scalextric model of a Type 56B made in France. The three British models are all of white metal, one a Type 56, the other two both Type 56Bs, one wearing the famous Gold Leaf Team Lotus livery and the other black and gold to represent the car entered by Worldwide Racing in the Italian Grand Prix at Monza.

PICTURE DETAILS

Model, Entex, Japan, plastic, 1/87th	
Model and box, MPC, USA, plastic, 1/25th	
Model Type 56, SMTS, GB, white metal, 1/43rd	
Model Type 56B GLTL, SMTS, GB, white metal, 1/43rd	
Model Type 56B Worldwide Racing, SMTS, GB, white metal, 1/43rd	
Model, Scalextric, France, 1972	
Press release, STP news, 1968	
Press release & photo, GLTL.	
Autosport, May 1971	
Cutaway drawing, Road & Track, 1969	

119

TYPE 57/58

Formula 1 & 2 1968

In reality little more than obscure design studies from the late-1960s, the confusion surrounding the Lotus Types 57 and 58 is perhaps best characterised by the fact that the latter one actually appeared first, in Formula 2 guise, before being comprehensively rebuilt as a Formula 1 prototype and hastily retro-named the Type 57. With its innovative De Dion suspension, the monocoque which formed the basis of both cars clearly underwent extensive testing at Hethel, evidence for which is provided by an original snapshot from the Classic Team Lotus archive shown here. But Graham Hill was never happy with the car and like Jochen Rindt he chose the Type 49T instead when contesting the Tasman Championship. As a result the monocoque was eventually abandoned in the Team stores and remained there until 1999 when finally the decision was made to finish the car, in June 2000 the press release shown here was issued marking the end of it's long restoration at the hands of Classic Team Lotus.

Formula 3 & 2 1969

Designed to compete in both Formula 2 and 3 (and later Formula Ford) the Type 59 in its various guises attracted some world class drivers, including Jochen Rindt, Andrea de Adamich before he went to Ferrari, John Miles Graham Hill and Emerson Fittipaldi. Even so, it's first race – Easter 1969 at Thruxton – was perhaps its finest, and saw Rindt battling through from the back of the field to overtake even Jackie Stewart before scoring the first of four wins in just eight races. Several mementoes of the car's 1969 season survive, including a signed photograph of a Formula 3 variant signed by works driver Bev Bond, an advertisement placed by Lotus Racing Sales in Autosport the same year for a works Type 59 F3, and another for all the works cars which appeared in the same magazine in November the following year. The works F3 team also made the cover of the same magazine in November 1969, while Gold Leaf Team Lotus also placed its own advertisements promoting merchandise associated with the team. The model, however, depicts the high wing F2 version of the car, a 1/43rd scale wooden model by RD Marmande in France, scratch-built and painted British racing green.

PICTURE DETAILS

Photograph, Classic Team Lotus archive, 1967

Press release, Classic Team Lotus, June 2000

Model Type 59, RD Marmande, France, wood, 1/43rd

Autosport, November 1969

Signed photo Bev Bond, GLTL F3.

Advert, Lotus Racing Sales, Autosport, 1969

Advert, GLTL, Autosport Nov 1970

Advert, GLTL, Gold Leaf merchandise, 1970

TYPE 59

TYPE 60

Seven S4 1969

Controversially styled by Peter Lucas and Alan Barrett, the 1969 Seven S4 may never have reached its somewhat optimistic targets but with sales of 15 a week at one time (leading to some 625 in total) it was by no means unsuccessful. In addition, thanks to an extensive and by Lotus standards relatively glamourous marketing campaign, 30 years on it is associated with some of the company's most distinctive and characterful memorabilia. Even the Type 60 technical specification sheet shown here has a decidedly 'Seventies' feel to it, whilst much the same can be said of the two advertisements for the car which appeared in the normally staid Autosport editions for July and August 1970. At the same time, the press were issued with photographs from the 'fashion shoot' which had produced these advertisements and their associated brochures – presumably all part of a concerted bid to make the S4 with its more spacious interior and optional hardtop one of the 'happening' cars of this frantic decade. More sober, perhaps, is the Lotus Seven Register newsletter dated Autumn 1970 using the new S4 on its cover, the press release issued by Lotus Components (soon to be renamed Lotus Racing) at the Earls Court Motor Show, and this other, more down to earth specification sheet for a similar car. Two different model

122

Seven S4 1969

PICTURE DETAILS

Model box, Nichimo, Japan, plastic, 1/20th, 1972

Model, Lesney 'Matchbox', GB, die cast, 1/63rd

Specification sheet, Lotus Cars, 1969

Advert, Autosport, July 1970

Advert, Autosport, August 1970

Model box, Nichimo, Japan, plastic, 1/20th, 1971

Press photo, Lotus Cars, 1970

Press release, Lotus Components, Earls Court Motor show 1971

Newsletter, Lotus Seven Register, Autumn 1970

Specification sheet, Lotus Cars, 1970

Specification sheets, Lotus Components Ltd, 1970

boxes are also shown, for the same Type 60 1/20th scale plastic kit made by Nichimo in Japan, and a memorably yellow die cast Type 60 made by Lesney Matchbox in the UK. In the final analysis the car was very much a child of its time, and it undoubtedly did well for Lotus even though there was little enthusiasm from the company's overseas dealers, particularly in the US. But when production switched from Lotus Racing to Lotus Cars late in 1971, Chapman had already marked its card. Clearly keen to push his company ever further upmarket, a stay of execution was granted for the S4 until stocks of chassis and other parts were exhausted, but by October 1972 the last Seven left the factory and Hethel looked forward to the bright new era of the Elite, Eclat and Esprit range.

TYPE 60

TYPE 61

Formula Ford 1969

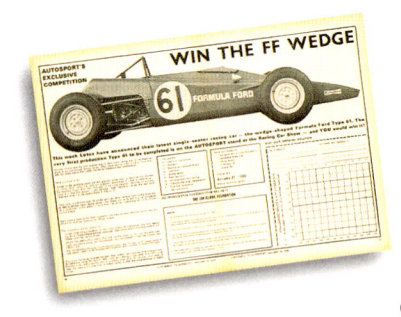

Launched at the 1969 Racing Car Show in London, and destined to sell nearly 250 units, the Type 61 was, like so many of its rivals designed to accept a range of different engines although it was offered with a 'preferred choice', namely the in-house Lotus-Holbay LH105 Ford 1600E. Evidently influenced by contemporary Indy car designs, the resin-bonded glassfibre body work with its tiny windscreen was clearly reminiscent of the foregoing Type 56 gas turbine car and as such brought a dash of international glamour to the Formula Ford arena – and at the same time more than a few successes. The star of the Type 61 show was definitely Emerson Fittipaldi's future Type 72/F1 partner, Australian Dave Walker, scoring nine victories in Formula Ford which was certainly impressive though never quite enough to topple its reigning Alexis and Merlyn rivals. To help sell the car, Lotus produced a surprisingly commercial brochure (for a pure racing car, that is) – the front and rear of which are shown here. The company also placed a higher than usual number of advertisements,

124

Formula Ford 1969

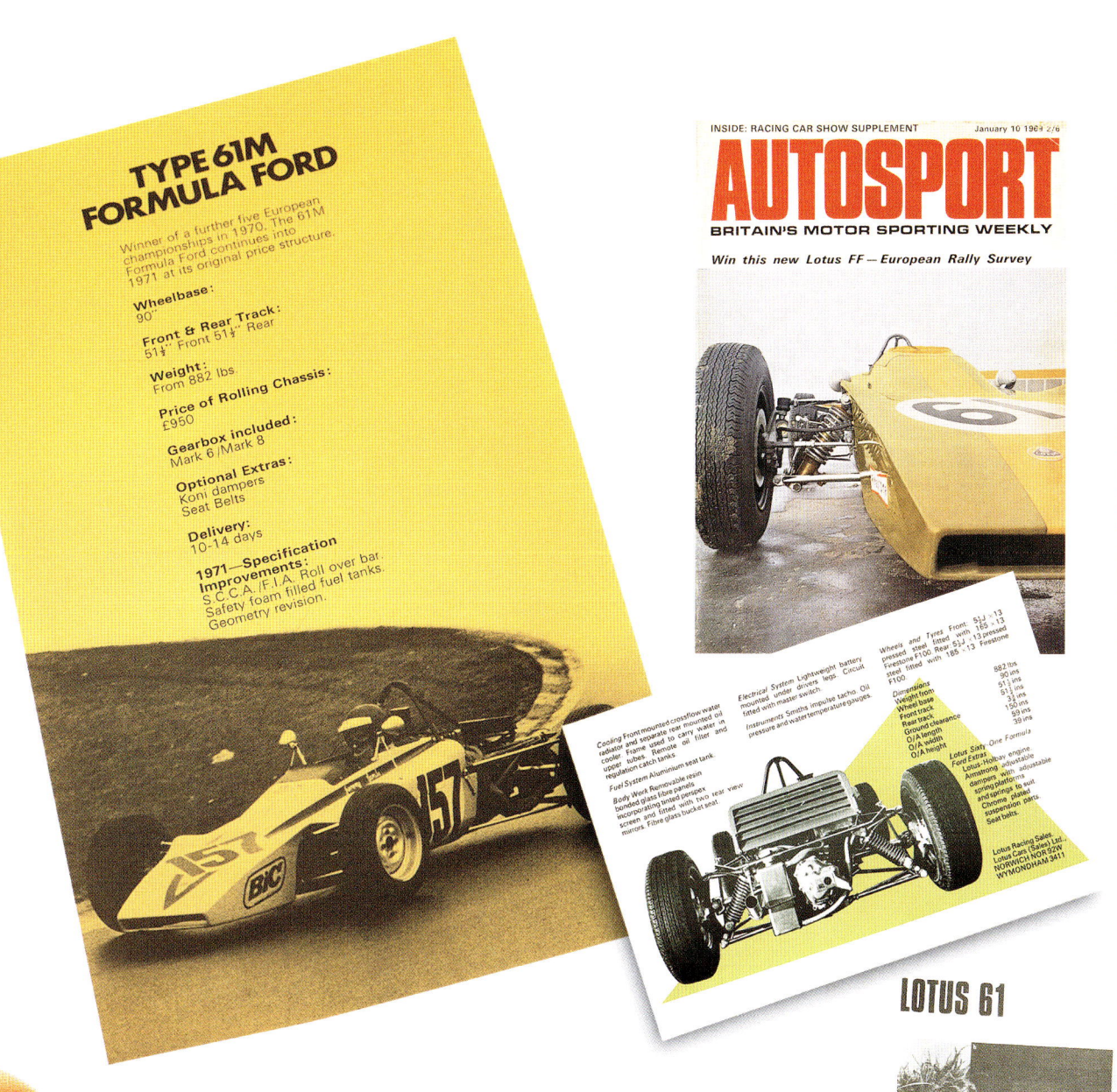

PICTURE DETAILS

Model, RD Marmande, France, wood, 1/43rd

Brochure, Lotus Racing Sales, front rear & inside, 1969

Advert, Dutch Lotus dealers.

Advert, Autosport, January 1969

Adverts, Lotus Racing Sales, Autosport, 1969

Lotus press news, with photo, Motor Show, 1971

Brochure / Information sheet, Lotus Racing Sales, 1971

Competition entry form, Autosport January 1970

those shown including no fewer than three from Autosport magazine. One of these, dated January 1969, heralds the new season and cheekily previews the 'winning car' – a Type 61, of course – whilst the other advertisement reproduced here was for the Dutch Lotus dealer network and uses the Type 61's image and record, merely as a way to sell the company's road cars. Rather more unusual is the Lotus Cars press release showing the lightweight single-seater as an armoured fighting vehicle, and the cover and spread from Autosport in January 1970 which gave readers the chance to enter a competition to actually win one of the most competitive racing cars of its time. Finally, the orange-painted model is another made by RD Marmande in France, scratch built from wood and to 1/43rd scale, and the very nicely produced information card is one referring to the later Type 61M – a variant with new front end bodywork and reduced frontal area.

TYPE 61

TYPE 62

Sports Prototype 1969

Gold Leaf Team Lotus offer for sale their two Lotus Europa 2-litre type 62 cars

Certain winners in the 2-litre Prototype Championship

Having completed the engine development programme for the LOTUS LV 240 2 litre twin overhead camshaft engine, these cars which won 7 out of ten races in 1969 are now released for sale. Full tubular chassis, Formula One suspension, Z.F five speed gearboxes, fuel injection engines developing 240 B.H.P. and full range of spares available. The fact that only two of these cars exist ensures excellent appearance money

Offers invited in the region of £6,000 each.

Team Lotus Ltd., Norwich, NOR 92W, Norfolk. Tel: Wymondham 2016

Whilst the Europa was for a while very much 'for export only', interest in a racing version came from home as well as abroad, especially after the Type 47 variant proved its worth repeatedly, most noticeably in the BOAC 500 World Championship where it won its class. The factory's response was to produce the Type 62, a much-modified Sports Prototype designed to compete in the short-lived but exotic Appendix J Group 6 class. It was powered by an early forerunner of the long-lived Type 907 engine, a 2.0-litre Vauxhall Victor-derived four cylinder unit with twin overhead camshafts and four valves per cylinder. Be-winged and be-spoilered but outwardly remarkably similar to its Europa ancestor, underneath the Type 62 was quite a different confection altogether. With massive flared arches to accommodate F1-style wheels and tyres, a complex multi-tubular spaceframe chassis in place of the expected backbone, and a suspension set up that was also much closer in design to that fitted to the company's fastest single-seaters. Often against small fields admittedly, in this form the car and it's sister Team car notched up several wins as well as a third place in the TT and a fourth in the Trophy of the Dunes at Zandvoort. Later sold for a seemingly modest £6,000 (the Autosport advertisement for which is reproduced here), the cars were also featured on a promotional advertisement 'Racing for

126

Sports Prototype 1969

TYPE 62

Britain' inviting readers to send away for a reproduction of one of Michael Turner's excellent paintings of the Gold Leaf Team Lotus cars in action. Two views are also shown here of a rare 1/43rd scale resin model made by Provence Moulage in France and painted in the colours of the Gold Leaf Team Lotus, along with an official press release and information card on the car and its new engine.

Initially the latter had proved to be the car's Achilles heel, but by revealing flaws early on which were subsequently amended, the Type 62 should be remembered as the car which laid the foundations for an engine which was to be the company's mainstay for nearly 25 years.

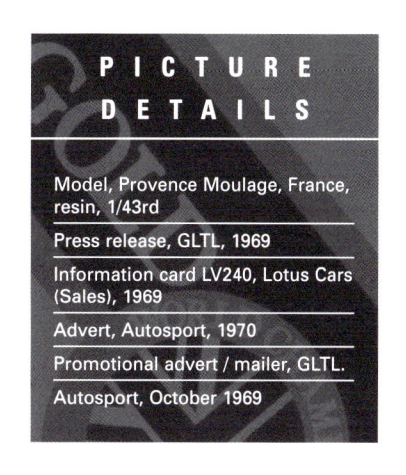

PICTURE DETAILS

Model, Provence Moulage, France, resin, 1/43rd

Press release, GLTL, 1969

Information card LV240, Lotus Cars (Sales), 1969

Advert, Autosport, 1970

Promotional advert / mailer, GLTL.

Autosport, October 1969

TYPE 63

Formula 1 1969

With time on his hands following the cancellation of the Belgian GP, Colin Chapman turned his hand to a new design borrowing ideas from both the Types 56 and 64 with a view to delivering a fourth Formula One World Championship – something, incidentally, which had never before been achieved.

Sticking with the superb 3 litre Cosworth DFV, he conceived a complex scheme to turn it around and, via a centrally-mounted gearbox and a system of transfer gears, power all four wheels whilst maintaining the optimum weight distribution for this striking new single-seater. In this form, the new Type 63 looked good and seemed to work effectively. But both Graham Hill and Jochen Rindt disliked the seating position and refused to drive, prompting Chapman to bring in John Miles who drove the car for its debut at Clermont Ferrand before retiring after completing just one lap. Later joined by Jo Bonnier, but with no more success, the baton then passed on to Mario

128

Formula 1 1969

PICTURE DETAILS

Model, Model Plus, Italy, white metal, 1/43rd

Rear wing, Classic Team Lotus.

Press release and photo, GLTL, 1969

Photo, Team Lotus promotional material.

Motor, Sept 1969

Model, white metal, 1/43rd

TYPE 63

Andretti, a firm fan of 4WD, who then crashed out badly after grounding the car in Germany. Eventually even Chapman was forced to admit his car was too heavy to win, but it was at least an interesting experiment and today is commemorated by a number of models including this Type 63 made by Model Plus in Italy. Shown from three different views, it is a 1/43rd scale white metal item painted with the colours of Gold Leaf Team Lotus and bearing the number 9. It is accompanied by another white metal model, built to 1/43rd scale, of the Gold Leaf Team Lotus car transporter which was used in late 1960s and early 1970s. Shown too is a variation of the Type 63 rear wing, available to collectors from Classic Team Lotus, and the Gold Leaf team's official press release and press photograph for the car's launch in 1969. From the same era, the black and white photographic print is also an original having been retouched by hand for use in the team's promotional material. Finally, the car also appeared on the cover of Motor magazine in September 1969, headlining an extensive feature titled 'The Lotus Story'.

TYPE 64

Indianapolis Car 1969

With a USAC ban, initially anyway, on cars like the Type 56 with four wheel drive and gas turbines, Chapman decided to modify his assault on the 1969 Indianapolis 500 and planned to do it with an all-new design destined to be the most powerful Lotus built so far: the 700bhp STP-Lotus-Ford Type 64 As was made clear in STP's own news release issued at the time (and reproduced here, with an official press photograph of the car's early development chassis) after an about turn by USAC on four wheel drive meant it was once more employed and again required the 3.0 litre Quad Cam Ford to be turned round in the chassis. Such a modification sounds complicated, but in fact allowed the most to be made of four-wheel traction by ensuring the most efficient disposition possible of the car's major masses. Even so, the car – which was unveiled to the world's press with an official Team Lotus press release dated March 25th and timed to coincide exactly with aforementioned US-only STP publicity – seemed ill-fated even before the start. In practice for the big day Mario Andretti posted a

130

Indianapolis Car 1969

massive 171mph before a hub overheated and sent him flying into the wall. For his part Jochen Rindt spun out completely, albeit without damaging the car, leaving only Hill to qualify and even then at a comparatively modest 160mph.

With no time to fix the problem the cars were withdrawn, leaving the Type 64 as one of the most complex Lotus designs ever constructed but one which, like the later Types 88 and 96, was never to actually contest a race. The box and car number 3 shown here are by Polistil, an Italian-made 1/25th scale die cast model with an engine cover but no engine, the metallic blue car is an unusual colour variation of the same model. That both versions lack an engine is strangely significant, for when the cars came back to Hethel beneath a swirling cloud of controversy the engines remained with Ford – and after three decades the two have yet to be reunited.

PICTURE DETAILS

Model and box, Polistil, Italy, die cast & plastic, 1/25th, 1974

Model, Polistil, Italy, die cast & plastic, 1/25th, 1974

STP Press News, March 1969

Team Lotus Press News, March 1969

Press photo, Ford USA, 1969

TYPE 64

131

SEVEN FILE 2
SUPER SEVEN FILE
THE LOTUS ELAN AND PLUS TWO BUYERS GUIDE
Lotus THE HISTORIC YEARS
RALLY LIBRARY
Talbot SUNBEAM-LOTUS
THE LOTUS ELAN AND PLUS TWO BUYERS GUIDE
LOTUS ELAN
Coupé, convertible, Plus 2
LOTUS SEVEN
TONY WEALE
Lotus turboesprit 1980-1986
Lotus Esprit 1975-1981
LOTUS 8
LOTUS SEVEN
Collection No.1
LOTUS ELAN 1963-1972
Collection No.2
LOTUS SEVEN
ROAD & TRACK ON LOTUS 1972-1983
LOTUS EUROPA 1966-1975
Lotus élite & éclat 1974-1981
practical CLASSICS & CAR RESTORER
on Lotus including Elan Restoration
Motor & Classic Cars
LOTUS 1979-1983
LOTUS SEVEN Super Profile
LOTUS ELAN Gold Portfolio 1962-1974
LOTUS HERITAGE
ROAD TEST LIMITED EDITION
LOTUS ELISE
Lotus
COLIN CHAPMAN'S LOTUS
Lotus Elise
The Complete Story
John Tipler
LOTUS
ALL THE CARS
Anthony Pritchard
The Single-Seat
LOTUS
Formula 1 & Indy Cars
Lotus story
LOTUS
THE THIRD GENERATION LOTUSES
ELITE, ECLAT, ESPRIT, EXCEL
TEAM LOTUS
LOTUS SEVEN
LOTUS107&107B FORD
Lotus Elan 1962-1973
LOTUS ELISE
LOTUS ELITE 1957-1964
LOTUS
Lotus élite & éclat 1974-1982
LOTUS CORTINA 1963-1970
LOTUS ESPRIT
Lotus
LOTUS
LOTUS ELAN Super Profile
LOTUS SINCE THE 70s
Illustrated LOTUS BUYER'S GUIDE
Graham Arnold
CLASSIC LOTUS FILE
Seven · Elite · Elan · Europa
THE ILLUSTRATED MOTORCAR LEGENDS
LOTUS ESPRIT TURBO
LOTUS ESPRIT
LOTUS Twin-Cam Engine
Miles Wilkins
Lotus 25
CLIMAX FWMV
A TECHNICAL APPRAISAL
THE MONOCOQUE REVOLUTION
LOTUS
SPORTS RACING CARS
ANTHONY PRITCHARD
THE LOTUS 1978
LOTUS: THE ELITE, ELAN, EUROPA
by Chris Harvey
SEVEN
The Lotus Elite
PROFILE PUBLICATIONS
AUTOSPORT FILE
Lotus
THE LOTUS
LOTUS SPORTS RACERS Gold Portfolio 1953-1965
LOTUS SEVEN AND CATERHAM
LOTUS 49
LOTUS
The Complete Story
Chris Harvey
LOTUS ELAN
MARK HUGHES
ロータス
LOTUS
The First Ten Years
IAN SMITH
LOTUS ELAN
The Complete Story
Mike Taylor
ロータス
The Lotus Elite
DENNIS E. ORTENBURGER
LOTUS SINCE THE 70s
LOTUS ELAN
ELAN PLUS 2
LOTUS SEVEN Gold Portfolio 1957-1973
CATERHAM SEVENS
LOTUS ELAN & SE 1989-1992
LOTUS ESPRIT
The Complete Story
Jeremy Walton
LOTUS ELAN
Collection No.1
Lotus Europa
Collection No.1
LOTUS ESPRIT TURBO
LOTUS FILE
THE ORIGINAL LOTUS ELAN 1962-1973
The Lotus Eleven
DENNIS E. ORTENBURGER
CORTINA
Workshop Manual 1969
LOTUS EUROPA Gold Portfolio 1966-1975
LOTUS ELAN
OWNERS WORKSHOP MANUAL
LOTUS
BRUCE GRANT-BRAHAM
LOTUS
9·11·15·17·19·23
LOTUS SEVEN Gold Portfolio 1957-1989
LOTUS
Chris Harvey
LOTUS Racing Cars
JOHN TIPLER
ROAD & TRACK ON LOTUS 1972-1983
LOTUS AND CATERHAM SEVEN

CHAPTER 3

68	Formula A	1969
69	Formula 3	1971
69	Formula 2	1970
69F	Formula Ford	1971
70	Formula A/5000	1970
72	Formula 1	1970
73	Formula 3	1972
74	Formula 2	1973
74	Europa twin cam	1971
75	Elite	1974
76	Formula 1	1974
76	Éclat & Éclat Sprint	1975
77	Formula 1	1976
78	Formula 1	1977
79	Formula 1	1978
79	Esprit S1 & S2	1976
80	Formula 1	1979
81	Sunbeam Lotus	1979

1970–1979

TYPE 69

Formula 2,3,Ford 1970

Another single-pronged assault on three different formulae – 2, 3 and Ford – the 1970 Type 69 grew out of a new requirement for F2 cars to be fitted with flexible aircraft-style rubber fuel tanks. Designed by Dave Baldwin, who had clearly learned many useful lessons from the Type 59, it made its debut at Thruxton for the first round of the European Championship. The colours were those of Jochen Rindt Racing, Rindt and his manager Bernie Ecclestone having taken over the factory F2 programme following the withdrawal of Roy Winklemann. The car was pitched against several other Type 69s including one driven by future F1 World Champion Emerson Fittipaldi. In the event, Rindt won – and won easily – a feat he repeated at Pau, Zolder and the Nürburgring during the same season: an impressive achievement, but still not good enough to put Lotus ahead of BMW and Tecno. The Team Lotus business card shown here dates from this period, and includes a very rare Jochen Rindt signature, whilst two of the cars modelled here represent the machines driven by Fittipaldi and Rindt himself. The first is a

134

Formula 2, 3, Ford 1970

TYPE 69

1/43rd scale scratch built model by RD Marmande in France, painted to represent Emerson's 1971 Team Bardahl car, whilst the second, also by RD Marmande and painted with the No.2, is an F2 Team Lotus car as driven by Rindt and Graham Hill.

The cover of Motor Sport magazine in August 1972 showed a particularly brilliant Emerson Fittipaldi performance – this time winning yet another race in the by then Moonraker-liveried Team Bardahl car. And finally three brochure/specification cars are reproduced here, showing the different formula variations of the Type 69. Some 65 cars were built in all, including those prepared for Formula Ford and F3, most using Cosworth FVA engines of 1,598cc initially and then of 1,980cc. Curiously, one car was also modified by Pete Lovely who cleverly grafted on the rear end of a Type 49B in order to contest the US and Canadian Grands Prix. He didn't win of course, but at least succeeded in adding another formula to the Type 69's impressive roster.

PICTURE DETAILS

Model, RD Marmande, France, wood, 1/43rd

Model, RD Marmande, France, wood, 1/43rd

Motor Sport, August 1972

Brochure/specification cards, Lotus Racing Sales, 1971

Business card, Team Lotus.

Advert, Team Lotus Ltd, Autosport, November 1970

TYPE 70

Formula 5000 1970

Chapman wanted his new car to be conceived, designed and built in just 10 weeks in order to make the Formula 5000 Series race at Riverside. In fact, however, the 1970 Type 70 didn't make it in time – not quite – but debuted instead at Sebring just a few weeks later, where it went pretty well for a dozen laps with Andretti before the engine blew up when he had a seemingly unassailable 18 second lead. Andretti walked out of the story there and then, but the Type 70 went on to win several races in the US, though curiously it never won a single race in Europe. Closer to home it proved consistently unequal to the challenge of its McLaren, Lola and Surtees rivals. The Team Lotus build cards for two of the (recently revised figure) nine Type 70 chassis constructed survive and are shown here. One, the show car, was never actually delivered to Bill Brack although he bought another. And the other, fitted with a 'tartan' seat was built for Jock Russell, the only private Type 70 entrant in the UK. The cars were also promoted fairly heavily both directly and in-directly using advertisements – like the one shown here for Lotus Racing Limited which appeared in several magazines and books such

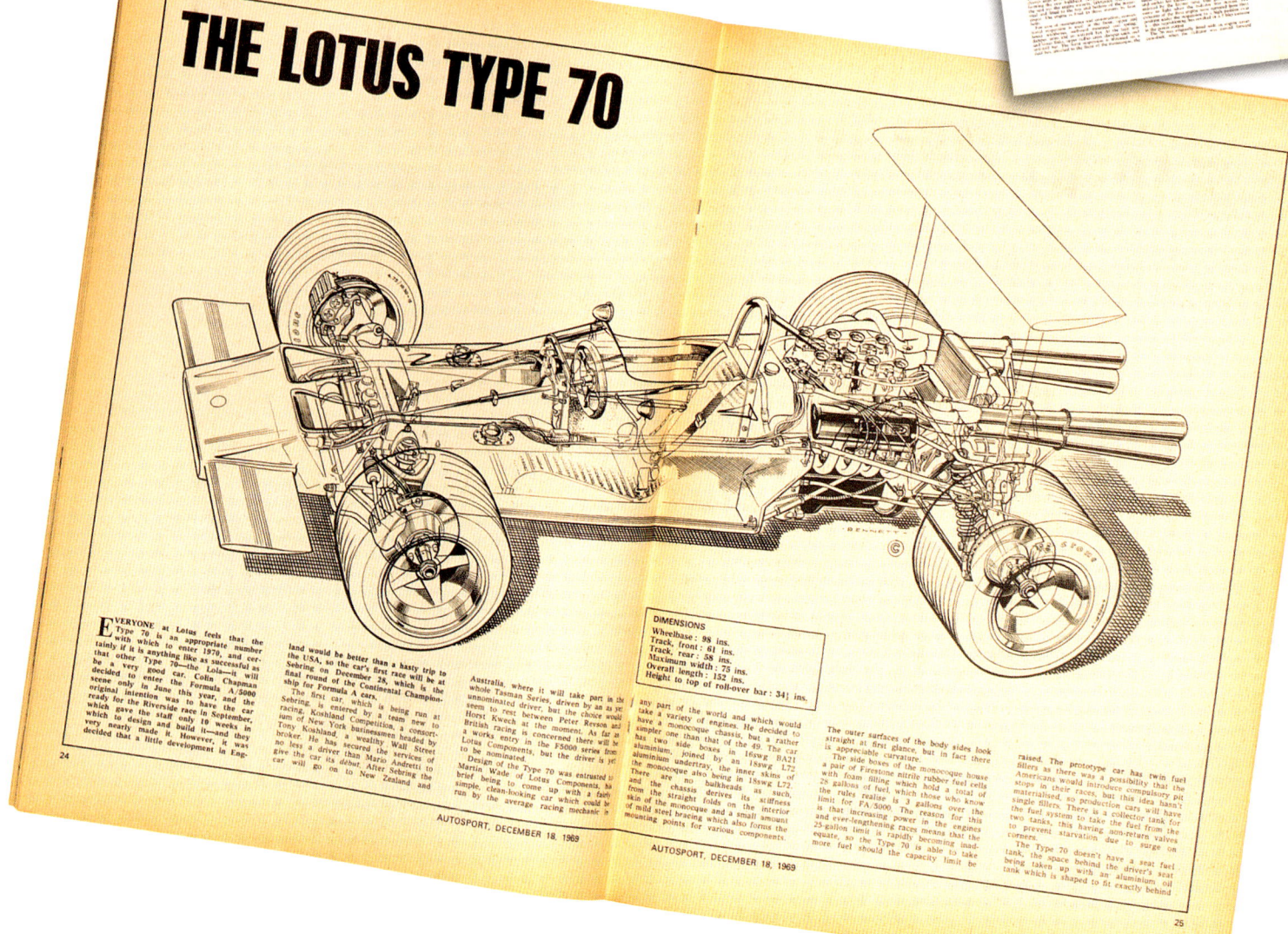

Formula 5000 1970

as Autocourse showing Lotus winning on the chess board – and with sales brochures and specification sheets like the one reproduced here which was actually aimed specifically at the US market. A sticker for the Lotus Racing Limited is also shown here, actually a very rare item now which appeared on all the customer cars sold at the time. In December 1969 Autosport in the UK published a nice cutaway drawing of the car, and it is seen here with another, more unusual illustration whose provenance is sadly unknown. Finally, reprinted on the left is a magazine article which appeared in Model Cars in May 1970. It shows a rare drawing of the Type 68 and 70 by Roger Taylor, the Type 68 being a one-off Formula A prototype for the finished car, cleaner in profile but beset with cooling problems until the rear mounted radiator was moved to the nose.

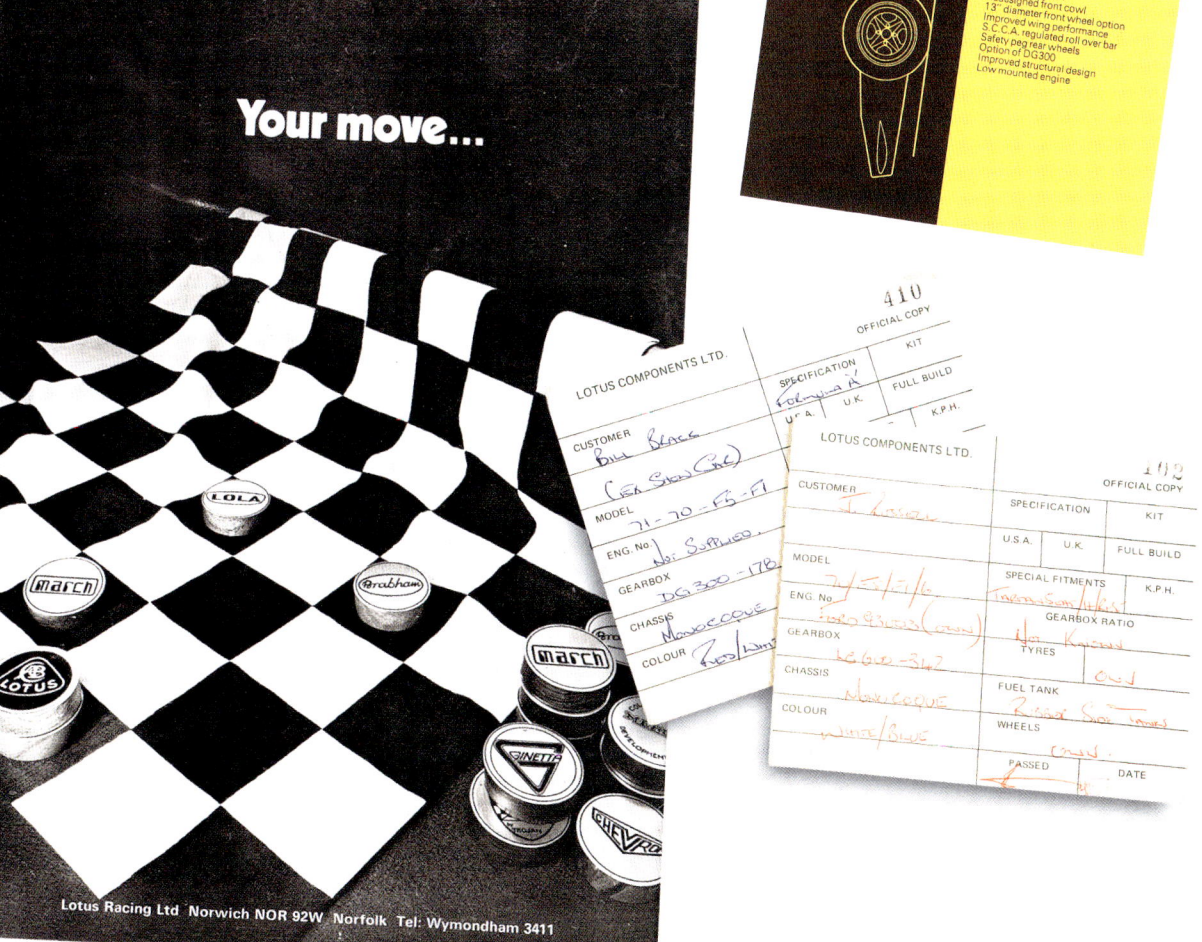

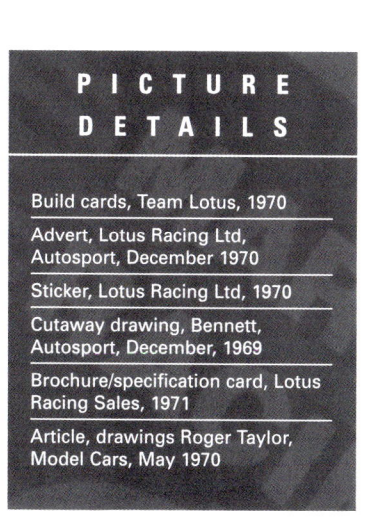

TYPE 70

PICTURE DETAILS

Build cards, Team Lotus, 1970

Advert, Lotus Racing Ltd, Autosport, December 1970

Sticker, Lotus Racing Ltd, 1970

Cutaway drawing, Bennett, Autosport, December, 1969

Brochure/specification card, Lotus Racing Sales, 1971

Article, drawings Roger Taylor, Model Cars, May 1970

TYPE 72

Formula 1 1970

Twenty victories to its name, three Formula 1 Constuctors Championships, and the first of a long and successful run of stylish John Player Specials, the elegant Lotus Type 72 is one of the greatest Grand Prix cars of all time and possibly even the most outstanding single racing car of the entire 1970s. Likened at its launch – and with good reason – to a high-speed hammerhead shark, the car made its debut in Spain still wearing Gold Leaf Team Lotus colours. It was immediately recognisable, its distinctive shape bearing witness to a raft of major new innovations which showed that impeccable attention had been paid to the overall aerodynamics. Most obviously, the twin radiators were located amidships to allow the profile to be even sleeker, and a carefully contoured rear section gave it the best possible penetration through the air. It was also, at exactly 530kg, possibly the lightest machine in its class. Surprisingly, for such an obviously brilliant design, the Type 72 made a slow start, unplaced in the Spanish Grand Prix and failing to really find its feet until Jochen Rindt took pole position in one at Zandvoort. He went on to win the race in fine style, quickly repeating the achievement in the subsequent British, French and German rounds. But the following season, even more surprisingly, the cars scored no race wins whatever – the first time this had happened to the team for a decade. The year after that, however, it was all change again as Emerson Fittipaldi, partnered now by the keen but outclassed Australian Dave Walker, streaked ahead of the field to take the 1972 Formula One World Championship. As well as winning two important non-Championship races, he took the flag in Spain, Belgium, Britain, Austria and Italy, and came in second at Clermont Ferrand and a good third on the streets of Monte Carlo. Significantly, 1972, of course, was also the year the cars were rebranded as John Player Specials – painted a super-cool combination of black and gold, a truly memorable livery, which at a stroke

Formula 1 1970

TYPE 72

Why Team Lotus?

GOLD LEAF Team Lotus – Constructors' and Drivers' Champions

PICTURE DETAILS
Model, Scale Racing Cars, GB, white metal, 1/43rd
Rear wing, Classic Team Lotus.
Airbox, Classic Team Lotus.
Booklet, inside and cover, Team Lotus, 1971
GLTL Press, British GP 1971
Advert, Gold Leaf cigarettes, Autosport, Nov 1970
Advert, Lotus dealers, Holland, 1970
Jacket, JPTL, G. Hadfield, 1972
Badge, John Player Grand Prix, Silverstone, 1975

TYPE 72

Formula 1 1970

made Colin Chapman's cars as identifiable around the world as any blood-red Ferrari. By the same token, the new sponsors' colour scheme was also something of a godsend to modellers, and the Type 72 soon became a firm favourite. Examples shown here of the many produced include a white metal model of the 72E made by Scale Racing Cars in Great Britain to 1/43rd scale and bearing the number 8; another shown with its box, made by Schuco in Germany to 1/12th scale, a die cast plastic model, painted with the number 4; and a third one, by an unknown maker in Hong Kong, a 4.5 inch-long slot racer carrying the champion's No.1. The number 5 car was also made in Britain by Scale Racing Cars, but this time representing an earlier iteration and so painted with the colours of Gold Leaf Team Lotus. Finally, the friction-powered toy shown here in its packaging is a real oddity: designed by Zee Toys in California but made in Hong Kong, the 1/24th scale plastic model is painted in a decidedly non-standard gold with a stripe. More interesting, perhaps, is the memorabilia associated with the car itself. The trophy shown here, for example, is the one presented to Emerson Fittipaldi for winning the 1972 Spanish Grand Prix – one of many – while the three sections of Type 72

140

Formula 1 1970

bodywork – the rear wing, airbox and front wing – are a selection of those available from Classic Team Lotus. Also shown is the front cover and a page from a little booklet produced by Team Lotus when it was trying to attract new sponsorship (prior to the arrival of John Player Special) and an official Gold Player Team Lotus press pack containing sought-after tickets for the 1971 British Grand Prix. The Type 72 also spawned some genuine rarities including the jacket given to George Hadfield of John Player and worn by him during 1972 – the straw boater is part of the same outfit – and the watch which is one of several presented to team members to mark the 1972 Championship season. Some of these goodies were also available to the fans at a price, as evidenced by the 1971 advertisement reproduced here for promotional goods or 'Super Supporters Gear', and this copy of 'Team Lotus Sings' – a (non-hit) single which was recorded to celebrate the Championship.

TYPE 72

PICTURE DETAILS

Model, Scale Racing Cars, GB, white metal, 1/43rd
Trophy, 1st Spanish GP 1972
Advert, GLTL promotional goods, 1971
JPTL Watch, 1972
JPTL promotional material, 1972
Badge, JPS World Champions, 1973
Advert, Brands Hatch, Autocar, June 1988

TYPE 72

Formula 1 1970

The words were printed on the back so we could all sing along with the lads. Naturally Type 72s also fulfiled another role, namely promoting cigarettes as per the Gold Leaf advertisement shown here (which appeared in Autosport in November 1970) and the John Player Special cigarette advertisement which pictured Emerson Fittipaldi's helmet well to the fore. Another tobacco brand, Lucky Strike, also ran two cars in the 1972 French, British and German rounds. Several other items of promotional material have survived and are reproduced here, including several John Player Team Lotus press releases for various Grand Prix – showing the results, driver profiles, race programmes and so on – two of the many sew-on badges which were produced to celebrate individual wins, and a photograph issued at the time of the car's launch and signed by Colin Chapman. With various tweaks along the way, the Type 72 also proved to be an especially enduring design. In 1973 Fittipaldi drove the car for another season, this time joined by Ronnie Peterson, between them notching up four more GP wins with a second at

Formula 1 1970

home for Peterson and a third at Monaco. And in 1974, by which time the Brazilian had switched allegiance to McLaren, Peterson was joined by Jacky Ickx who quickly made his mark by taking the flag at the Brands Hatch Race of Champions. For his part, Peterson took the Type 72 to three more victories – in Monaco, France and Italy – a truly remarkable achievement for a four-year-old design. Incredibly, the cars came back again for more the following year, and although outright victory was not to be this time around, the Type 72 – or as it was always better known, the John Player Special – was by then well-established after a working life of nearly half a decade as one of Formula One's supreme designs.

PICTURE DETAILS

Model & box, Schuco, Germany, die cast, plastic, 1/12th

Model, unknown, H.Kong, plastic, 4 1/2"

Front wing, Classic Team Lotus.

Press photo, signed by Colin Chapman, 1970

Straw Boater, JPTL, G.Hadfield, 1972

Lucky Strike promotional material, French, British German GP's, 1972

Record, 'Team Lotus Sings'.

JPTL promotional material, 1972

Advert, JPS, 1973

Model Type 72D, Exoto, Japan, die cast, 1/18th, 1998

143

TYPE 72

TYPE 73

Formula 3 1972

Technically less of a tour-de-force than the Type 72, but still visually impressive and with a sophisticated chassis for its class, the Formula Three Type 73 was also, crucially, presented in the same stunning black and gold JPS livery. Only two were completed, one each for Tony Trimmer and Bernard Vermilio, along with one spare monocoque. Trimmer, involved in the early testing, debuted the car coming sixth at Mallory Park in March 1972 after which some revisions were made to the car's complex design. Subsequent results included a second place at Monaco and on his return attempt, a first at Mallory Park.

Shown here is a rare promotional leaflet for the car, an official press photograph of the team assembled for the 1972 season, and two ashtrays, a water jug, some watch stickers and a few badges – the latter items being John Player promotional goodies given away at various race meetings. Rather confusingly, given that they sponsored the F1 & F3 cars, John Player Special also sponsored the F2 series, thus the rare sticker shown above.

Formula 2 1973

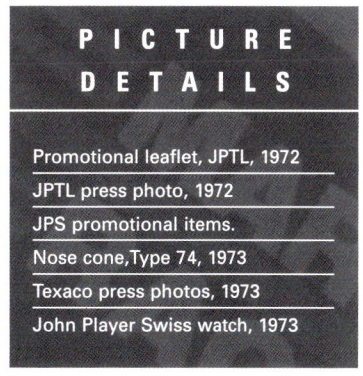

The fact that they shared the same type-number as the Europa Twin Cam and Special might have caused confusion for the factory's 1973 Formula Two challengers were it not for the fact that, in recognition of their lead sponsor, both cars were simply known as the Texaco Stars. Shown here in two contemporary photographs, the Type 73 used an extensively modified version of the Novamotor GM/Vauxhall Victor block, a relatively large engine by F2 standards, and one whose power output failed to reach the original target despite numerous revisions, both cars failed to shine as a result. Also shown here is a real collectors item, one of the Type 72 style nose cones the car ran at some parts of the season. In the hands of Emerson Fittipaldi, Ronnie Peterson and eventually Dave Morgan, they were instead repeatedly relegated to 'also rans' – a 5th at Karlskoga the best result – and by the end of '73 Lotus finally pulled out of the class completely in order to focus its efforts more effectively on Formula One.

PICTURE DETAILS

Promotional leaflet, JPTL, 1972
JPTL press photo, 1972
JPS promotional items.
Nose cone, Type 74, 1973
Texaco press photos, 1973
John Player Swiss watch, 1973

TYPE 74

TYPE 74

Europa Twin-cam & Special 1971

A musical toy Europa from Hong Kong, a novel model speedboat made from a Europa bodyshell, and an understandably triumphant press release confirming the completion of the 25,000th Lotus Twin Cam engine – it takes only a cursory glance at some of the more unusual memorabilia associated with the final iteration of the Lotus Europa to reveal just what a huge impact this car had on the motoring world in the 1970s, given its uncompromising and specialist nature. The new type number for the car came about when Renault announced it was ceasing production of the standard Renault 16 engine, leaving Lotus to re-engineer the car to accept its own 1,558 cc Lotus-Ford Twin Cam. It continued to use the Renault-built 4-speed gearbox, however, eventually replacing it with another Renault product in 1972 when the time came to add another cog. Performance was impressive, even with only four speeds: 120mph, 7.5 seconds to 60mph, and a reasonable 30mpg under normal driving conditions. Externally the new car looked much the same as the Type 46, although Lotus had sensibly paid attention to critics of the earlier design and made numerous detail modifications to the basic shape. The most obvious was to the rear deck, where the characteristic buttresses or fins were cut down by several inches in a bid to improve the car's three-quarter rear vision. In fact the jury is still out on the question as to whether or not this single objective was achieved, but to many eyes the finished shape was an improvement on the old one while the lowered floorpan and new seats were certainly a welcome modification. At the same time a small chin spoiler helped to freshen the car's frontal aspect, two new fuel tanks totalling 12.5 gallons improved its range, and the optional 'Spider' wheels (shown an the advertisement) served further to distinguish the Type 74 from the Renault-engined Type 46. Selling well, in late 1972 the car received another boost after it was fitted

Europa Twin-cam & Special 1971

PICTURE DETAILS

Model box, Yodel, Japan, plastic kit, 1/24th

Model, Yonezawa 'Diapet', Japan, die cast, 1/40th

Styling drawings, Lotus Design dept.

Owners handbook, Europa Special, 1973

Owners handbook, Europa Twin Cam, 1971

Models & box, Tomica, Japan, die cast, 1/59th

Brochure, Europa Special

Advert, Auto Garden, Japan.

Information sheet with dealers, Lotus Cars.

Colour chart, Lotus Cars, 1973

with the new 'Big Valve' engine from the Elan and renamed the Europa Special. Inevitably, given this new name and the track cars' stunning performance at this time, it was also offered for the first time with its own version of the sensational black-and-gold livery of the John Player Specials. Sales rose and rose – and no wonder – reaching a grand total of 9,230 by the time production ceased in 1975, and of course in this guise the car proved even more irresistable than the last to the model makers. Shown below are several reminders of the many offered at the time, including from Japan the box from a 1/24th scale 'Supercar' model made by Yodel and a rather unusual navy-blue JPS 1/40th scale model made by Yonezawa Diapet. The aforementioned yellow speedboat was actually made by established modelmaker Provence Moulage in France, while the three smaller 1/59th scale cars shown here with an appropriate box are again from Japan where the

147

TYPE 74

TYPE 74: Europa Twin-cam & Special 1971

diminutive car was clearly a huge hit as evidenced by the advertisement for Auto Garden, a leading Japanese Lotus specialist.

Given a relatively long production life of more than four years, plenty of promotional material for the car has survived including an advertisement for the Europa Special which appeared in Autosport in 1972, a lavishly produced brochure for the same car, and two editions of Lotus Press News covering the Europa Twin Cam and Special. Three original styling drawings done in pastels are also shown, a real rarity, along with a two genuine owners handbooks for the Europa Special and Europa Twin Cam, a single sheet Europa Twin Cam information and specification chart, and a colour chart for those cars offered for sale by the factory in 1973. From a marketing perspective the synergy between the racing cars in JPS black-and-gold and the matching road cars was obvious, giving enthusiasts a chance to buy a car in the same strip as a genuine F1 championship winner. And with the 'Big Valve' engine shaving half a second off the 0-60 time and adding another 5mph to the top-end, JPS Europa Specials have unsurprisingly remained one of the most memorable sports cars of the early 1970s.

Europa Twin-cam & Special 1971

PICTURE DETAILS

Musical toy, Hong Kong, plastic, 10"

Model speedboat, Provence Moulage, France, resin, 1/43rd

Advert, Brand Lotus, Autosport, February 1971

Lotus Press News, 25,000th twin cam engine, October 1970

Lotus Press News, Europa TC

Card brochure, 6-page, Lotus Cars, 1972

Lotus Press News, Special.

Advert, Autosport, 1972

TYPE 74

TYPE 75

Elite 1974

A completely new look, a new engine, and representing in every way a quantum leap up-market for the company, the Type 75 Lotus Elite used a familiar name and retained the factory formula of a steel backbone chassis and GRP bodywork, the Elite was supplied only as a complete car and with a price, which by Lotus standards, was a relatively high £5,445 for January 1975. Powered by the new Lotus 907 engine, a die-cast alloy block of 1,973cc derived from the Vauxhall slant-four, Oliver Winterbottom's fashionably razor-edged wedge effectively disguised the fact that underneath there was more than a passing resemblence to the outgoing Europa. But even so, with its highly distinctive sports-hatch styling, the car was a new departure for Lotus and saw the

PICTURE DETAILS

Model set, Corgi, GB, die cast, 1/43rd, 1974

Models, Tomica, Japan, die cast & plastic, 1/63th

Model box, Tsukuda, Japan, plastic, 1/24th

Brochures, Lotus Cars.

Owners handbook, Lotus Elite

Price list, Lotus cars, September 1974

Brochure, Don Safety Trophy, 1974

Press pack, Lotus Cars, 1974.

Advert, Autocar, 1974

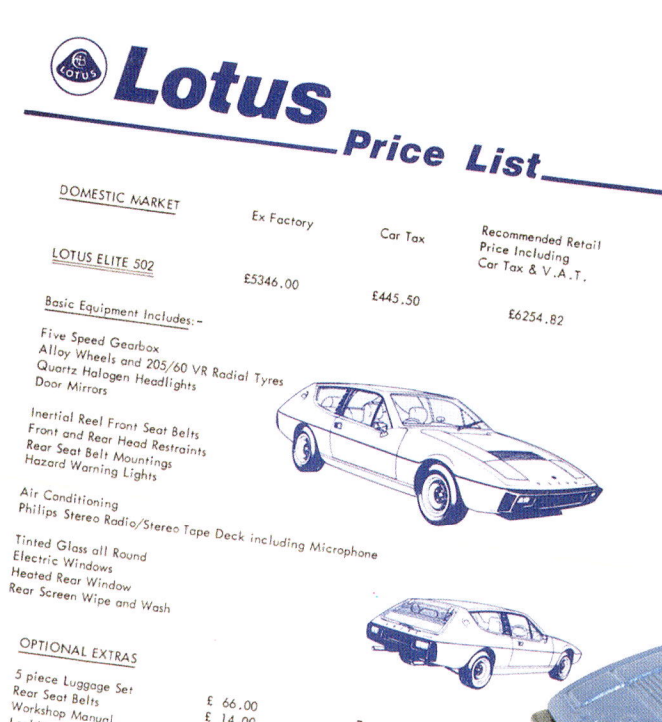

Elite 1974

Norfolk company reaching for something sleeker, safer, more sophisticated and above all more stylish than anything it had produced in the past. It also proved the value of Chapman's latest innovation, a way of circumventing the time-consuming and costly process of hand-laying glass fibre by instead using a procedure known as Vacuum-Assisted Resin Injection in which the body was produced in two halves and then bonded along the centreline. The join then cleverly concealed by a lateral rubbing strip – a trick employed at Chapman's two boat-building operations – this same process was later to be employed on the Eclat and of course on the Esprit which continues in production more than quarter of a century later. That the new technology worked there was no doubt, and fitted with steel beams in the doors to comply with the stringent new US regulations, the Elite also proved to be an extremely safe design and one which went on to win the prestigious Don Safety Trophy in 1974, as per the cover and spread from the awards brochure shown here. Similarly, the car's aggressively upmarket intentions were signalled by an advertising campaign in The Sunday Times the same year – an example from which is shown here – along with a contemporaneous Lotus Cars press pack headed 'Interim report on the Elite' – a machine soon to be flagged by the company as 'Britain's most exclusive car'. Spotting a clear winner British toy-maker Corgi got in on the act too, producing a

TYPE 75

TYPE 75

Elite 1974

model of the John Player Special racing team, complete with a die-cast 1/43rd scale Lotus Elite and a matching Type 72 racing car. Tomica in Japan also modelled Chapman's latest effort, two versions of which are shown here – one in white and one in blue, both to 1/63rd scale and of die-cast plastic. And in the US Airfix produced a so-called Elite 'Rally', a moulded 1/24th scale plastic kit (whose box is pictured here) while another Elite 'Rally' was issued by Pilen in Spain to 1/40 scale, of die-cast plastic and painted white with the number 10. The same company was responsible for the blue-painted 1/43rd scale car, while the remaining box art relates to a model Type 75 made by Tsukuda in Japan, a 1/24th scale plastic kit car. Otherwise, among the more official memorabilia shown here are both sides of a specification and price list effective from 1st February 1977 – in this guise the car actually remained in production until the end of the decade – along with a Lotus

152

Elite 1974

TYPE 75

PICTURE DETAILS

Model box, US Airfix, USA, plastic, 1/24th

Model, Pilen, Spain, die cast, 1/43rd

Model, Pilen, Spain, die cast, 1/43rd

Specification & price list, 1st February 1977

Folding brochure 6 page, Lotus Cars, 1974

Folding brochure 8 page, Lotus Cars, 1978

Elite owners handbook, an earlier version of the Lotus Cars price list from September 1974, and two spreads from one of the first combined Elite, Eclat and Esprit brochures. Another two versions of the same folding brochure are also pictured, showing the reverse. A substantial machine – at nearly 2,600lbs it is almost twice the weight of the Europa – the Elite was also heavier than many steel-bodied saloons of the period. Nonetheless Autocar magazine were impressed and reported enjoying 'typical Lotus excellence of handling combined with a good ride'. Over the next six years the factory sold 2,398 units all told, before the Elite was freshened up and refitted with the larger 2.2 litre Type 912 engine giving the car several more years of life.

153

TYPE 76

Formula 1 1974

Dubbed the John Player Special Mark I, the 1974 Lotus Type 76 is numerically confusing, not just because the same type-number was assigned to the forthcoming Eclat the following year but also because it represented an attempt to produce an even lighter version of the all-conquering Type 72, a car which was already known to the fans and factory alike as the John Player Special. Distinguished by its novel four-pedal arrangement – the two linked centre pedals were for right- and left-foot braking – and electronic clutch, the car was certainly technically inspired but appealed neither to Jacky Ickx (who asked for the extra pedal to be removed after testing) nor to Ronnie Peterson (who persevered with it for the first few races). After several unsuccessful outings, however, even he rebelled and the car was relegated to little more than a source of spare parts for the ageing Type 72s which were hastily brought out of retirement. Peterson reportedly also found the car – seen here in a series of press photographs showing it testing and at its first race – too heavy, and indeed after considerable lobbying he eventually persuaded Chapman to ditch the design and start something new. The car was nonetheless an extremely attractive design and

154

Formula 1 1974

one which was modelled by Polistil in Italy – whose two 1/55th scale Type 76 cars are here shown with a JPS Transporter in their in original box, by Stombecker in Canada (which in 1974 produced this Type 76 slot car fitted with its characteristic early-spec. double-decker rear wing) and also in 1/24th scale with a single rear wing as shown in this anonymous die-cast model. Three original badges have survived from the unsuccessful 1974 season, along with a , John Player Team Lotus silk scarf and a rather smart official John Player Team Lotus mechanics shirt. The best result for the car itself, however, was a fourth place – and even then not for the whole car but merely for the monocoque and front suspension components which were incorporated into a sort of motorised mongrel after Ickx's car had been destroyed the night before the German Grand Prix.

PICTURE DETAILS

Model set, Polistil, Italy, die cast, 1/55th	
Slot car, Strombecker, Canada, plastic, 1974	
Model, Scale Racing Cars, GB, die cast, 1/24th	
Press photos, Lotus Cars.	
Badges, JPTL, 1974	
Ladies silk scarf, JPTL.	
Mechanics shirt, JPTL.	
Advert, Duckhams Q Magazine, 1974	

TYPE 76

TYPE 76

Eclat 1975

Originally conceived as a cheaper version of the range-topping Elite, but by no means a less attractive or desirable design as a result, the Type 76 Lotus Eclat S1 was similar in numerous respects to the aforementioned car. It sold extremely well – 1,299 units between 1975 and its replacement in 1980 – but rather surprisingly was completely ignored by both toy- and model-makers who preferred to direct their energies towards its sister car and (from 1976) the even more striking Type 79 Esprit. Shown here, however, are two versions of the same Eclat 6-page folded brochure – one from 1975 depicting a red car and another from two years later depicting a yellow one. The cover and information page from the Lotus range brochure are also from that year, while the information sheet reproduced below is a real rarity – describing what was to become the Eclat when it was still officially known as the Elite Sprint. Although this was soon changed, the Sprint tag was to reappear two years later

Eclat 1975

PICTURE DETAILS

Brochure, 6-page, Lotus Cars, 1975
Brochure, 6-page, Lotus Cars, 1977
Brochure, 8-page, Lotus Cars, 1975
Information sheet, Lotus Cars, Elite Sprint, 1975
Advert, Autocar, Eclat Sprint.
Advert, The Sunday Times, 1975
Advert, Autocar, 1975

when in 1977 it became apparent that most Lotus buyers preferred a higher specification for the car even if this meant paying a higher price. This of course had not been the company's original intention as the Eclat was always meant to be a more basic and cheaper buy than the Elite. But in a world where the customer is king, the response was predictable and various new features were quickly incorporated into the design – as per the advertisement shown here – including a lower axle ratio, wider alloy road wheels in place of the original steel ones, and a distinctive white livery with black striping. The other advertisements are from Motor Magazine dated 1975, and another showing the car outside Harrods, part of the continuing process of reinforcing the company's new upmarket image.

157

TYPE 76

TYPE 77

Formula 1 1976

Actually F1's third JPS Lotus, the John Player Special Mark II or Type 77 took a bow in mid-September 1975. Very much an interim model at a time when Lotus was slipping behind several of its rivals, it was designed to hold the fort whilst work continued on the radical new Mark III Type 78.

Nicknamed 'Confusacar' after a failed attempt by Chapman to explain its complex variable suspension in an airport hotel car park, the car's other role of course was to eradicate memories of the ill-fated Type 76 while providing the team with a workable replacement for the ageing Type 72. Some of the material issued at the time is shown here, and the car certainly looked impressive enough in the cut-away by Tony Matthews, in the original John Player Team Lotus race set up sheet for chassis no. JPS 11, and in the set of original press photographs handed out at the launch with the accompanying press release. But early impressions were not auspicious: coolant leaked from Ronnie Peterson's car in practice for Brazil, and a collision between his car and his temporary team mate Mario Andretti's during the race took both cars out and prompted

158

Formula 1 1976

Ronnie's departure to rival March. Thereafter it was a sorry tale of exploding engines and spin-offs before eventually Andretti struggled on to take the flag at Mount Fuji – the team's first win (and only one that season) since Monaco in 1974. Shown here is a die-cast plastic model of the car fitted with its early short side pods, still in its original 'race track' packaging and made by Inca Plas in Spain to 1/40th scale. A similar car, also painted with the number 5, is by Britain's Scale Racing Cars and built to 1/43rd scale in white metal. And the remaining pair are a later long-pod version of the car by Nikko in Japan, die-cast to 1/28th scale and a 1/24th scale Scalextric toy. Rather more unusual however is the large flat-pack DIY press-out cardboard model, fitted with wooden axles and made by Tandem Products Ltd of London and the John Player Team Lotus Type 77 beermat.

PICTURE DETAILS

- Model, Inca Plas, Spain, die cast & plastic, 1/40th scale
- Model, Scale Racing Cars, GB, white metal, 1/43 scale
- Model, Nikko, Japan, die cast, 1/28th
- Model, Scalextric, GB, plastic, 1/24th
- Beer mat, JPTL.
- Cut-away drawing, Team Lotus, Tony Matthews, 1976
- JPTL press photos.
- Cardboard model, Tandem Products Ltd, 1/16th
- JPTL race set up sheet, January 1976
- Press release, JPTL.

TYPE 77

TYPE 78

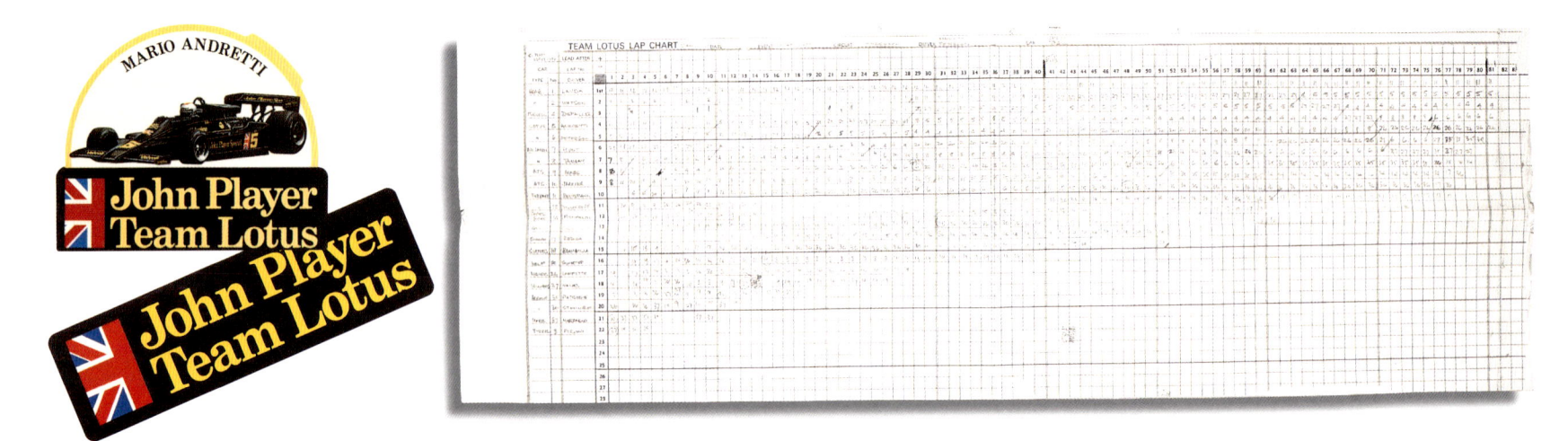

Formula 1 1977

With only one F1 win the previous season, it must have been a relief – not just to the driver in question, but to the whole JPS/Lotus entourage – when Mario Andretti described the handling of his new John Player Special Mark III as like being 'painted to the road'. Chapman's solution to the Type 76/77 debacle was to closet himself away for much of the summer and direct his attention toward creating a machine in which the entirety functioned as an aerodynamic whole rather than one onto which aerodynamic aids were bolted. Inspired by the light and elegant DeHavilland Mosquito of World War II, his solution, his 'wing car', was the Type 78, a device which literally sucked itself onto the track and used wings and fins merely for additional stability. Powered once again by the redoubtable Ford DFV, and driven by Mario Andretti and Gunnar Nilsson, the car's first victory came at Long Beach and was quickly followed by a win in Spain (Andretti's), at Zolder (Nilsson, who also set the fastest lap time), and in France and Italy (both Andretti's) leaving Lotus trailing only the Ferrari 312T-2 in the 1977 Constructors' Cup. The two drivers are represented in the official postcards reproduced here along with another John Player Team Lotus beermat, the team's original press release for the new car, and one of the team's handwritten lap charts from the USGP West held on April 2, 1978. With another two wins in its second season, but with Nilsson retiring due to ill-health and both Andretti and

160

Formula 1 1977

PICTURE DETAILS

Model, Eidai-Grip, Japan, die cast, 1/43rd

Model, Quartzo, USA, die cast, 1/43rd

Model, unknown, die cast 1/24

Sticker, Rebaque F1 team.

Beer mat, JPTL.

Postcards, JPTL.

Press release, JPTL.

Stickers, JPTL, 1977

Wind tunnel model, Team Lotus 1977

Cut-away drawing, Team Lotus, Tony Matthews.

Model box, Tamiya, Japan, plastic kit, 1/20th

Lap chart, Team Lotus, USGP West, April 1978

Peterson moving onto its successor, time was almost up for the Type 78. One soldiered on, however, with Hector Rebaque – whose team sticker is shown here – but without any real success. Also here and wearing the number 5 is a model by Eidai-Grip in Japan, one of the Team Rebaque car by Quartzo in brown and gold for the 1978 German GP, a Tamiya plastic kit in 1/20th scale, and an unidentified die cast 1/24th scale model. Most interesting, however, is the original wind-tunnel development model, and another fine cut-away drawing commissioned by Team Lotus and drawn by Tony Matthews.

TYPE 78

Esprit S1 & S2 1976

First seen as an Ital Design concept at Turin in 1972, Giorgetto Giugiaro's Europa-based Lotus M70 design study took four years to reach fruition but was destined to become the longest-lived of all Lotus production sports cars. Hethel's financial difficulties at this time were well known and explain much of the delay between show-car and showroom; but when deliveries finally began in late-1976, the finished car looked every bit as stunning as that first M70 prototype. Performance was perhaps another matter – Autocar, to name just one, singularly failed to achieve the performance figures claimed by the factory – and there were complaints too about the mid-engined car's noise and vibrations. But in its favour, it was a clean, fresh design – visually very much of a kind with the Elite and Eclat – but more rakish and far more spacious than its spiritual predecessor the Europa had been. By anyone's reckoning it was also a more aggressively upmarket machine – and a good job too, one might say, given that the price had risen from a projected £5,844 at launch to £7,883 by the time it actually went on

Esprit S1 & S2 1976

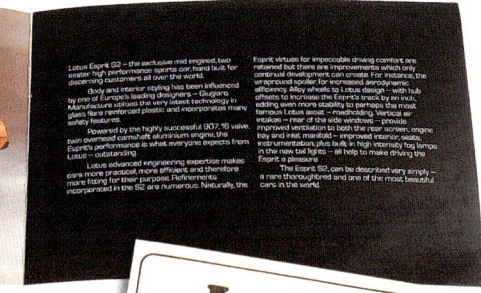

PICTURE DETAILS

Model, Western Models, GB, white metal, 1/43rd

Presentation model, Corgi (Mettoy), GB, Gold plated plastic, 1/43rd, 1977

Model and box, Eidai Grip, Japan, die cast & plastic, 1/28th

Advert, Wolfrace wheels.

Brochure, 6-page, Lotus Cars, 1975

Brochure, 6-page, Lotus Cars, 1976

Brochure S2, 8-page, Lotus Cars, printer Monitor Advertising Ltd, London.

Long may Lotus blossom

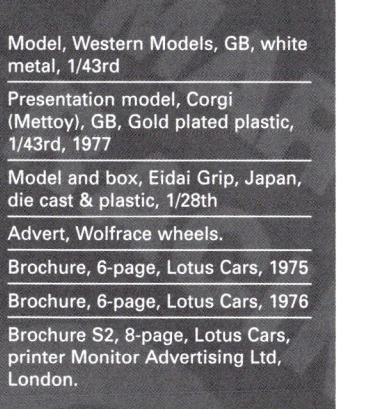

wolfrace

Wolfrace Wheels Ltd.,
Elms Industrial Estate,
Shuttleworth Road,
Goldington, Bedford.
Telephone: 0234 62535/6/7
Telex: 825483

sale. Of the promotional material issued at the time, the two Esprit S1 brochures shown here are essentially the same, that depicting the red car being a version printed in late 1975, and that showing the white car appearing a year or two later. The other brochure, an eight-page item with a silver cover, was produced by Monitor Advertising in London following the announcement in December 1977 of the new Esprit Series 2 or S2 – designed as much as anything else to silence critics unhappy with the power and performance of the original car, which had nevertheless still managed to shift 718 units without too much difficulty. As can be seen from the Esprit S2 advertisement reproduced here and dating from early 1978, the new version was distinguished by the use of Speedline wheels in place of the original Wolfrace cast alloys

TYPE 79

TYPE 79

Esprit S1 & S2 1976

(which are also shown here, in their own advertisement featuring an early Esprit). Other modifications included a new front spoiler and rear valance, but the real S2 eye-opener appeared the following year when Lotus announced that it was building a genuinely limited run of just 100 S2s in its distinctive JPS livery of black and gold. Conceived to commemorate the performance of the other Type 79 – Mario Andretti's, that is – with yet another victory for Lotus in the World F1 Constructors' Cup, the car also now carried a discrete but significant plaque describing its maker as the World Champion Car Constructors. Shown here with a genuine Series 1 Esprit owners handbook from 1976 are several models of the car including two very special ones presented to Colin Chapman. The first of these is a handbuilt Esprit given to 'the Guvnor' in Paris in 1975 by the workers engaged on the Esprit project, which we can see in the photograph alongside had pride of place on his desk. And the second, whilst less impressive from a detailing standpoint, is at least gold-plated – a 1/43rd scale 007 Esprit made by Corgi (Mettoy) and presented to Chapman on July 7, 1977. The others are more commercial models, the yellow car being a die cast model made by Asahi Tsusho Sigma in

164

Esprit S1 & S2 1976

Japan to 1/43rd scale. The other gold car is a white metal item made by Britain's Western Models, also to 1/43rd scale, and the final white 007 car shown here with its original box is also from Japan, made by Eidai Grip to 1/28th scale. Fitted originally with the canted-over 1,973 cc Lotus Type 907 engine – identical to that which powered both the Elite and Eclat, and delivering a respectable 160bhp through a combined 5-speed 'box and final drive unit from the complex Citroën SM – the Esprit itself received yet another boost in 1980 when it was fitted with the larger (2.2 litre) Type 912 engine. Now known as the Esprit 2.2, by 1981 it had sold another 88 units bringing the total so far to 1,866 – a startling achievement for such a specialised device, and yet another boost for Chapman's enduring combination of backbone chassis and GRP body.

PICTURE DETAILS

Model, Asahi Tsusho Sigma, Japan, die cast, 1/43rd

Model, Lotus Cars factory, resin, 1975

Advert, Autocar, 1978

Owners handbook, 1976

Information sheet S2, Lotus Cars, 1977

Model, Testors, USA, plastic, 1/20th

TYPE 79

TYPE 79

Formula 1 1978

Having fought back so well with the Type 78, Colin Chapman sealed his success a year later and watched his John Player Special Mark IV win six races in the one season thereby making him the most successful racing car designer in the history of Formula One, beating the record of Mercedes-Benz which had stood since 1955. Eschewing honeycomb material in favour of sheet aluminium for the Type 79, Chapman's return to traditional materials certainly didn't indicate that he was abandoning innovation; indeed, by using massive sidepods, each acting as a huge venturi, he was seeking to perfect his 'wing car' and to recapture the 25% of aerodynamic effect which had been lost between the planning and execution of the earlier car. Still with the Hewland 'box and Cosworth DFV, the new machine made its debut in early 1978 at the non-Championship International Trophy at Silverstone. Succcess eluded it, however, until Zolder in mid-May where Andretti took pole and won the race – a perfect birthday present for Chapman, 50 two days earlier, especially as Ronnie Peterson followed him home in second place. It was a feat the duo repeated weeks later at Jarama, then at Paul Ricard and again in Holland, after which some Team members were seen wearing the now legendary T-shirt bearing the lines 'John Player Team Lotus won two one two'. By the season's end, Lotus had 86 points to Ferrari's 58 with Andretti clinching the Driver's Championship and Ronnie Peterson

166

Formula 1 1978

taking second place. The team's suppliers naturally made the most of it – witness these three advertisements for Valvoline, AP & Goodyear – and NGK presented the team itself with a commemorative plaque. The model-makers did too, depicting it both as the original JPS 'Black Beauty' and in its later Martini guise: the aerial view is of an English 1/43 scale model by Scale Racing Cars; the others are by Hobos in Italy, a white metal Martini car with the number 1, by Scale Racing cars, painted in black and gold, and by an unknown Japanese manufacturer, a childrens pedal car circa 1980.

The other mementoes are rarer still, being a Type 79 front wing end plate from 1978, a rear wing end plate in Martini colours from 1979, and a programme from the 1978 John Player British race featuring the Type 79 on its cover.

TYPE 79

PICTURE DETAILS

Model, Hobos, India, white metal, 1/43rd

Model, Scale Racing Cars, GB, white metal, 1/43rd

Model, Scale Racing Cars, GB, white metal, 1/43rd

Pedal car, Japan, c.1980

Front wing end plate, 1978, Classic Team Lotus.

Rear wing endplate, 1979, Classic Team Lotus.

Programme, John Player British GP, 1978

JPTL News, March 1978

Beer mat, JPTL.

Poster, artwork John Hostler

Commemorative Plaque, NGK spark plugs, 1978

Adverts, Valvoline, AP & Goodyear, 1978

TYPE 80

Formula 1 1979

What became known as Colin Chapman's 'wingless wonder', the Type 80 represented his best attempt yet to secure the greatest possible download by utilising giant ground-effect side pods and sliding skirts. Just as significantly, by abandoning wings in favour of small trim tabs for minute aerodynamic fine tuning, its creator was confident he could liberate the equivalent of 50bhp for his star driver Mario Andretti. Unveiled at Brands Hatch in March 1979, the car looked fantastic and radically new but in early testing it became clear that so-called porpoising – pitching of the long nose, a problem which affected the rival Brabhams just as badly – was damaging the skirts and effectively switching the downloading effect on and off with complete unpredictability. The solution was to add small nose wings, then later a rear wing (an endplate for which is pictured here), and then eventually to dispense with the skirts themselves, thereby ruining utterly the purity of the original concept. Worse still, Carlos Reutemann refused to drive the car preferring the older Type 79 and effectively splitting the team in two, with one half of the squad supporting the older car, and the other willing Andretti's Type 80 to work more effectively. It never did, however, its best place

168

Formula 1 1979

being a third at Jarama and eventually Chapman called it a day. He retired the wingless wonder, but not before Polistil in Italy had commemorated the ill-fated equipe with two die-cast Type 80s – rather than one of them and a Type 79, which would have been more life-like – and a matching 1/55th scale transporter in the team's striking green Martini livery. The car was also modelled by Mini Racing in Italy to 1/43rd scale, and by Polistil again in 1983 to 1/40th scale (shown here with and without its stickers). Also reproduced is a copy of the original Martini Racing Team Lotus press release issued at the time of the car's launch, and the accompanying photograph of the wind tunnel model. The final photograph shows this same wind tunnel model as it is today – without its wheels and suspension which were probably re-used on a subsequent model.

PICTURE DETAILS

Model set, Polistil, Italy, die cast, 1/55th

Model, Mini Racing, Italy, white metal, 1/43rd

Press release & photo, Martini Racing Team Lotus.

Wind tunnel model, Team Lotus, 1978

Rear wing endplate, 1979, Classic Team Lotus.

Model, Polistil, Italy, 1/40th, 1983.

TYPE 80

TYPE 81

Sunbeam Lotus 1979

Appealing to the Chrysler and Talbot dealer network, which welcomed the opportunity to retail something a little more interesting, and certainly important to Lotus which had recently lost a good customer for its engines following the collapse of Jensen, the Sunbeam Lotus was primarily an homologation special. Built for rallying, it proved to be a superb road car as well and a real winner for the Norfolk-based company at a time when F1 victories were somewhat thin on the ground. Very much in the mould of the Ford Escort RS1600 and Vauxhall Chevette HS2300, this was the car which was to defeat the mighty Audi Quattro to win the World Rallying Championship and as such was felt to be the ideal machine for the young executive – keen to drive something different but not yet quite up to the job of securing his own Lotus Esprit. Its aspirational image belied the raw material – the Sunbeam was OK for its day, but it was certainly no star – and as such formed the basis of numerous glamorous advertisements including the double-page spread shown here which appeared in several magazines at the time, and the three single page items produced by Talbot. Also shown here is the brochure cover and an inside spread for the new Talbot Simca Sunbeam Lotus – produced by Talbot Cars in October 1979 at which time only a limited number of dealers were permitted to sell and service the car – and the cover and spread of a later, more lavish brochure.

PICTURE DETAILS

Model, Mini Racing, Italy, white metal, 1/43rd

Model, Polistil, Italy, plastic, 1/40th, 1982.

Brochure, Talbot Simca Sunbeam Lotus, Talbot Cars, Oct 1979

Advert, Autocar, 1980

Brochure, Talbot Cars, 1980

Advert, Talbot Cars, 1979

Sunbeam Lotus 1979

Fast if flawed – although as one roadtest pointed out it was usually the Talbot bits which fell off not the Lotus ones – the car was destined to remain a rarity with fewer than 2,300 produced of the 4,500 which were originally planned. It was also modelled by several different companies including Mini Racing in Italy which produced this 1/43rd scale representation of the Sunbeam works Team rally car (number 2) and also by Polistil in Italy which was responsible for the even more extreme rally version – a 1/40th scale plastic model of this strangely charismatic little car.

TYPE 81

MOTOR SPORT
LOTUS FOUNDERS DAY
SUNDAY 21st AUGUST
Lotus World
MANY HAPPY RETURNS!
SLIPSTREAM
LOTUS
Fast Lane
Lotus World
1984 LOTUS WEEKEND
Flash Black
LOTUS
Latest Lotus Logo Launched, Labeled Loser
Autosport
F1: Lotus test Dumfries
car
NEW LOTUS V8!
AUTOSPORT
Lotus: We're not dead yet!
GRAND PRIX INTERNATIONAL
CHICANE
Classic cars
HISTORIC LOTUS REGISTER
CHRISTOPHER NEIL
ROAD & TRACK
FIRST LOOK!
AUTOCAR
THE FUTURE AT LOTUS STRAIGHT TALK FROM THE TOP
LOTUS OPEN DAY 85
Classic cars
Lotus Elan
PARTS CATALOGUE
Christopher Neil Ltd
CAR
IS THIS THE LAST LOTUS?
Motor
LOTUS EATER?
CLASSIC
COUPE CLASS
NEWS
Motor
ESPRIT TURBO HC
AUTOSPORT
RIO F1 TESTS
MOTOR SPORT
RIO REHEARSAL FOR F1 ACES
CLASSIC
WIN AN ELAN!
AUTOSPORT
ACTIVE SENNA
FAST LANE
ESPRIT BACK ON TOP?
AUTOSPORT
SENNA STREETWISE
Motor
SHOW '87
COMPLETE GUIDE TO MOTORFAIR
NEW LOTUS ESPRIT
Motor
SHOWSTOPPERS
FULL MOTORFAIR REPORT
Fanauto
LOTUS ESPRIT TURBO
HISPANO et le SPORT
AUTOCAR
WIN THE NEW LOTUS
Lotus ~ Duxford '88
Club Team Lotus - Anglian Area
THE LOTUS FESTIVAL
LOTUS DRIVERS CLUB
CHICANE
LOTUS
DRIVERS CLUB
Motor
NEW LOTUS ELAN REVEALED
Lotus World
AUTOTECH SUCCESS
car
ALL YOU NEED TO KNOW ABOUT NEXT YEAR'S LOTUS ELAN
CAR AND DRIVER
ESPRIT DE CAR!
NEW LOTUS TURBO
Lotus World
NELSON THIRD AT IMOLA
SPORTS CAR ILLUSTRATED
British Car
ESPRIT TURBO
Lotus World
A GREAT SHOW!
TEAM LOTUS
Lotus Concours '89
LOTUS '89
DONINGTON PARK
PRIX EDITIONS
£1000 QUIZ!
Lotus LETTERS
The Power of Innovation
Classic cars
HISTORIC LOTUS-CORTINA RESTORED
automotive engineering
AutoWeek
POWER
Lotus World
RIO '89
Lotus World
EXHILARATING NEW ESPRIT TURBO SE
Lotus World
OUR 400TH GRAND PRIX
LOTUS NEWS
LOTUS NEWS
Lotus World
CAMEL'S LOTUS OWNERS PARTY
SUPER TEST
performance CAR
Lotus Get It Right
1990 CAR OF THE YEAR
MOTOR TREND
Beyond Miata
AUTO
LOTUS OMEGA
AUTOCAR &Motor
WE DRIVE THE LOTUS CARLTON
AUTOSPORT
LOTUS IS SAVED: HAKKINEN SIGNS
AUTOCAR &Motor
MEET THE NEW
LOTUS CARLTON
& LOTUS ESPRIT
CLASSIC
LOTUS SEVEN
CHICANE
HISTORIC LOTUS REGISTER
Newsletter
CLUB
INFO
elite LOTUS
elite LOTUS
elite LOTUS
CLASSIC
LOTUS ELAN
LOTUS NEWS
Classic cars
elite LOTUS
MOTOR SPORT
Jim Clark
CHEQUERED FLAG
elite LOTUS
RACE RALLY
elite LOTUS
PAUL MATTY SPORTS CARS
BIL MAGASINET
LOTUS
LOW FLYING
MERRY CHRISTMAS
Club of Great Britain
LOTUS NEWS
MICHELIN
elite LOTUS
AUTOCAR &Motor
NEW LOTUS Elan
LOTUS IN GEAR
July 1994
car
Back from the dead
Lotus POSITION
Future Events - News & Views
London

CHAPTER 4

81	Formula 1	1980
82	Esprit Turbo	1980
82	Esprit Turbo HC	1986
82	Esprit Turbo se	1988
82	Esprit V8	1997
83	Elite S2	1980
84	Éclat S2	1982
85	Esprit S3	1981
86	Formula 1	1980
87	Formula 1	1981
88	Formula 1	1981
88B	Formula 1	1981
89	Éclat / Excel	1982
91	Formula 1	1982
92	Formula 1	1982
93T	Formula 1	1983
94T	Formula 1	1983
95T	Formula 1	1984
96T	Indy Car	1985
97T	Formula 1	1985
98T	Formula 1	1986
99T	Formula 1	1987
100T	Formula 1	1988
100	Elan	1989
100	Elan SE & S2	1989
101	Formula 1	1989

1980-1989

TYPE 81

Formula 1 1980

Martini having withdrawn its sponsorship following the debacle the previous year, it was perhaps understandable that for the 1980 season Chapman offered up a revised version of his outgoing car rather than another wholly new or wildly experimental design. What Mario Andretti called 'a very straight car' faced particularly stiff competition at its debut in Argentina, and not just from the dominant Williams team but also from Ligier and Brabham. Indeed, it wasn't until the Interlagos race that the team had anything to celebrate – a second place for Elio de Angelis – but even this was no portent of what was to come and the Type 81's final tally included just two fourths, in Italy and Watkins Glen, and a sixth place there, and in Austria. Faring rather better than the Type 80, but still along way short of good, the Type 81 is more kindly remembered as the car in which Colin Chapman discovered Nigel Mansell. Keen, but still stuck back in F3, Mansell was still some way off from the big time but

174

Formula 1 1980

TYPE 81

PICTURE DETAILS

Model, Western Models, GB, white metal, 1/43rd

Model pack, La Ilusion, Spain, plastic, 9.5"

Rear wing end plate, 1980, Classic Team Lotus.

Booklet, Essex promotion, The Lotus Story, 1980

Essex Team Lotus press release, 1980

Essex race report, 1980

Artwork, Team Lotus archive, 1979

Essex / JPTL race report, 1981

Chapman recognised his talent immediately and he soon made his F1 debut sitting in a Lotus. With Martini's money gone – artwork shown here from the Team Lotus archive pictures the new car with no livery as a sponsorship deal had yet to be struck. – The Type 81 saw the beginnings of the relationship with Monaco-based Essex Petroleum. The new sponsorship at least gave the cars an excellent new livery, as seen in the 1/43rd scale white metal item shown here made by Britain's Western Models and by the rear wing end plate from a 1980 model. By still being used the next season the Type 81 also managed to see the return of John Player as a sponsor. The packaging of the larger yellow car is even more curious, however, and made by La Ilusion in Spain unwittingly pre-empts the period of Camel sponsorship. Also shown is the cover of 'The Lotus Story' produced as part of the Essex promotion, and a press release for the new Type 81 printed on the lavish trademark silver foil letterhead. Finally an insert featuring driver histories and race reports from the season says it all: by no means the team's worst year, but still with plenty of room for improvement.

175

TYPE 82

Esprit Turbo, HC & Essex 1980

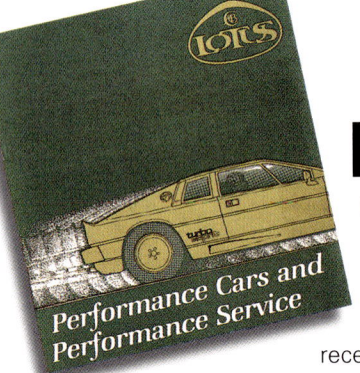

Delayed by work on the DeLorean project, it was not until 1980 that Lotus finally felt able to unveil the much needed new Type 82 Esprit Turbo. Built around the new longer-stroke 2.2 litre 910 engine it also received a heavily revised version of the original Giugiaro body, the most obvious characteristics of which were a new wrap-around front bumper and spoiler assembly, new sideskirts, a kick-up rear spoiler and twin NACA-type ducts beneath the doors to improve engine-bay cooling. Lotus were naturally keen to stress that this was no mere bolt-on turbo, rather 'a fully developed and redesigned motor car in its own right'. Accordingly, and to further remove it from its forebear, it also gained black louvres over the engine bay and a set of 15-inch alloys, mostly BBS but with a few cars getting three-piece Compomotive wheels instead. The launch party at the Royal Albert Hall having been funded by F1-sponsor Essex Petroleum, the appearance of a colourful and more luxurious 'Essex' version (reproduced here in 1/43rd scale by Western Models, along with the appropriate sales sheet) came as no surprise, nor that produced to commemorate the car's role alongside 007 in For Your Eyes Only – an appearance which did much to boost sales against the recessionary background of the early 1980s. In fact the car proved to be one of the fastest selling the company had ever produced (and the fastest, hence this Quickest off the Marque advertisement for the Esprit Turbo HC from 1987), helped in no small part by a welter of promotional material including this square green dealer brochure for 'Performance and Performance Service' from 1986, a 6-page brochure

Esprit Turbo, HC & Essex 1980

featuring a red Turbo and a yellow S3 (from 1982), and a 1988 brochure which used the previous season's F1 car, the Type 98T. The car was also used to promote JPS designer label clothing, photographed on location in the South of France, by Lotus Cars USA which with a favourable exchange rate could undercut the rival Ferrari 308 by almost 20%, and as the centrepiece of a rare and rather trendy poster produced in 1984 by Grey Publications.

PICTURE DETAILS

Model, Western Models, GB, white metal, 1/43rd

Brochure, Lotus Sales & Service, 1986

Sales / specification sheet, Essex Turbo, 1980

Brochure, 6-page, Lotus Cars, 1982

Brochure spread, JPS designer label, 1983

Advert, Lotus Cars USA.

Advert, US dealer, El Camino Real, California

Poster, Grey Publications, 1984

Folder, USA dealers.

Advert, Lotus Cars, 1982

Advert, Autocar, 1987

TYPE 82

177

Esprit Turbo & SE 1988

With no new type-number despite a substantially new shell, the Peter Stevens reworking of the Giugiaro original was one of the most significant changes to the Esprit line-up and contributed in no small part to its incredible longevity. Rechristened the Turbo SE, its more rounded profile was reminiscent of the rival Ferrari 328GTB although there was never any mistaking the essential Esprit-ness of the new car. The truth was that financial constraints precluded any wholesale redesign but with electronic fuel injection replacing the Dellorto carbs, and a new Renault 'box in place of the venerable Citroën-Maserati unit, even the 910 engine got a new lease of life and was now producing a healthy 265bhp. In Turbo form at least – once again a normally-aspirated car was also offered – it was, however, by now becoming an alarmingly expensive car. Cheaper than a Ferrari, but as the press were beginning to point out, hardly a bargain for what was still only a four-cylinder car.

Advertising kept sales reasonably healthy, however, examples shown here including a full page advertisement for the SE which appeared in the Sunday Times in 1991, a particularly imaginative Dutch offering asking 'What combines British luxury with Forza Italiana?' (answer: the Lotus Esprit Turbo), and two advertisements placed by Lotus Cars, one

Esprit Turbo & SE 1988

for the official Lotus Used Cars register which, it has been suggested, may provide a hint that new car sales were finally suffering. Also shown are various Lotus cars specification sheets for different variations on the new car – Esprit, Esprit Turbo, Esprit SE and the Esprit Turbo SE – three different spreads from the 1989, '40 years of Excellence' brochure, and finally a leaflet produced for the Turbo Esprit by Lotus Cars USA.

PICTURE DETAILS

Specification sheets, Lotus Cars.

Brochure, 12-page, Lotus Cars, 1988/9

Leaflet, Lotus Cars USA

Advert, Lotus Cars, Holland.

Advert, The Sunday Times, 1991

Adverts, Car magazine, 1990

TYPE 82

Esprit Turbo S4 & Sport 300 1994

A more or less continual process of modification and refinement – in the absence of any real development budget, the only way of keeping such an old design in the showrooms – meant that before long the Esprit SE – blown or otherwise – had morphed again, this time emerging as the S4 and later S4S. Tweaks to the front suspension geometry, a new anti-roll bar, and new springs and dampers on all four corners – it was all welcome and even slightly overdue, but it came at a price which soon saw the Esprit selling – if not exactly like hot cakes – at a towering £47,000. Once again the advertising department did its best to keep things moving – witness this full page Car magazine advertisement, 'The car will take your breath away', and another showing a bungee jumper as one of the few ways (presumably) in which Sunday Times readers could rival the sheer experience and thrill of driving a Lotus S4. Eventually however, the development engineers had to come to their assistance, and before long a limited-edition 'high wing' version called the Sport 300 was wheeled out, based largely on the US-only X180-R and with its power output raised to 300bhp and everything that could be stripped out hastily stripped out. Some of the promotional material for this car and the S4 was pretty standard, like the folded brochure wallet and inserts shown here, but some was a little bit more

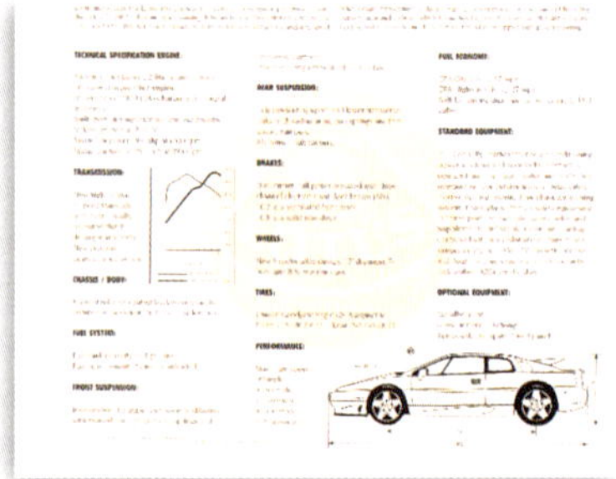

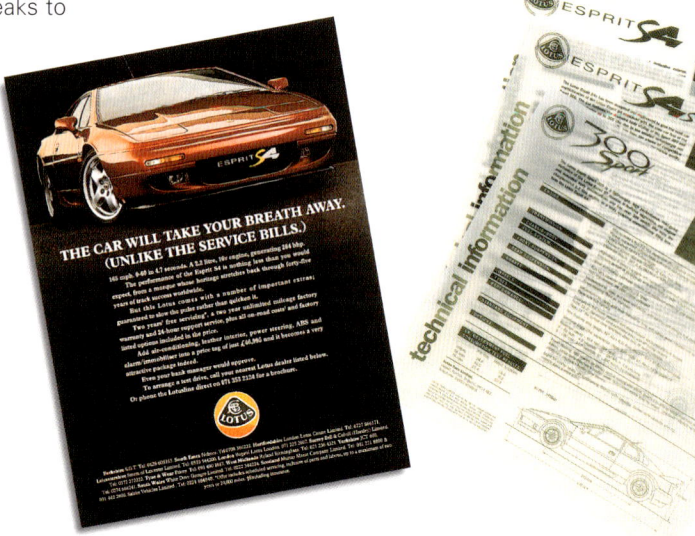

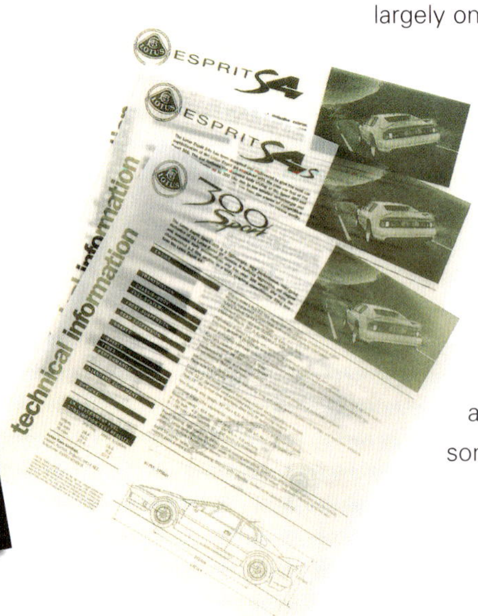

TYPE 82

180

Esprit Turbo S4 & Sport 300 1994

PICTURE DETAILS

Model, SMTS, GB, white metal, 1/43rd

Specification sheets, Lotus Cars.

Advert, Car magazine, September 1984

Advert, The Sunday Times, 1995

Brochure, wallet and specification sheets, Lotus Cars.

Brochure Sport 300, 6-page, Lotus Cars.

Brochure, 8-page, Lotus Cars.

Brochure S4S, 6-page, Lotus Cars

Brochure, Lotus Cars, France.

offbeat, like the one entitled 'The true definition of performance lies in the fusion of sensation and function', and another which invited drivers to Satisfy Your Driving Ambition. Also shown here is a model of an Esprit S4, made by SMTS in Great Britain to 1/43rd scale and of white metal, and various Lotus specification sheets for the S4 and for the Sport 300.

TYPE 82

Esprit Turbo V8 & Sport 350 1996

Whilst no-one was in the business of actually knocking the Esprit publicly, repeated calls for what one motoring hack called 'a more euphonious driveline' – more cylinders, in other words – could not be ignored for ever and although the four cylinder car was to remain in production a while longer (charge-cooled now, and renamed the Esprit GT3), a V8-engined production Esprit was finally unveiled in 1996. The big news came in the form of the new 32-valve Type 918 engine, a 3.5 litre unit capable of meeting all existing emissions criteria and outputting a phenomenal 350bhp at 6,500rpm. What Lotus justifiably called 'the exclamation marque' – as per this 1998 brochure – gave the model line-up precisely the sort of shot in the arm it had long been missing and it is not hard to be swept along with the enthusiasm of the related promotional material from the time such as this 6-page brochure

'Celebrating 50 Years of Engineering Excellence.' Certainly, after staying in production for more than half of this timespan, the Esprit had never looked better nor moved as quickly: 0-60mph in well under five seconds, 0-100mph in only 10, and with a top speed of around 175mph. And of course racing versions had an extra 200bhp to play with.... For Lotus customers more was to come in the shape of the sensational Sport 350 – 'the most extreme and focused development so far of this classic 21-year old formula' – and although the Esprit was by no means any longer necessarily the bargain supercar it had once been (see the price lists shown here for the Esprit V8 and Esprit GT3) it was still capable of holding its own

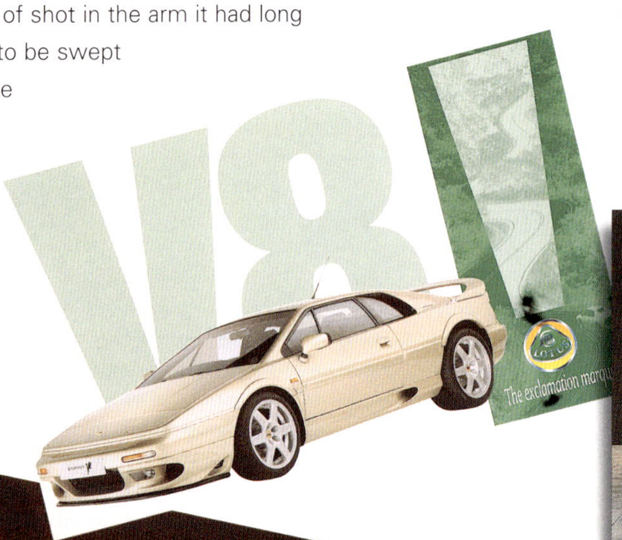

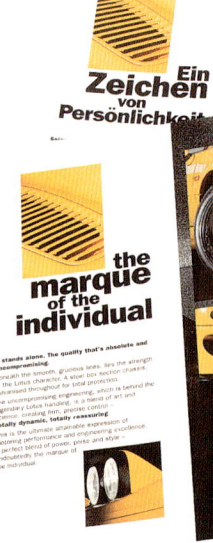

Esprit Turbo V8 & Sport 350 1996

PICTURE DETAILS

Brochure, Lotus Engineering 1996
B: Spread from Sport 300 brochure
Brochure, 6-page, Lotus Cars, 1998
Brochure, 8-page, Lotus Cars, 1998
Brochure V8 engine, 4-page, Lotus Cars, 1999
Price list & brochures, 1999
Specification sheet, Lotus Cars, Sport 350, 1998
Brochure V8, Lotus Cars, English & German.
Brochure, Lotus Cars, 1999

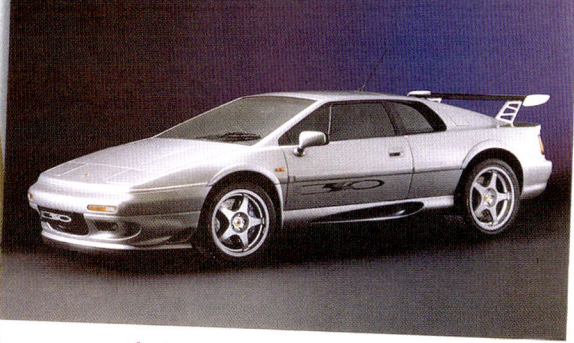

Lotus Esprit V8 Sport 350

against the stiffest and most contemporary competition. Rebodied, re-engined and reengineered it might have been, but what we see today is still essentially that stunning concept car that was wheeled out by Ital Design back in 1972. What is thus one of the all-time great automotive survivors, the Type 82 Esprit is, nevertheless, still by any standards very much a thoroughly modern machine and phenomenally desireable piece of kit.

TYPE 82

Elite S2 1980

Time spent on the Delorean and finalising the Sunbeam Lotus hatchback for Talbot delayed any improvements to the company's own line-up but in 1980 Lotus finally announced the latest iteration of the Elite. Known both as the Elite S2 and as the S2.2 which utilised the longer-stroke 2.2 litre Type 912 engine, giving the car much improved torque values and fuel economy. Corrosion protection was uprated too, the car also gaining a new Getrag 5-speed with the option of a 3-speed automatic. At the time several advertisements appeared optimistically describing the new car as a business alternative to the usual company car, one of these being shown here along with another for the Riviera option – a removable roof panel offered at the time – and numerous different brochures for the S2.2 range, including one which cleverly converts to an Eclat as the reader turns the page. The model is a Corgi die cast toy in 1/43rd scale and is believed to be a Series 2 car (it's hard to tell). The handbook certainly relates to the later car, however, as does the acetate copy of the Lotus Cars colour chart for all the S2.2 models and the colour range card from 1981.

TYPE 83

184

Eclat S2 1980

The car which was eventually to kill off the Elite, the Eclat's development precisely mirrored that of its parent, so that in May 1980 it too received the long-stroke Type 912 engine with a corresponding improvement in torque and fuel consumption. Like the Elite, it too was confusingly known as both the Series 2 or S2 and the S2.2 – but then confusion over names was nothing new at Lotus. This, after all, was the car which had originally been tagged the Elite Coupé, then briefly the Elite Sprint, and was to become at various times the Eclat 3, the Eclat Excel and, finally in 1982, the Excel. Whatever, for the S2.2 the popular coupé also gained new spoilers, a new rear bumper assembly, more reliable pop-up headlamps and the option of a removable 'Riviera' roof panel. Naturally the price rose too, to a heady £16,751, before eventually falling back to a recessionary £14,850 in October 1981 in a bid to ride the downwave as sales of Elites and Eclats together fell to as low as just two or three units a month.

PICTURE DETAILS

Model, Corgi, GB, die cast, 1/43rd

Hand book, Lotus Cars.

Colour range cards, Lotus Cars, 1981

Colour chart, Lotus Cars, 1981

Advert, Lotus Cars, Autocar, 1981

Leaflet, Lotus Cars, Lotus range & dealer list.

Advert, Lotus Cars, 1980

Brochure, 12-page, Lotus Cars, 1980

TYPE 84

Esprit S3 1981

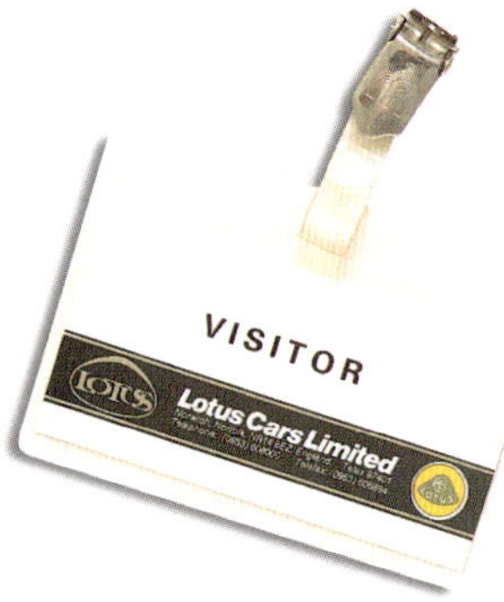

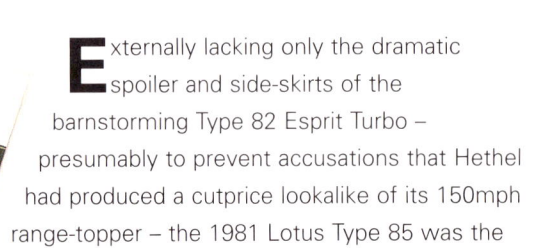

Externally lacking only the dramatic spoiler and side-skirts of the barnstorming Type 82 Esprit Turbo – presumably to prevent accusations that Hethel had produced a cutprice lookalike of its 150mph range-topper – the 1981 Lotus Type 85 was the first fruit of a concentrated effort by the factory to rationalise its model ranges, components and manufacturing methods in a bid to put the company back on a more secure footing financially. Called the Esprit S3, the new car still used the same 912 engine as the outgoing S2.2, and the same Citroën SM gearbox, but in a clear bid to boost flagging sales it was substantially cheaper – saving buyers 12% overall or a hefty £1,800. At the same time it gained colour-coded bumpers, sills and spoilers – to further distinguish it from the Turbo – and the same car's new Momo steering wheel as part of a modest interior upgrade. Motor magazine called the result 'the Esprit's coming of age, with reducing production costs and improving quality...this is a much better product all round.' The first brochure for the new car is reproduced here, showing a gold car on the cover, and was printed by Haig-McAlister Limited in 1981. It is accompanied by an extra-large fold-out brochure for the S3 and Turbo models from 1983, a colour chart dating from around 1982, and (with the green cover) a later 10-page brochure featuring a very large and controversial 'Wickens' badge and the entire Lotus range. The other two brochures are from 1986 (for just

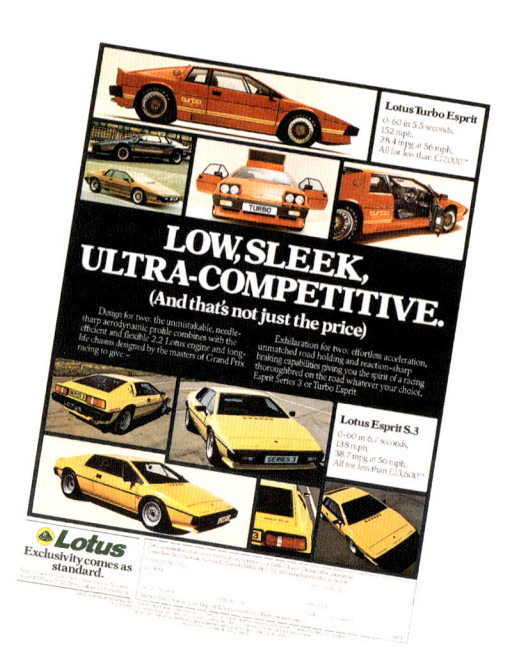

Esprit S3 1981

PICTURE DETAILS

Model, Eugene Van Herpen, Holland, metal, 1/43rd

Brochure, Lotus Cars, printer Haig-McAlister Ltd advertising, 1981

Brochure, 8-page fold out, Lotus Cars, 1983

Visitor badge, Lotus Cars, 1986

Brochure, 10-page, Lotus Cars, 1985

Brochure, 8-page, Lotus Cars, 1986

Brochure, 8-page concertina, Lotus Cars, 1987

Leaflet, USA dealers.

Poster, Autosport, ICS racing.

Colour chart, Lotus Cars, 1987

the S3 Esprit) and a 1987 redesign concertina type brochure for the whole range of Lotus cars. Also shown is a solid metal scratch-built model of the Type 85 on wooden plinth, made by Eugene Van Herpen in Holland to 1/43rd scale, an official Lotus Cars visitors badge from 1986, a promotional leaflet produced for the factory's dealers in the USA, and a poster for the ICS racing version of the car which was issued free with Autosport magazine.

187

TYPE 85

TYPE 86

Formula 1 1980

By late 1979 it was clear that what Lotus conceived, its rivals would perfect. Rather than seeking merely to refine the elegant Type 80, Chapman decided to take another quantum leap in order to reconcile the conflicting requirements of a suspension system which had to insulate the driver from road shocks while optimising the vehicles overall aerodynamic functionality. His solution, twin but separate chassis, had something in common with a modern HGV with stiff suspension carrying the load and a sprung cab to insulate the driver. As such it was more accurately described at the time as a 'technology demonstrator' rather than a full-on racing car, and indeed was announced as such in the Essex Team Lotus press release reproduced here which refers to its development and launch as 'a racing secret'. In the event, however, Chapman's racing secret didn't last long and whilst the Type 86 underwent testing with Mansell and de Angelis, the FIA 'clarified' its existing regulations to effectively outlaw the new design.

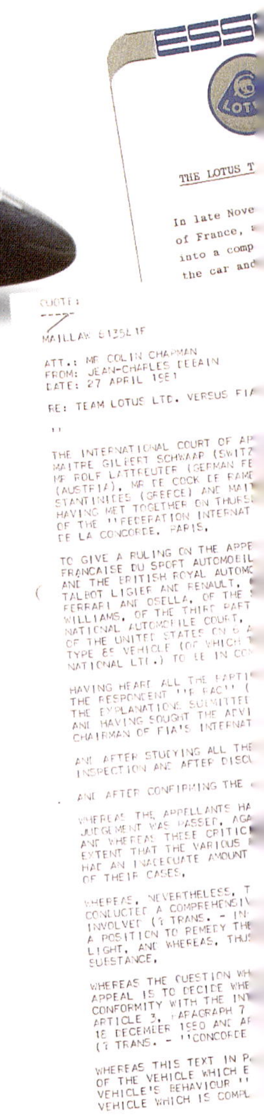

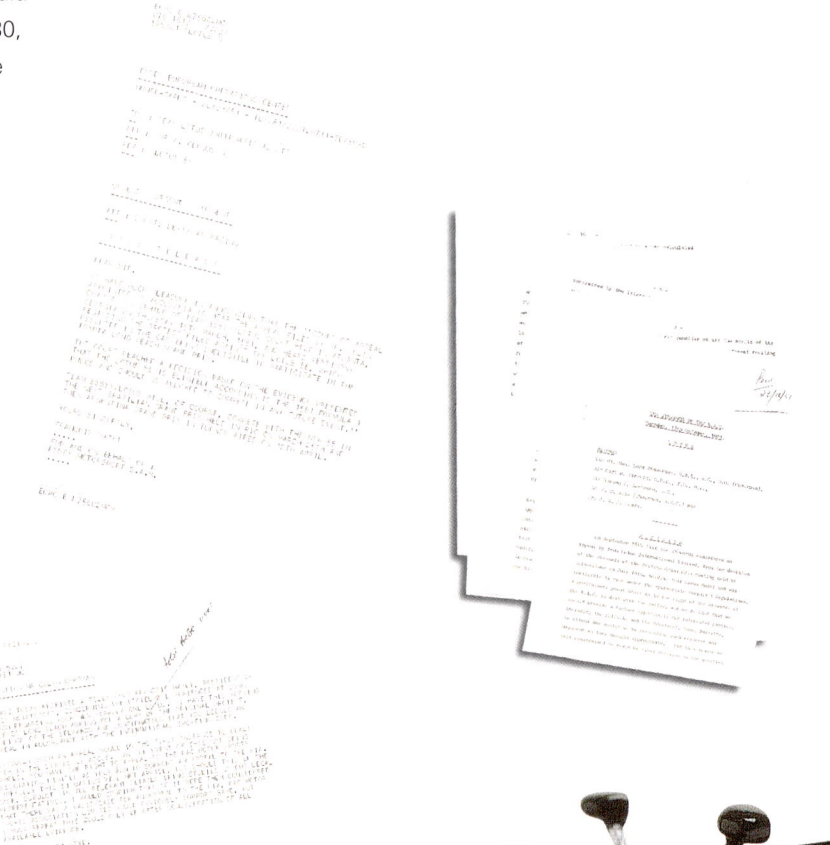

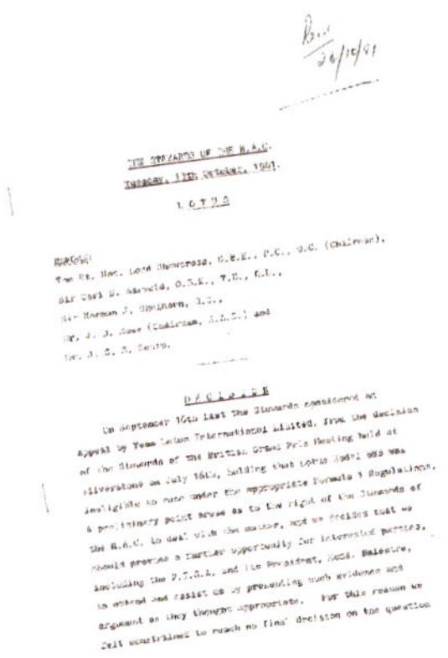

One of the early development wind tunnel models made by Team Lotus is shown here, along with two views of a commercial model of the Type 86 made by Cogy in Italy to 1/43rd scale and of white metal.

188

Formula 1 1981

Despite problems with FIA over the Type 86 'technology demonstrator', Chapman pressed ahead with a 'production' version, building two Type 88s to contest the 1981 season. Controversy naturally attended its every appearance with the car passing scrutineering then attracting a hail of protests from the season leaders Ferrari and Williams and several other rivals. Confusion reigned – as per these telex messages between Team Lotus and the FIA, banning the car, re-instating it and then banning it once more - before Chapman announced his withdrawal at San Marino, the first time Lotus had been absent from the grid since 1958.

The model shown here is a later Type 88B made of white metal by Scale Model Cars to 1/43rd scale, and along side it a page from Autocar dated June 1981 when John Miles was given the rare opportunity to drive and write about Type 88 and an original front wing from an Essex-liveried version of the car.

TYPE 88

PICTURE DETAILS

Wind tunnel model, Team Lotus, 1980

Model, Cogy, Italy, white metal, 1/43rd

Press release, Essex Team Lotus, Feb 1981

Model, Scale Model Cars, GB, white metal, 1/43rd

Article, Autocar June 1981

Telex messages, Team Lotus / FIA, March / April 1981

Front wing, 1981, Classic Team Lotus

TYPE 87

Formula 1 1981

In reality another in a growing line of stop-gap cars, the Type 87 was nevertheless the most sophisticated of the conventional Lotus ground-effect cars produced so far. It was wheeled out at a time when the team's preferred machine – the inspired but understandably controversial Type 88 – was denied the chance to run despite having yet to be 'proved to be ineligible'. Disappointment over the Type 88 was balanced to some degree – for the fans at least – by the news that the cars were to race once again in the black and gold livery of the old John Player Specials. A multi-million pound deal having been struck at Brands Hatch with Imperial Tobacco, and with Mansell joined by Elio de Angelis, the new car also used much of the running gear of the Type 88 so there was an understandable air of optimism around the pits at the start of the 1981 season. Despite a promising start at Monaco, however, it soon became clear that this was not the car to put Lotus back in front. The best result – Mansell, 4th, Las Vegas – was far from typical and although in revised 'B' form the car went on to contest a second season, it was an uphill struggle all the way and the podium remained as distant a prospect as ever. The model of Type 87 shown

Formula 1 1981

here was made in Britain by Scale Racing Cars, and is shown with a pre-JPS signing Essex Team Lotus press release and photographs. On June 15th another release was issued confirming the return of John Player Team Lotus, and this same release was issued again the following year with only minimal changes for the slightly longer, lighter and larger-wheeled Type 87B. The remaining press release is somewhat more mysterious. Obviously written after the close of the Type 87's racing career and citing the car's first and last appearances – Monaco 1981, Las Vegas 1981 – it is printed on an earlier style of JPS letterhead, perhaps suggesting the team was using up old stocks of paper.

PICTURE DETAILS

Model, Scale Racing Cars, GB, white metal, 1/43rd

Press release and photos, Essex Team Lotus, Feb 1981

Press release, JPTL, June 1981

Press release, JPTL, Type 87B, 1982

Rear body work, 1982, Classic Team Lotus

TYPE 87

Excel 1982

Originally known as the Eclat 3, then as the Eclat Excel, as the M55 (at least within the factory walls) and eventually simply as the Excel, what was to prove the final iteration of this once popular and now much modified model was announced to the press in October 1982. At the time new-car sales were in free fall – with a recession on the one hand and rising prices on the other resulting in a drop from around 1,200 annually to just 380-odd – a situation Lotus hoped to reverse with a shrewd raid on the parts-bin of it's partner Toyota in order to update the ageing four-seater coupé.

Externally the aerodynamics received a major tweak and a 7% improvement thanks to a new front spoiler and softer edges all round. At the same time a number of Toyota components popped into the make-up including door handles and a new filler cap which was at least discretely hidden beneath the large trademark green and yellow 'ACBC' company badge. This reliance on the Japanese – a shortlived solution as Group Lotus was soon to be purchased by General Motors – continued under the skin too. The car stuck with its well-proven Type 912 16v dohc 2.2 litre engine, but a number of other modifications were made to enable the Excel to use Toyota running gear wherever possible. The most significant components thus employed were a version of the Toyota 5-speed gearbox – essentially the same as that

Excel 1982

PICTURE DETAILS

Brochure, 8-page, Lotus Cars, 1986
Brochure, Lotus Cars, Eclat Excel, 1983
Brochure, Lotus Cars, Excel, 1983
Brochure, Lotus Cars, Excel SE, 1986
Colour charts, Lotus Cars, 1986 & 1987
Advert, Lotus Cars, 1984
Advert, Lotus Cars, 1986
Advert, Car magazine, May 1990

fitted to the Supra, and said to be 6% more efficient than the old one – and a new final drive unit which brought more refinement to the car and markedly reduced noise levels. The ventilated disc brakes were Toyota's too, as were the driveshafts, but whilst the chassis was finally galvanised to improve its longevity the interior remained largely as before with a little extra headroom and the option of a new three-spoke wheel. But perhaps the most significant improvement of all was a price reduction of more than £1,000. That took the car down to a more competitive £13,787 at a time when affordability was precisely what the market was demanding.

That said, what Autocar's testers called 'a completely different and dramatically improved car – a paragon of poise' was never

TYPE 89

Excel 1982

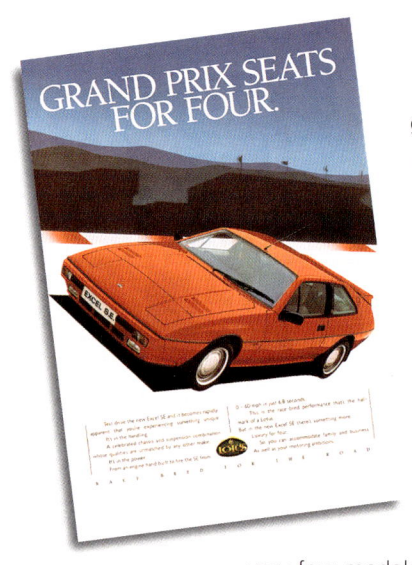

going to be quite enough to halt the decline of a company still very much in shock from the sudden loss of its founder. The Excel certainly achieved one important thing, however, and selling a respectable 2,159 units all told, it and the later Excel SE managed to keep things ticking over until 1989 and the launch of the much-vaunted new Elan. Surprisingly, given those largely respectable sales figures, very few models of the car were ever produced, although pictured here is one by by Alezan of France of a 1/43rd scale resin model of an early car.

Also shown is a considerable amount of factory literature produced at the time including a 4-pager for the 'Hethel Celebration Excel', another from 1991, an 8-page brochure featuring the complete range and another for the Excel (both from 1986), the very first 'Eclat Excel' brochure from 1983 and, from the same year, the first edition referring to the new car as simply the Excel. Also, several single-page specification sheets for the 1988 Excel, the 1989 Excel SE, and – with an illustration – the 1989 Excel. The identical design was used for the brochure for the 1986 Excel SE, with just a few changed images and specifications to take account of the improvements which included blisters over the front wheel arches and a rear spoiler. The two Lotus colour charts are from the same period, whilst various advertisements show the early Excel on a full page and, in an

Excel 1982

attempt to foster a more obviously upmarket image, a 1987/88 version photographed outside Ketteringham Hall in the company of one of the team's famous racing car transporters. Finally two of a series of advertisements promoting secondhand Lotus cars – 'as good as new' – through the official dealer network are shown here, along with an advertisement for the new 1986 model, 'hot off the test track'.

PICTURE DETAILS

Model, Alezan, France, resin, 1/43rd

Brochure, 4-page, Lotus Cars, 1991

Brochure, 8-page, Lotus Cars 1986

Specification sheets, 88 Excel, 89 Excel SE, 89 Excel.

Brochure, Lotus Cars, 1986

Brochure, Lotus Cars, 1985

Advert, Autocar, April 1990

Advert, Car magazine, June 1990

TYPE 89

TYPE 91

Formula 1 1982

Essentially a revision of the Types 87B and 88, what became known as 'Colin Chapman's Weight Watcher' was actually the first car to be completed after Peter Wright took the helm at the team, leaving Chapman more time to deal with more pressing Group Lotus issues. As such, the Type 91 – the 'missing' Type 90 was a still-born Elan successor – retained the earlier Kevlar monocoque but was fitted with even stiffer suspension and an 'underpod' to provide the last word in tuneable aerodynamics. Wright also claimed to have shaved 10% off the weight of 'everything' – a necessity if the Cosworth 3.0 litre was to stand a chance against its new turbocharged rivals. The original press release for the car's launch is shown here with a menu from the Hotel Nelson, Norwich, dated February 16, 1982, and two rather more unusual mementoes: a special bottle of wine from the 9th Historic Festival,

Formula 1 1982

1994, at Zandvoort, and some Republic of Madagascar stamps showing the car, Chapman and Elio de Angelis. De Angelis also made it onto a Tissot-sponsored poster which also featured a young Nigel Mansell, the Swiss watchmaker being a subsidiary sponsor although the cars retained their 'traditional' gold and black livery as can be seen in these two models, one an Italian Hotwheels toy, the other a 1/43rd scale model made by Hi-Fi in Italy of white metal. Also shown is a rear wing endplate from 1982, two different front wings (from Classic Team Lotus), a Club Team Lotus sticker, and an 'official' beermat featuring the car. The Type 91 also formed the centrepiece of a 1982 brochure for the new JPS 'designer label' clothing range which had models draping themselves over the car. No amount of glitz could disguise the facts, however, and in the final analysis the Type 91 did little to relieve Chapman's gloom about circuit racing: de Angelis won in Austria, the team's first chequered flag for four years, but the turbos were coming and the Lotus/Cosworth combination was more than showing its age.

PICTURE DETAILS

- Model, Hi-Fi, Italy, white metal, 1/43rd.
- Model, Hot Wheels, Italy, plastic, 1/25th
- Rear wing endplate, 1982, Classic Team Lotus.
- Front wing, 1982, Classic Team Lotus
- Dinner menu, JPTL press release, Feb 1982
- Wine bottle, 9th Historic Festival, Zandvoort, 1994
- Lotus stamps, Republic of Madagascar, 2000
- Club Team Lotus sticker, 1982
- Beermat, JPTL
- Tissot poster, Autosport, 1982
- Advert, JPS, Autosport, July 1982
- Advert, various sponsors, Autosport, Feb 1982

TYPE 91

TYPE 92

Formula 1 1983

Actually the final flourish of the enduring Lotus-Cosworth relationship (and despite the JPS cigarette advertisement shown here) Nigel Mansell's Type 92 was a normally-aspirated car designed to run alongside his team-mate's Type 93 which already had the turbocharged Renault engine. This strange situation arose because the agreement between Lotus and the French provided only sufficient V6 engines for the one car. And whilst the Cosworth could never prove competitive in such company, Chapman went to great lengths to enhance its chances by incorporating his latest secret ingredient: computer controlled active suspension. Unfortunately the reactions of the equipment were never equal to the task – particularly given the extra weight burden (as per the specification sheet shown here) – and after just two outings (and two 12th places) the secret ingredient was stripped out leaving Mansell to battle on without it. With no wins to its credit as a result, the Type 92 is instead commemorated by another John Player Team Lotus beermat and a child's pedal car best described as 'almost' a Type 92.

198

Formula 1 1983

TYPE 93T

PICTURE DETAILS

Childrens Pedal Car, 1985?

Beermat, JPTL

Specification sheet / press release, JPTL

Advert, JPS, Autosport, July 1983

Sticker, Club Team Lotus, 1983

Front wing endplate, 1983, Classic Team Lotus.

Press photos, Team Lotus.

Programme, European GP, Brands Hatch, 1983

Press pack with spread, European GP, Brands Hatch, 1983

Press release, spec sheet & photo, JPTL.

Press release, JPTL.

Promotional leaflet, JPS, 1983

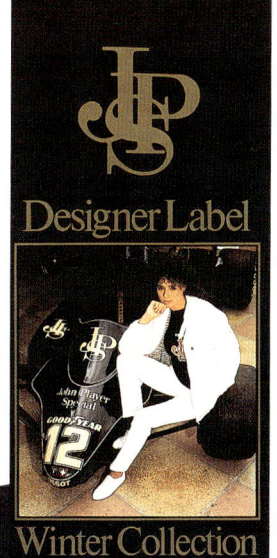

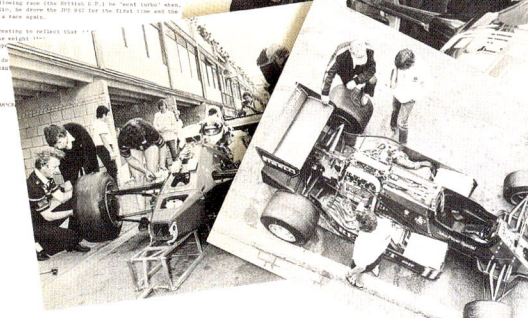

The first Lotus since the founder's death, the company's first turbocharged F1 contender, and also the first to be built using the company's massive new Kevlar-curing oven, the Type 93T – literally 'baked to perfection' at 125°C – was primarily the work of Birmingham University graduate Martin Ogilvie. Launched with all due pomp and circumstance, but with the team still clearly reeling from Chapman's sudden death, the car is seen here on the cover of the programme for the 1983 Brands Hatch European Grand Prix, on an official Club Lotus Team sticker, and in a set of three team photographs showing early testing. The press pack for the race at Brands Hatch also included a cutaway of the car, and two press releases were issued showing de Angelis at the wheel and announcing a new car 'for Nigel'. In neither's hands was it a success, however, and with too much to learn too quickly, team boss Peter Warr was soon persuaded to abandon both cars and to start again from scratch.

199

TYPE 94T

Formula 1 1983

From conception to reality in just five weeks with the factory working double shifts seven days a week, Gerard Ducarouge, the new Chief Engineer, somehow managed to produce two new cars for the team and in time for the all-important 1983 British Grand Prix. With new suspension, new bodywork, a new gearbox and even new pedals, the Type 94T retained a few elements of the aforementioned Type 91 but had radically different weight distribution of a calibre which apparently left de Angelis feeling 'wildly enthusiastic' about his new car's feel and attitude although Mansell was still somewhat less forthcoming.

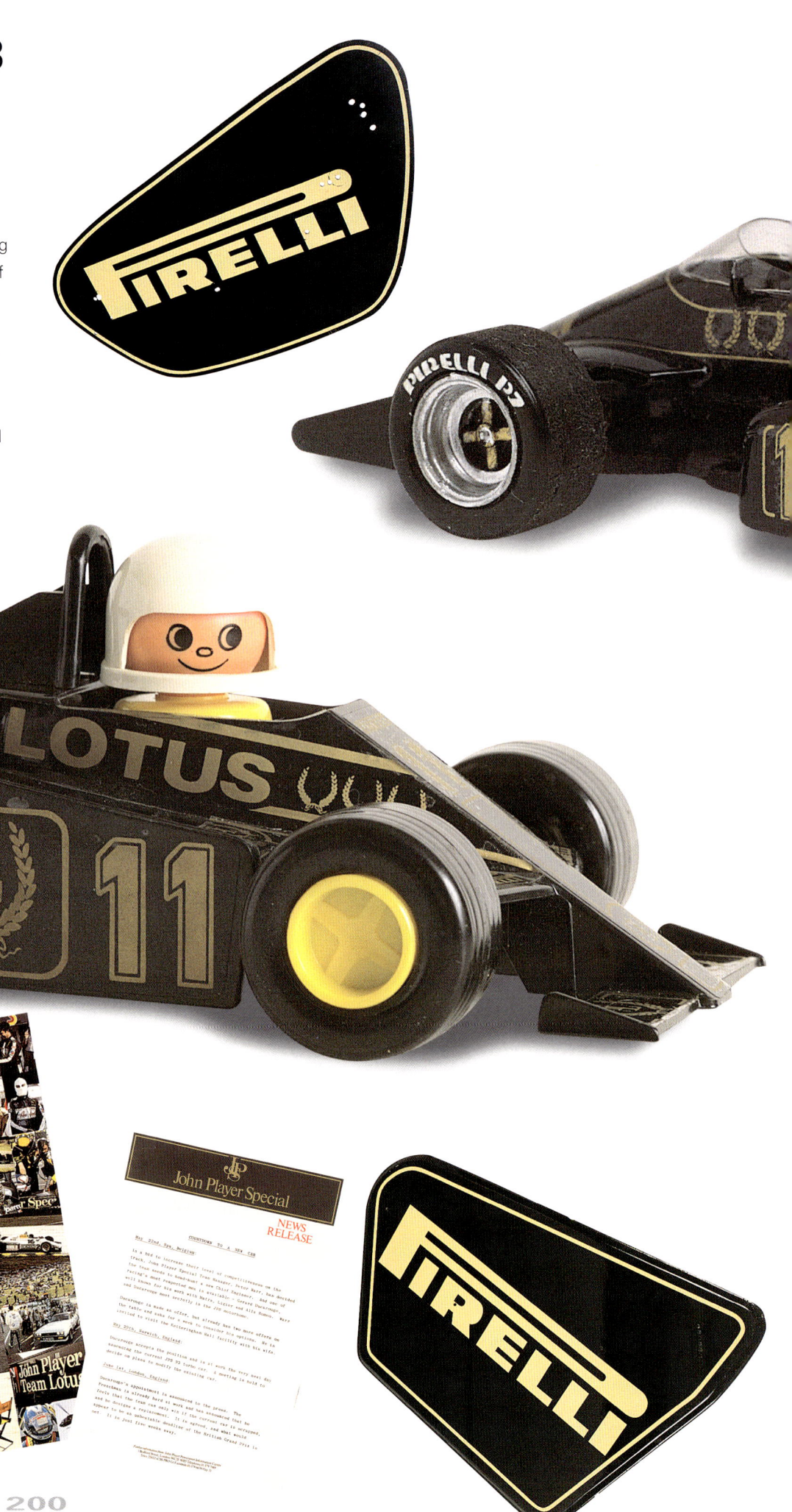

Formula 1 1983

TYPE 94T

Inevitably as the season progressed, various tweaks and so on were tried, the two different versions of a single-element rear wing end plate used in 1983 shown here being employed as an alternative to the earlier four-tier version. Such modifications paid off in the end too, with de Angelis securing pole position and Mansell storming home in third place before his home crowd in the Brands Hatch Grand Prix of Europe. A John Player poster for that event is reproduced here and whilst for Lotus it wasn't exactly the greatest race ever, it was to be the best result the team enjoyed all year and as such proved sufficient to justify Mansell's place in the team, to thank Imperial Tobacco and John Player for sticking with Lotus throughout the long years of no wins, and above all – as Elio de Angelis put it – to prove that here at last was a new car, and one which worked as Chapman would have wanted it to work. "It's a pity the Old Man is not here," he said, "he would have loved this." The car also reappeared later as a die cast model in 1/43rd scale, and as a rather groovy plastic toy which on close examination reveals couldn't really be any other Type No. The final exhibit is the original driver's race suit from 1983 as worn by Nigel Mansell – like the turbocharged Lotus not quite yet a champion, but with luck and perserverence well on his way.

PICTURE DETAILS

Model, Tameo, Italy, die cast, 1/43rd

Toy, plastic, 4"

Drivers race suit, Mansell, 1983

Rear wing endplates, 1983, Classic Team Lotus.

Poster, John Player Grand Prix, Europe, 1984

Press release, JPS, July 1983

Press release, JPTL, July 1983

TYPE 95T

Formula 1 1984

Smaller and slimmer than before, the third turbocharged Lotus F1 car also exhibited incredible survivability with all four cars still intact after 16 races, two pole positions and six front-row starts. Once again power came from the Renault V6 which was now supplied to no fewer than three F1 teams – indeed the French were eventually to sign on for another three seasons with Lotus – and whilst Ducarouge's new design was never quite enough to win the 1984 World Drivers' Championship, de Angelis finished no fewer than 12 races and took third place for the year, despite having never actually been first past the chequered flag. The car was the last Lotus Mansell was to drive (it is his car modelled here, by Hi-Fi in Italy) but significantly the first to welcome Ayrton Senna to the team – also Britain's Johnny Dumfries, who made the cover of Autocar prior to signing in 1986. The 95T itself appeared in an advertisement for Simpson Racewear, on a John Player Team Lotus postcard – cheap and cheerful, in black and white, on some stamps produced in 2000 for Madagascar, and in another splendid Tony Matthews cutaway published by the team.

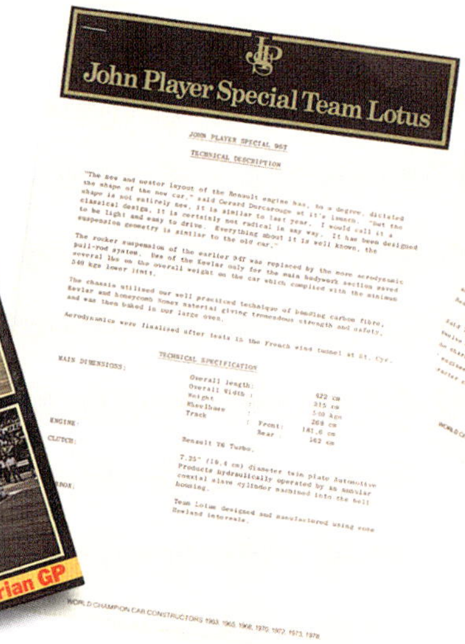

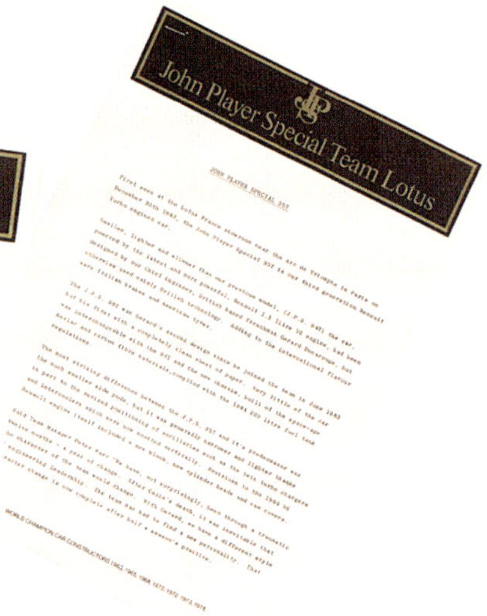

John Player Special Team Lotus Type 95T

Indianapolis Car 1985

Two decades after Jim Clark had triumphed in the Indianapolis 500 came a request from the erstwhile F2 team boss Roy Winklemann who fancied seeing Lotus take its chances in the US PPG/CART series. The invitation was irresistible – and not just because the only four drivers ever to win the Indy 500 and the F1 World Championship were all Lotus drivers – and work began immediately on the stunning 720bhp Type 96T which was announced to the press via the Camel Team Lotus press release reproduced here and with the accompanying official photographs. Team Lotus design drawings – front, side and aerial elevations – show a more substantial machine than contemporary F1 designs, but the essentials were much the same and looked promising. Politics intervened, however, and with hostility from the established teams the car remained a non-starter. Elegant, full of potential, (as shown in the official Team Lotus press photo, taken outside Ketteringham Hall) but never any more than that.

PICTURE DETAILS

Model, Hi-Fi, Italy, white metal, 1/43rd

Advert, Simpson Racewear, Autosport, March 1984

Poster, Team Lotus, cutaway drawing by Tony Matthews, 1984

Postcard, JPTL.

Autosport, January 1985

Press release & spec sheets, JPTL, Feb 1984

Lotus stamps, Republic of Madagascar, 2000

Press release, Camel Team Lotus.

Third angle projection, Team Lotus.

Press photo, Team Lotus, 1985

TYPE 96T

Formula 1 1985

With the Team's new driver leading the field at Imola, Detroit, Silverstone, the 'Ring, Brands Hatch and Adelaide, and taking pole position seven times in his first season with Lotus – de Angelis, the seasoned veteran, managed only one pole – it is perhaps scarcely surprising that the image of Ayrton Senna driving the 1985 Lotus Type 97T has remained so well etched onto the memories of race-goers around the world. A logical progression from the Type 95T, but with new wings to meet the changing race regulations and an altogether more sophisticated approach to driver safety, the new car also paid particular attention to limiting aerodynamic interference around the front wheels using means which were soon copied by all the leading teams. Power still came from Renault, but with the older EF4 engines being used only for qualifying sessions before the cars were switched over for the races themselves to the new Mecachrome-supplied EF5 – an engine whose durability was such that none averaged more than just 270 miles. On race day itself the young Brazilian completely and consistently

Formula 1 1985

TYPE 97T

overshadowed de Angelis (whose overalls are pictured here), winning at Estoril and Spa, although the Italian at least managed one last flourish for the team and took the flag in San Marino after the disqualification of Alain Prost's McLaren. (A sad end, many thought, for such a Lotus stalwart.) As expected as a result, the model shown here is of Senna's car not Elio's, made by Tameo Kits in Italy, to 1/43rd scale and of white metal. It is accompanied by an Olympus Camera promotional fact sheet about the car, and an extremely rare and valuable Olympus poster which has been signed to Peter Warr, the team manager, by his new star driver. Also shown are three of the differently-shaped rear wing endplates which the team evaluated during this landmark season, showing how hard they were trying, one which saw Lotus not just back in the running after so long in the F1 wilderness but with its clever carbon-composite chassis actually winning races too. With Ayrton and the 97T, Team Lotus was at last very much back in business.

PICTURE DETAILS

Model, Tameo kits, Italy, white metal, 1/43rd

Overalls, deAngelis, 1985

Factsheet, Olympus Camera, 1985

Poster, Olympus Cameras, 1985

Rear wing endplates, 1985, Classic Team Lotus.

Press Releases, JPTL, 1985

TYPE 98T

Formula 1 1986

With the French now out of F1 on their own account, Lotus found itself in a role akin to being the Renault works team. That meant it received all the benefits of the latter's really massive R&D budget, whilst the company's other two engine customers (Ligier in France and Britain's Ken Tyrrell) had to look to its subsidiary Mecachrome for engine service and supply. Accordingly, for the new season Lotus obtained the brand new EF15B twin-turbo, designed to give better fuel economy in line with changing race regulations which limited fuel tank size to just 195 litres. This in turn enabled Ducarouge to design an even smaller, lighter chassis, the hugely experienced designer also taking the opportunity to fit an all-important electronic fuel gauge to avoid the most frustrating sort of F1 disaster. For the 1986 season Senna (whose race suit is shown here) was joined by future Le Mans winner Johnny Dumfries. Both are pictured here, along with the outgoing de Angelis and the new car, on a series of postcards issued by the team. Also shown is a trophy presented to

Formula 1 1986

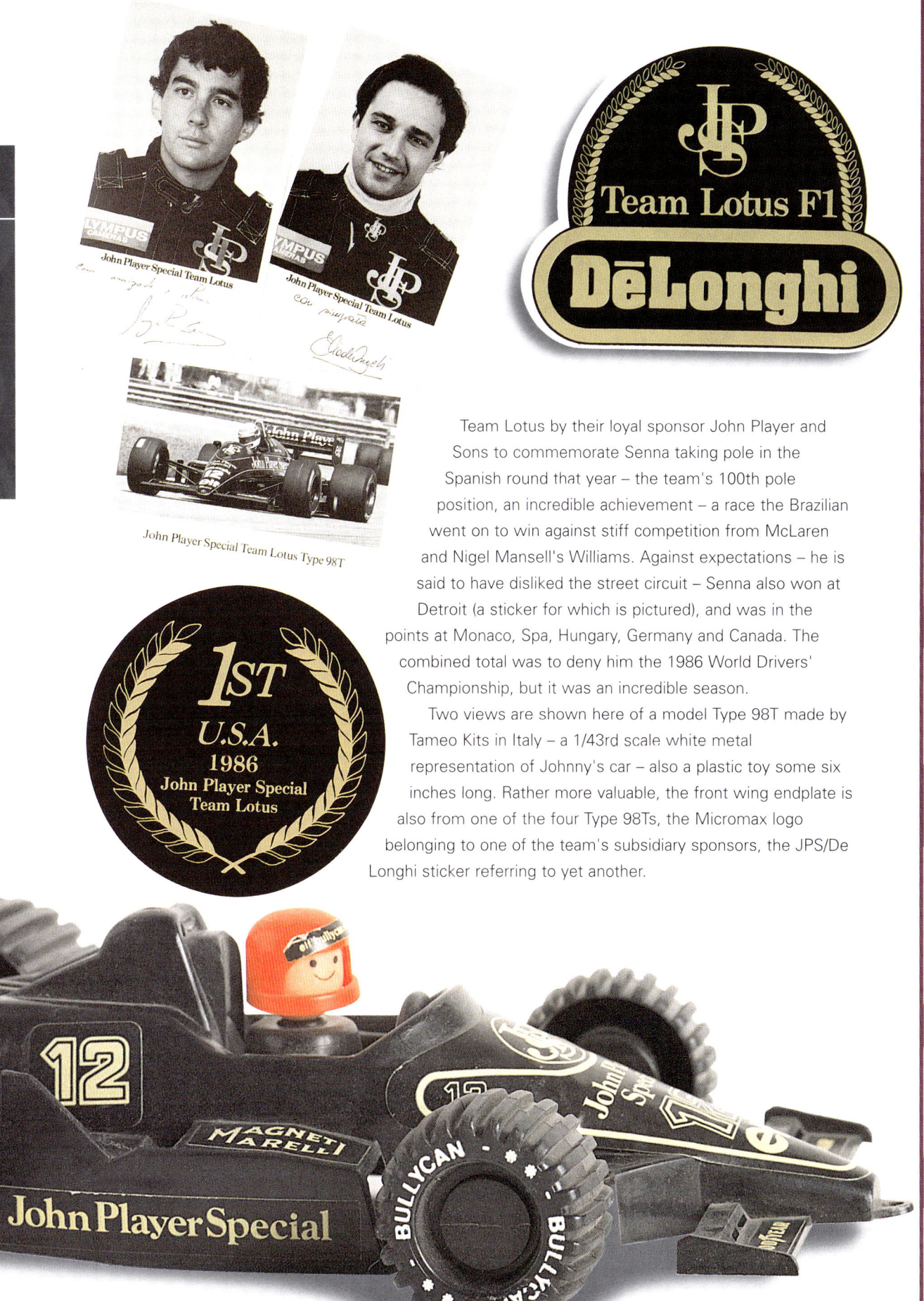

PICTURE DETAILS

Model, Tameo kits, India, white metal, 1/43rd	
Toy, H.Kong, plastic, 6"	
Trophy, John Player & Sons, Spanish GP, 1986	
Race suit, Senna, 1986	
Front wing endplate, 1986, Classic Team Lotus.	
Sticker, JPS/DeLonghi.	
Sticker, JPTL, USGP, 1986	
Postcards, JPTL	

John Player Special Team Lotus Type 98T

Team Lotus by their loyal sponsor John Player and Sons to commemorate Senna taking pole in the Spanish round that year – the team's 100th pole position, an incredible achievement – a race the Brazilian went on to win against stiff competition from McLaren and Nigel Mansell's Williams. Against expectations – he is said to have disliked the street circuit – Senna also won at Detroit (a sticker for which is pictured), and was in the points at Monaco, Spa, Hungary, Germany and Canada. The combined total was to deny him the 1986 World Drivers' Championship, but it was an incredible season.

Two views are shown here of a model Type 98T made by Tameo Kits in Italy – a 1/43rd scale white metal representation of Johnny's car – also a plastic toy some six inches long. Rather more valuable, the front wing endplate is also from one of the four Type 98Ts, the Micromax logo belonging to one of the team's subsidiary sponsors, the JPS/De Longhi sticker referring to yet another.

TYPE 98T

TYPE 99T

Formula 1 1987

A turbocharged V6 from Honda instead of Renault, and vivid yellow and blue Camel branding in place of the long-established JPS black and gold, Gerard Ducarouge may have hinted at similarities by describing his latest F1 design as merely 'a classic car based on the previous three' but to fans of Lotus racing cars the new Type 99T must have seemed startlingly different to much that had gone before. For a start, the construction method harked back to pre-1986 practices – the car's monocoque being once more built up using a single, folded carbon-fibre/Kevlar sheet – and the engine was completely new to the team, the admirably wide powerband of Honda's extremely high-revving RA166-E also necessitated the use of a new Lotus/Hewland six-speed 'box and – because of its tendency to vibrate ferociously – a general strengthening of the entire car. Re-named Camel Team Lotus Honda, the equipe also acquired a new driver, Satoru Nakajima from Japan, although even then it must have been clear that he would never do much more than shadow the team's star performer, Ayrton Senna. Even with Senna, however – who Ducarouge described as 'probably the best driver in the world' – the season got off to a poor start with a retirement in Brazil, second place to Mansell at San Marino, and a collision with the Englishman which removed him from contention at Spa. For Monaco, though, he came up trumps winning the race, and repeating the feat shortly

208

Formula 1 1987

afterwards at Detroit for the team's 79th and – though no-one knew it yet – final Grand Prix win. Shown here are two steering wheels from the six cars assembled – that with the flat bottom edged coming from from chassis 99/5 which Senna drove in the French round, and that with the round profile coming from the same chassis which he took to Detroit for the US GP. Other original components which have survived from the cars include a complete rear wing assembly from the 99T with 'Lotus' signwriting for use at circuits where tobacco sponsorship was banned, two quite different front wing endplate designs from 1987, and a computerised dashboard assembly – a reminder, were one

TYPE 99T

PICTURE DETAILS

Model box, Heller, plastic & metal kit, 1/43rd

Model, Guisval, Spain, die cast & plastic, 4"

Steering wheel, Senna, USGP, 1987

Front wing endplate, 1987, Classic Team Lotus.

Computerised dashboard, Camel Team Lotus, 1987

Advert, Team Lotus, 1988

Champagne, Camel Team Lotus, Brazilian GP 1987.

Postcard, Camel Team Lotus.

TYPE 99T

Formula 1 1987

needed, that the Type 99T had even more wiring and plumbing than any of its predecessors thanks to the host of ancillaries which came with the sophisticated new engine. The car was also modelled quite extensively but, as is often the case, with varying regard for accuracy as can be seen from the quartet shown here.

The first was made in Britain by Formula One, a nice 1/43rd scale white metal model painted yellow and black and wearing the appropriate Camel motifs. Also shown, with its box, is a 1/20th scale plastic kit car made by Tamiya in Japan, and a noticeably unrealistic four-inch long yellow die cast and plastic model made by Guisval in Spain. The 1/43rd scale plastic & metal kit made by Heller is rather better, however, and again is shown here with its original box. The official Team Lotus calendar for 1988 also featured the car with a selection of pictures from the previous season, and the same year the advertisement shown here was produced as part of the Team Lotus drive to attract additional sponsorship. Otherwise the memorabilia relating to this, the last winning design Lotus was to produce for Formula One, is a Team Lotus specification sheet for the car,

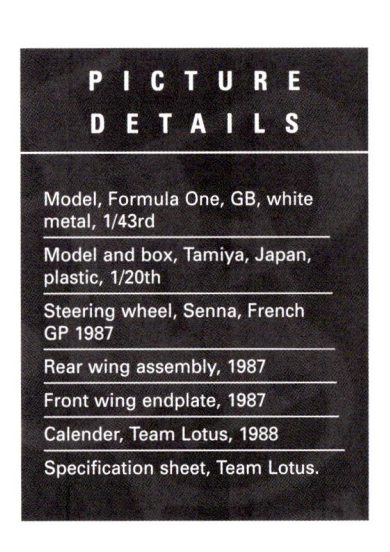

PICTURE DETAILS

Model, Formula One, GB, white metal, 1/43rd

Model and box, Tamiya, Japan, plastic, 1/20th

Steering wheel, Senna, French GP 1987

Rear wing assembly, 1987

Front wing endplate, 1987

Calender, Team Lotus, 1988

Specification sheet, Team Lotus.

Formula 1 1987

an attractive boxed Camel Team Lotus presentation set of Champagne and champagne glasses given to the team mechanics to mark the car's (admittedly, less than impressive) performance at the Brazil Grand Prix in 1987, and an official Camel Team Lotus postcard depicting Ayrton Senna with information about him printed on the reverse. In the final analysis, the Type 99T was by no means a bad car. Senna also took it to second place at Imola, in Japan and in Australia, coming third in Britain and in Germany, and fourth in the French Grand Prix. A fifth in Austria was sufficient to leave him third overall which was hardly the best performance in the team's long history. But – as time would tell – neither was it the worst.

TYPE 99T

TYPE 100T

Formula 1 1988

Another track car sharing its type number with a road-going machine – this time the long-awaited new Elan – the 100T was charged with the task of delivering a fourth World Drivers' Championship for Nelson Piquet, Satoru Nakajima's new No.1. At its launch at Paul Ricard, the World Champion – whose racing overalls are shown here – was bullish, acknowledging the 'stiff competition, as always', but saying that with the new car he saw no reason why he couldn't pull it off. Slightly less bulky than the previous season's car, but with another Honda V6, the new car's distinctive nose-and-wing assembly was a consequence of yet more rule changes – not to mention many hundreds of hours spent in the wind tunnel at Comtec in the Midlands with models like the Team Lotus-manufactured carbonfibre tub shown here. It was indeed data from these very tests and others which were to be called into question when the bones were picked over at the end of a largely unsuccessful season.

True, both drivers had scored some points in the 100T – though never coming higher than third – but neither had ever looked in any danger of winning the Championship (and indeed Piquet's performance seemed almost to deteriorate as each race slipped by). Some racegoers blamed the team's over-reliance on possible misleading data, others said Lotus had set too much store by its principal driver – but either way it was a disappointing season for Lotus and, what was worse, the trend seemed definitely to be heading downward. The model of Piquet's No. 1 car pictured here is actually Italian, by Tameo Kits, a 1/43 scale white metal item, a similar car also being produced by Onyx model cars with Nelson Piquet shown

Formula 1 1988

seated behind the wheel. For its part, Camel Team Lotus featured the car in numerous press releases and on one of its official postcards, whilst also handing out mini sweetie packs with all the major sponsors' names for the 1988 season. Also shown is a host of other promotional material produced at the time, including postcards, stickers, and race report cards for both the cars and drivers.

PICTURE DETAILS

- Model, Tameo kits, Italy, white metal, 1/43rd
- Model, Onyz, Portugal, white metal, 1/43rd scale.
- Press release & postcard, Camel Team Lotus
- Mini sweet packs, Camel Team Lotus, 1988
- Drivers overalls, Piquet, 1988
- Postcards, stickers, race reports, 1988
- Wind tunnel model, Team Lotus, 1987
- Front wing assembly, 1988

TYPE 100T

Elan 1989

TYPE 100

Long awaited, some say overpriced, and certainly controversial in its choice of engine (Japanese) – not to mention the fact that it put the power through the front wheels – the Type 100 Elan was nonetheless a crucial car for Lotus. Along with the ageing Esprit it would steer the company through a difficult half-decade. The takeover by General Motors had predictably scuppered any plans for a Toyota-powered sports car, and casting around for a replacement engine design director Colin Spooner felt Isuzu's 1.6 litre 'four' would suit a new generation which had grown up with a succession of front-wheel drive hot hatchbacks. Clothing the chassis – inevitably yet another variation of the tried and tested steel backbone – fell to Peter Stevens who, later to reinforce his already impressive credentials with the incredible McLaren F1, successfully beat off rivals including Ital Design's Giorgetto Giugiaro and even GM's own Chuck Jordan. With a drooping bonnet and hourglass shape, his vision for the car was perhaps surprising. Unveiled at the 1989 London Motor Fair, it drew its fair share of praise as well as winning a major award from the British Design Council and plaudits from the motoring press. One journalist even exhorted his readers to 'sell your grandmother to buy the new Elan'. Thereafter pent-up demand for the evocatively-named new car ensured it got off to a roaring start – but only at home. Throughout its life overseas sales remained a problem for the Elan

214

Elan 1989

and for a variety of different reasons. In the US, for example, it was simply too expensive and actually found itself in competition with the Corvette. While in Japan, the choice of an Isuzu engine meant it was perceived as a rival for Mazda's Miata/MX5, which was far, far cheaper, rather than for the 944 which had always been Hethel's intended target. Eventually, GM lost patience with the situation and pulled the plug on the project when total sales had reached just 3,800 or so. That was a long way short of the projected target of up to 5,000 cars annually. Although eventually revived (as the Elan S2) following the company's acquisition by Artioli's Bugatti concern, it was finally left to Kia to soldier on with the car after the latter acquired the tooling and rights to the design in 1995. Of the models shown here, the first, by Britain's SMTS, is a 1/43rd scale white metal road-going Elan. Also shown is a Chinese-made toy, 1/36th scale and branded as part of the Shell UK sports cars series which was manufactured to be

TYPE 100

PICTURE DETAILS

Model, SMTS, GB, die cast, 1/43rd

Press release, Lotus Cars, M200 February 1992

Brochure page, Lotus Engineering, Vox Ingeium no.4, 1991.

Brochure, Lotus Cars, 1991

Colour Chart, Lotus Cars, 1988

Advert, Sunday Times, 1990

Press release & photo S2, Lotus Cars, Oct 1989

Brochure, 12-page, The Elan Story

Elan 1989

given away free with petrol, and (rather more unusual) a 1/43rd scale model of the M200 design concept which was based on the standard Type 100. The one-of M200 was also the subject of a press release issued by Lotus Cars in February 1992 and of a feature in the Lotus Engineering house magazine Vox Ingeium, Issue No.4 from 1991, a page from which is reproduced here. Also shown is a 1991 brochure for the Elan entitled 'Ten Reasons for Owning the Lotus Elan – reading time ten minutes', and various Lotus Cars specification sheets for the Elan, the higher specification Elan SE and the final post-GM Elan S2. A Lotus colour chart from 1988 is also reproduced here along with a copy of the Lotus Engineering type approval regulation brochure. Throughout its life the car was advertised fairly widely, including an expensive full-page advertisement which appeared in the Sunday Times in 1990 – 'Nothing drives like an Elan' – and which used the same pictures and copy as that used in at least two brochures produced the same year. The Lotus press release and official photograph show the new Elan immediately prior to its launch – it is dated 8th October 1989 but was not released for another 10 days – while the three spreads are from a 12-page Elan

Elan 1989

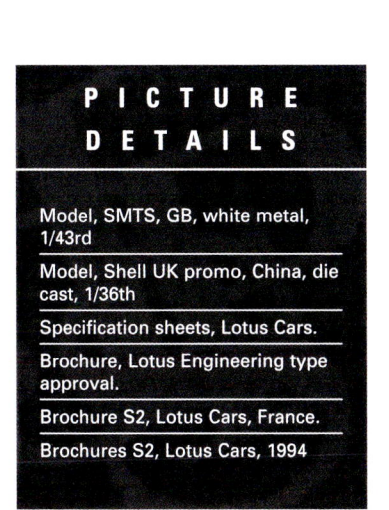

TYPE 100

PICTURE DETAILS

Model, SMTS, GB, white metal, 1/43rd

Model, Shell UK promo, China, die cast, 1/36th

Specification sheets, Lotus Cars.

Brochure, Lotus Engineering type approval.

Brochure S2, Lotus Cars, France.

Brochures S2, Lotus Cars, 1994

booklet-type brochure telling the 'The Elan Story'. Some continental promotional material has also suvived, including this cover from a French-language Elan S2 brochure for Elan S2. The same car also forms the subject of the remaining memorabilia pictured here, namely the complete range of Elan brochures, price lists and details specification sheets from 1994.

217

Formula 1 1989

TYPE 101

With Ducarouge gone, and indeed shortly afterwards Honda with it's turbocharged 1.5 litre engines, the Type 101 and its quad-valve Judd V8 was very much a new car for a new era. The Judd wasn't the engine of first choice, but once it became apparent that the intriguing 5-valve Tickford head commisioned to use with the engine by Team Lotus was going nowhere, Lotus found itself a mere 'customer' for the Judd CV – the more advanced EV being reserved for the rival March team. Camel was still on board, however, and with a new designer called Frank Dernie joining from Williams the team soon found itself with a car which was so small that, as Peter Warr put it, 'you don't have to walk round it, just step over it.' With Nelson Piquet testing the car at, appropriately enough, the Autodromo Nelson Piquet in Rio, the team was shaping up nicely for the 1989 season. Dernie was certainly pleased with the car ('enormously'), and Piquet expressed his delight too, saying driving it he even forgot the pain from his injured ribs. But it was to be another matter once the season got underway with one failure after another and no points at all until the Canadian and British rounds, at both of which Piquet managed fourth place. He came fourth in Japan too, fifth in Germany and sixth in Hungary. Nakajima finished fourth in Australia, his only result all year, and that despite shearing off the front wing shown here in an incident with Nigel Mansell. One of the team's bespoke Momo steering wheels

Formula 1 1989

TYPE 101

is also pictured with the driver's pitstop notes attached to the centre – they were especially small to prevent drivers scuffing their knuckles on the sides of the diminutive car's cockpit – the other mementoes being of a more commercial nature like the 1989 keyring, 1990 team calendar, and the race report cards which were produced for every race. Two advertisements are also shown here, illustrating the benefits of sponsorship according to Team Lotus, and a model made by Tameo Kits in Italy of a 1/43rd scale white metal car painted with the number 12.

PICTURE DETAILS

Model, Tameo kits, Italy, white metal, 1/43rd

Adverts, Team Lotus, 1989

Steering wheel, 1989

Front wing, Australian GP 1989

Keyring, Camel Team Lotus, 1989

Calender, Camel Team Lotus, 1990

Sticker, Camel Team Lotus, Piquet.

Sticker, Team Lotus Associates.

Promotional folder, Team Lotus Associates.

Race report cards, Camel Team Lotus, 1989

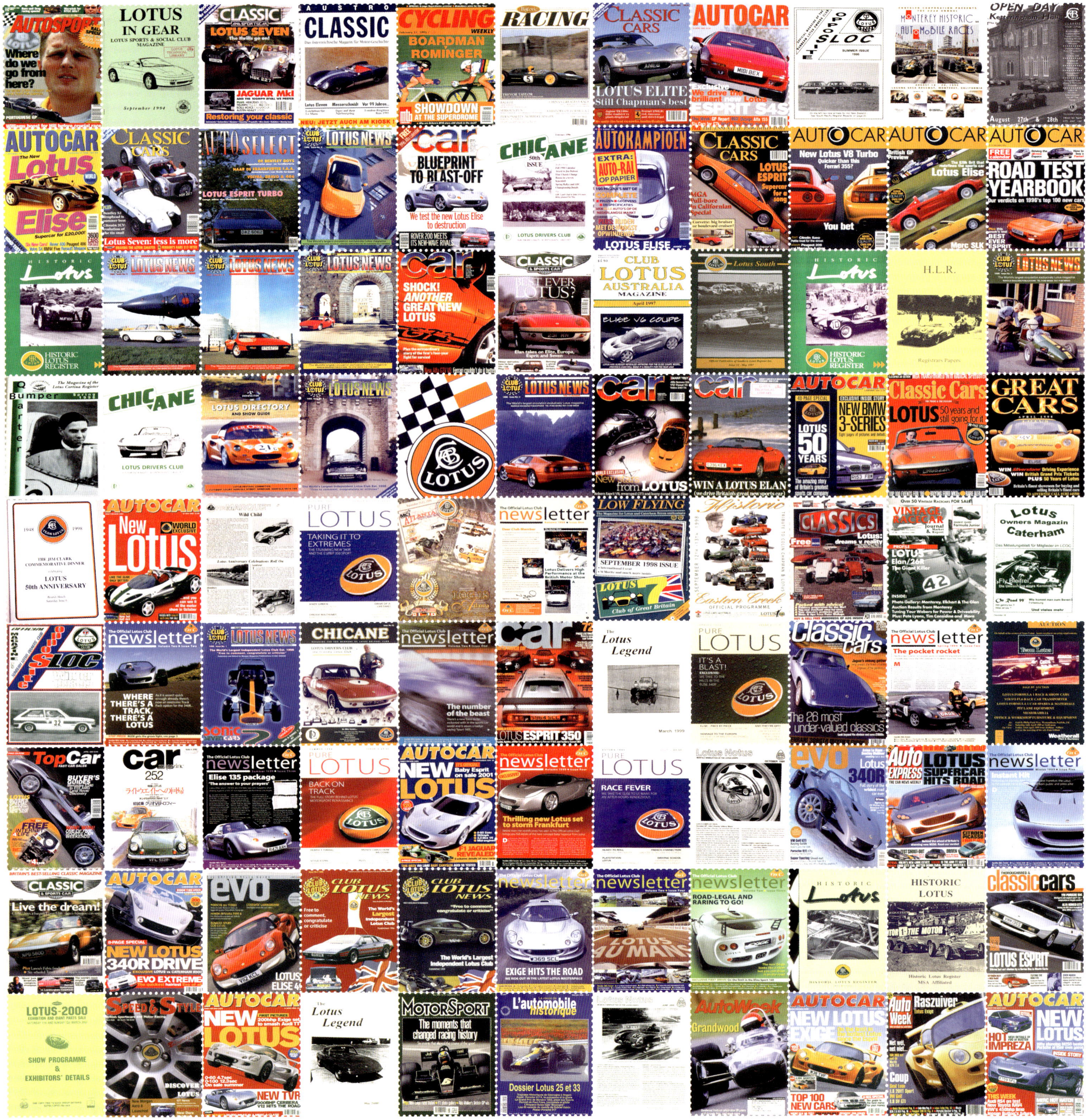

CHAPTER 5

102	Formula 1	1990
102B	Formula 1	1991
104	Lotus Carlton	1990
105	Esprit SCCA race & roadcar	1990
106	Esprit X180R race car	1991
107	Formula 1	1992
107B	Formula 1	1993
108	Pursuit bike	1992
109	Formula 1	1994
110	Road bike	1993
111	Elise	1996
114	Esprit sports GT	1995
115	GT 1 car	1997
118	M250 Project car	2002

1990-2000

TYPE 102

Formula 1 1990

Frank Dernie called the Type 102 'an evolutionary progression' but in one major respect it differed markedly from its predecessor and that was in its choice of engine. In place of the Judd V8 was a 3.5 litre Lamborghini V12, making the new car heavier but more powerful and – like its two new drivers, Martin Donnelly and Derek Warwick – also slightly taller than what had gone before. The new car made its debut at Phoenix in 1990 – an invitation to the Camel party there was autographed by Derek Warwick – but the race itself was not auspicious. Donnelly suffered a component failure which prevented him even making the startline, and whilst Warwick at least started he was soon out when his suspension collapsed. Indeed finished no higher than fifth all season despite some determined and occasionally truly heroic driving. Donnelly's record was worse still, and came to a finish after an horrific career-ending 'off' during qualifying at Jerez. He was replaced by the personable but relatively inexperienced Englishman Johnny Herbert, and once more it was clear that this was not going to be a vintage year. Team manager Rupert Mainwaring had predicted a minimum of 40 championship points – 'and we would like a win' – but the final tally was just three points, the lowest score for Lotus since its first season back in 1958. The two cars pictured here were made by Onyx in Portugal, to 1/43rd scale – complete with miniature Warwick and Donnelly dolls. The suit is one of Warwick's, who also

1990 Camel Team Lotus Driver, Martin Donnelly

Formula 1 1990

signed the postcard of himself, whilst the other autographed items are official photographs of Donnelly and of Johnny Herbert pictured towards the end of the season when he took over for the last two races. The other mementoes include a press release from the unveiling, dated February 19, an ashtray, badge and drinks stirrer, and a pamphlet entitled 'The living Legend', a brief history of Lotus and 'The Future', containing a third angle projection of the ill-fated 103. More interesting perhaps is the real thing: front- and rear-wing endplates and the engine air intake scoop internals from one of the five Type 102s produced.

TYPE 102

PICTURE DETAILS

Model, Onyx, Portugal, die cast, 1/43rd, Warwick.

Model, Onyx, Portugal, die cast, 1/43rd, Donnelly.

Press release, Camel Team Lotus, Feb 1990

Ashtray, Team Lotus, 1990

Signed postcard, Warwick, Camel Team Lotus.

Badge & drinks stirrer, Camel Team Lotus.

Drivers suit, Warwick, 1990

Signed driver photos, Team Lotus.

Front wing endplate, Classic Team Lotus.

Rear wing endplate, Classic Team Lotus.

Engine air intake scoop internals, Classic Team Lotus.

Signed invitation, Camel party, Phoenix GP, 1990

Booklet, Team Lotus, 1991

223

Formula 1 1991

TYPE 102B

A return to Judd engines, this time the EV V8 previously used by Leyton House and Brabham, and a two new drivers, the Type 102Bs driven by Julian Bailey and Mika Hakkinen were also to be run under the auspices of an entirely new outfit, the team having been taken over before the 1991 season by an independent consortium headed by Peter Wright and Peter Collins. The big tobacco money had gone too which spelt an end to Frank Dernie's never-to-be-seen 'Type 103' so instead the team set to work with a substantially modified version of its predecessor – tagged the 102B, as per the Type 25 precedent set in the early 1960s – which despite using 800 new parts is not conventionally considered to be an entirely new car. It did look remarkably different, however, particularly after a thorough testing in Honda's windtunnel at Imperial College. What's more, after initial problems qualifying at Imola for the San Marino race it turned in performances which seemed to suggest the dreadful ghost of 1990 may have been laid to rest: a fifth place for the 'flying Finn' and a sixth for Julian Bailey. Six races later, however, neither driver had managed to finish a race and little else changed when Herbert replaced Bailey, although he at least managed seventh place in Canada before handing over his seat to Michael Bartels who didn't even manage that. Johnny Herbert's racing suit is shown here, along with a postcard signed by Mika Hakkinen. More telling of the team's tough year though is the Team Lotus press release showing

224

Formula 1 1991

TYPE 102B

PICTURE DETAILS

Model & box, Tamiya, Japan, white metal, 1/20th

Model & box, Tamiya, Japan, plastic & metal, 1/28th, 1992, Hakkinen.

Drivers suit, Herbert, 1991

Press pack, Castrol Team Lotus, 1991

Advert, OZ Wheels, December 1990

Signed postcard, Castrol Team Lotus, Mika Hakkinen.

Sticker pack, Team Lotus/Tamiya.

Press release, Team Lotus

Press release & drawings, Type 103, Team Lotus.

drawings for the Type 103 which should have replaced the Type 102 but didn't, and an advertisement for OZ Wheels which shows its replacement, the Type 102B, but in plain green as no sponsorship deals had yet been finalised.

Tamiya eventually stepped in and one of their sticker packs is illustrated here along with the boxes and built up models of two of its kits, one to 1/20th scale and another produced in a slightly smaller 1/28th scale of plastic and metal and showing Mika Hakkinen in place.

225

TYPE 104

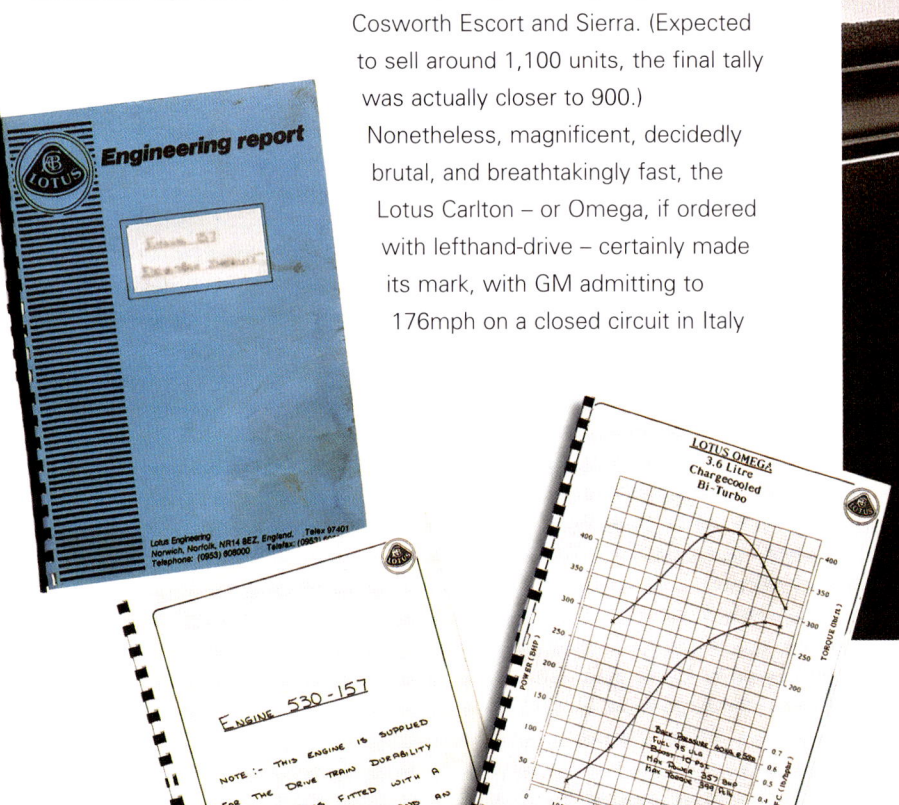

Lotus Carlton 1989

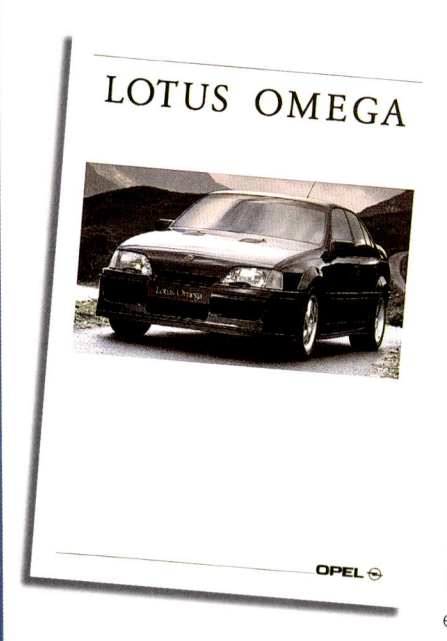

Quite unlike anything seen before – comparisons with the Cortina and Sunbeam are inappropriate as the Type 104 was conceived strictly as a road car – the creators of the 1989 Lotus Carlton had one principal objective: to build the world's fastest saloon. For Lotus the appeal of a project which was financially attractive and technically challenging was understandable. And the objectives ascribed to Bob Eaton of General Motors were equally obvious: to produce something which would enable Opel and Vauxhall to shed their humdrum image and which would do for them precisely what the Cosworth range had done for their rival Ford. That the fruits of the cooperative venture achieved this there is little doubt, although sales were never in any danger of eclipsing the Cosworth Escort and Sierra. (Expected to sell around 1,100 units, the final tally was actually closer to 900.) Nonetheless, magnificent, decidedly brutal, and breathtakingly fast, the Lotus Carlton – or Omega, if ordered with lefthand-drive – certainly made its mark, with GM admitting to 176mph on a closed circuit in Italy

Lotus Carlton 1989

with a 0-62mph time of 5.4 seconds. Even on the road the car achieved 'over 174mph', and for the first time in its long history one British motoring magazine recorded in-gear acceleration for 140-160mph. The 1/43rd scale white metal model shown here in its distinctive dark green livery is by British model-maker SMTS. Also reproduced is one of the original Lotus Carlton handbooks, a 6-page Lotus Carlton brochure from Vauxhall Motors Limited in September 1990 (first seen in Geneva, it took a full year before the first customer cars were actually delivered) and a 4-page preview brochure for the same car which was issued the previous October. Somewhat rarer is this copy of the original Lotus Cars Engineering report on the development of the 3.6 litre twin-turbo engine, showing the cover and several pages with a graph of the projected power output (377bhp @ 5,200rpm, 419lbs of torque from 4,200rpm). Finally the press pack is one produced in 1989 by Opel in Germany for its version of the car, and is shown here with several pages of information about the engine and a Lotus Omega leaflet.

TYPE 104

PICTURE DETAILS

Model, SMTS, GB, white metal, 1/43rd
Handbook, Lotus Carlton.
Brochure, 6-page, Lotus Carlton, Vauxhall Motors Ltd Sept.1990
Preview brochure, 4-page, Vauxhall Lotus Carlton, Oct 1989
Development engine report, Lotus Engineering.
Press pack, Lotus Omega (Opel), 1989
Engine information pages, Lotus Omega, 1989
Leaflet, Lotus Omega.

Esprit SE (SCCA) 1990

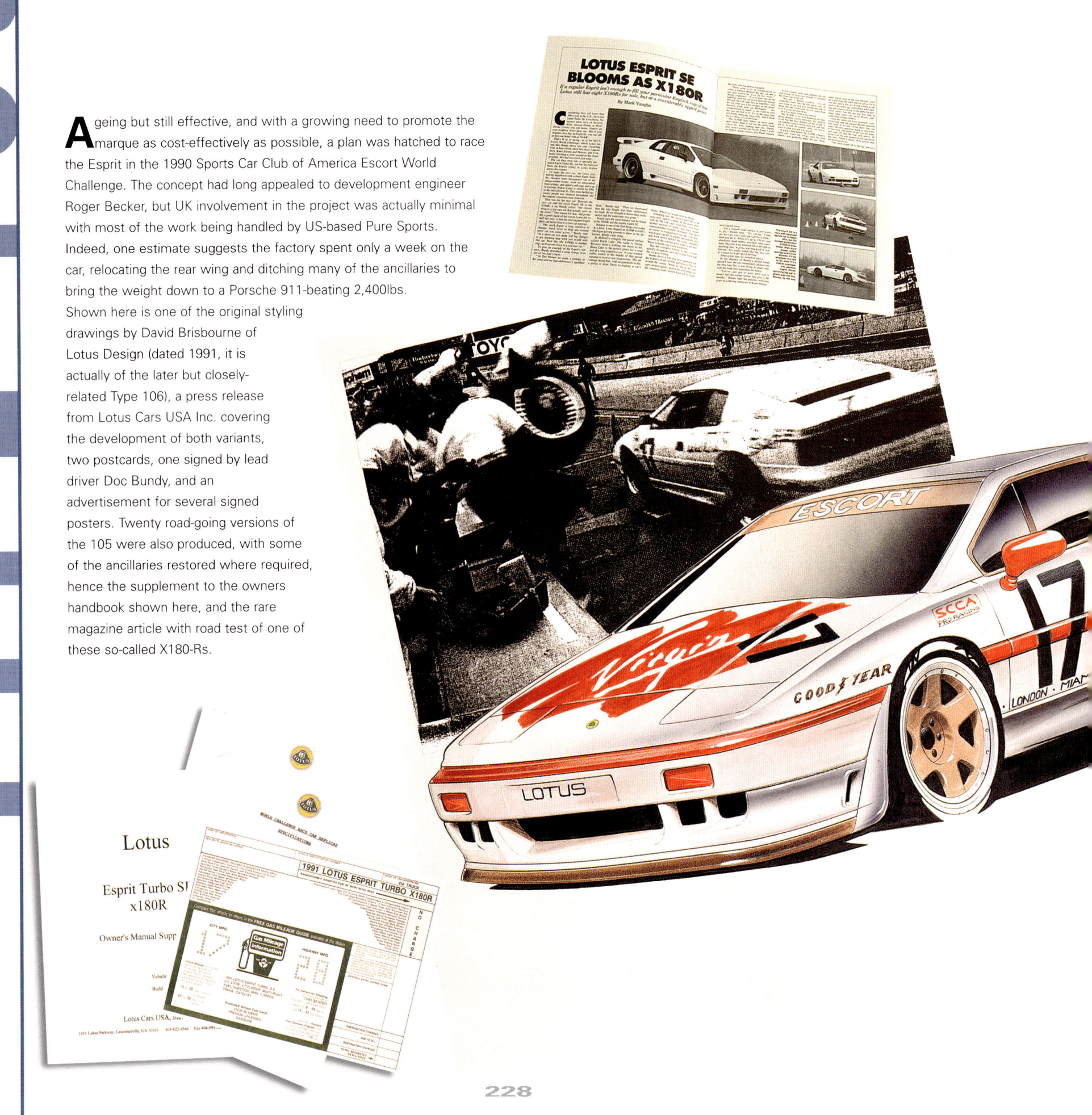

TYPE 105

Ageing but still effective, and with a growing need to promote the marque as cost-effectively as possible, a plan was hatched to race the Esprit in the 1990 Sports Car Club of America Escort World Challenge. The concept had long appealed to development engineer Roger Becker, but UK involvement in the project was actually minimal with most of the work being handled by US-based Pure Sports. Indeed, one estimate suggests the factory spent only a week on the car, relocating the rear wing and ditching many of the ancillaries to bring the weight down to a Porsche 911-beating 2,400lbs. Shown here is one of the original styling drawings by David Brisbourne of Lotus Design (dated 1991, it is actually of the later but closely-related Type 106), a press release from Lotus Cars USA Inc. covering the development of both variants, two postcards, one signed by lead driver Doc Bundy, and an advertisement for several signed posters. Twenty road-going versions of the 105 were also produced, with some of the ancillaries restored where required, hence the supplement to the owners handbook shown here, and the rare magazine article with road test of one of these so-called X180-Rs.

228

Esprit X180R 1991

TYPE 106

PICTURE DETAILS

Styling drawing, Lotus Design Department, David Brisbourne, 1991

Press release & postcard, Lotus Cars USA Inc, Nov 1991

Signed postcard, Doc Bundy, 1991

Advert, Lotusport Inc.

Owners handbook supplement, fuel consumption figures

Lotus Engineering magazine, Voxingenium, 1992

Article, US magazine, road test Type 105.

Three more Esprit-based race cars were built for the 1991 SCCA World Challenge series, to be raced by Lotusport Inc. and once again with Doc Bundy as the team's lead driver. With money still very tight, they were clearly intended to continue the successes of the previous season which on a shoestring budget had seen no fewer than four victories for Lotus, including a brace of 1-2s, and six poles positions in just eight races Similar to the outgoing Type 105 but developed to comply with the new series regulations, each car gained a strengthened chassis with a redesigned FIA-approved rollcage, revised suspension with greater geometry adjustment, larger wheels and a new front bib spoiler similar to that created for the road-going X180-R. And as the page reproduced here from the Lotus Engineering magazine 'Voxingenium' makes clear, the cars once again came up with the goods. Successful in both 1992 and 1993, and with Bundy winning the drivers' title in '92, the Type 106 provided a flicker of hope for Lotus fans at a time when there was precious little cheer to be had from the cars' performance in Formula One.

229

Formula 1 1992

TYPE 107

'Contemporary but conventional', the first all-new Lotus F1 car of the Collins/Wright era was also the first in a long time to use a Ford engine – prompting more than a few hopes that the team would see a return to the sort of form it had enjoyed back in June 1967, the first time they were in alliance with the blue oval. Memories were well to the fore of Jim Clark's win at Zandvoort – the first of 155 wins for the DFV and its derivatives, and of an incredible 159 wins for Ford-engined cars – with Ford hoping to repeat the magic with its new HB, the fastest revving V8 in motor racing history, producing 730bhp at a staggering 13,500 rpm. For his part new designer Chris Murphy created a car which was classically Lotus: simple and light, with state-of-the-art aerodynamics honed in the team's own windtunnel, and a switchable system of active suspension to give Johnny Herbert and Mika Hakkinen – seen here in a Castrol Team Lotus poster – the best possible chance against the all-conquering cars of Frank Williams. Shown here is a Tameo Kits model of the car made in Italy to 1/43rd scale of white metal, and a rechargeable racing toy made in 1992 by Tomy in China. In Japan Tamiya also modelled the car, producing in 1993 a plastic 1/20th scale kit, but by far the most interesting representation of the car is the 1/4 scale model shown here which was produced – complete with miniature sponsor decals – by the mechanics at Team Lotus. As the

230

Formula 1 1992

TYPE 107

PICTURE DETAILS

Model, Tameo kits, Italy, white metal, 1/43rd

Model, Team Lotus, 1/4 scale, 1991

Racing toy, Tomy, China, plastic, 1992

Model box, Tamiya, Japan, 1/20th, 1993

Plastic stopwatch & binoculars, Team Lotus, made in Japan.

Posters, Team Castrol Lotus, Mika Hakkinen

cars themselves were rebuilt as Type 107Bs, this is the nearest thing we have to a genuine Lotus Type 107. Also associated with the car is this pair of Japanese binoculars and a Team Lotus plastic stopwatch, both given to guests of the team during a season which, whilst ultimately unsuccessful in terms of points-won, finished with Lotus in decidedly better shape than it had been at the start – and with useful funding from its major sponsor, Castrol.

231

Formula 1 1993

Launched at Claridges in London (with the 'B' suffix saying all that needs to be said about the team's continuing financial strictures), the modifications to the previous season's car were at least such that Johnny Herbert – now partnered by Alessandro Zanardi – could report that the car was much improved and that he would be happy to drive it to its limit. In retrospect, one can say the team was probably mistaken in concentrating its strictly finite resources on developing an active suspension set up instead of pursuing semi-automatic gearboxes at a time when its rivals were streaking ahead with various highly sophisticated traction control systems. In any event despite a good start to the season which saw Herbert coming home fourth in three races – including two in front of his home crowd at Donington and Silverstone – as the year wore on it became apparent that with little money for technical innovation and development Lotus was in trouble. For a while Herbert was the hero – celebrated in a 1996 calendar with artwork by Michael Turner, congratulated by the The Independent Club Lotus, and with sponsor Loctite offering free Johnny Herbert models – but it was clear that while the Ford HB was certainly better than the Judd V10 (which had been mooted originally) it was also hugely more expensive than the Lamborghini V12 and left Lotus with precious little resources and no real chance of beating the leaders. Fans were delighted then when a deal was signed with Mugen-Honda, something which saw yet another stop-gap version of the Type 107 being created for the 1994

Formula 1 1993

TYPE 107B

PICTURE DETAILS

Model, Tameo, Italy, white metal, 1/43rd

Calendar, Sept 1996, artwork Micheal Turner.

Model set, Corgi Autocity, GB, plastic, 1/64th

Leaflet, Loctite, free model offer.

Steering wheel, Team Lotus, 1993

Invitation, Team Lotus launch, 1993

Model box, Tamiya, Japan, plastic, 1/20th

Sticker, Team Castrol Lotus.

Promotional leaflet, Club Lotus / Team Castrol Lotus.

Postcards, Castrol Team Lotus.

season, namely the Type 107C, another rejig designed to accept the ZA5C Mugen-Honda V10 and to comply with yet another change in the regulations. Shown here is a model of the earlier car, made by Tameo Kits in Italy, a box for a Japanese Tamiya kit, and a Corgi Autocity set featuring a transporter with two Type 107Bs. The damaged steering wheel is from also from 'B', crashed by test driver Pedro Lamy at Silverstone, and the various posters, stickers and postcards were produced for Team Castrol Lotus.

TYPE 108
Pursuit bike 1992

By far the most widely known of the factory's non-car projects, the two hi-tech Lotus bicycles – the Type 108 Olympic pursuit bike and the Type 110 Lotus Sport Bike – hit the headlines in the early 1990s largely through the efforts of Chris Boardman who used the former to smash several long-established bicycling records at the 1992 Barcelona Olympic Games. Boardman is seen here in a later race on the front cover of Cycling Weekly dated February 11th 1995. 'A World Championship showdown' with rival Tony Rominger, just one of many events which saw the radical design trouncing its more conventional machines and which for a short while brought the 'cinderella sport' of cycling into the homes of millions of TV viewers around the world. Lightweight, aerodynamic and quite unlike anything else seen at the time, the Type 108 concept was the work of an independent inventor Mike Burrows but Lotus joined the project once a ban on the machine had been lifted by sport's authorities. Thereafter the aerofoil-section composite monocoque quickly became 'the most famous bike in the world', Bryan Steel shaving five seconds off his time for 2000m at one race meeting and Lotus eventually producing 12 of them including eight 'replicas' which were sold to competitors for around £15,000 apiece. At the same time the publicity surrounding Chris Boardman's gold medal – Britain's first in the sport for almost three-quarters of a century – prompted Lotus to consider developing a true production version, the

234

Sport Bike 1993

Type 110, which was designed to sell for a rather more achievable £1,650 (plus taxes) – an impressive price for a machine which went on to score a unique 1-2 in the 1994 Cycling World Championships with Boardman again taking gold. Various brochures and so forth were produced for both bikes and are shown here, including Lotus Cars specification sheets, a pair of Lotus Sport-branded cycling gloves made under license by Eagle Cycle Works in Wales, and an eight page brochure for complete range of bikes and accessories.

PICTURE DETAILS

Specification sheet, Lotus Sport Pursuit Bike.

Specification sheet, Lotus Sport 110.

Cycling gloves, Eagle Cycle Works, Wales.

Cycling Weekly, February 1995

Brochure, 8-page, Lotus Sport Cycles 1994

TYPE 110

TYPE 109

Formula 1 1994

The cover of Autosport dated September 1994 says it all: We're not dead yet – the end of Team Lotus? The mere fact that such a question is being asked suggested that the writing was already on the wall by the time the Type 109 made its final, fruitless appearance. The team was clearly happy with its new Mugen-Honda deal, but there was no escaping the fact that the 'new' car was in reality actually a substantially reworked Type 107. A stop-gap version of the latter, the 107D, had already made an appearance at the start of the season whilst the 109 was being readied, but even with Herbert qualifying in fourth place on the grid at Monza, many observers had already worked out that even with a new car on its way the team was not shaping up well. In fact, the car in question was to be the last ever Formula One Lotus, the last gasp from a team which – irrespective of its founder's famous motto, crescit sub pondere virtus, in adversity we thrive – looked finally as though it had lost the fight. With nearly forty seasons behind it, 79 Grand Prix wins, six driver's World Championships, and seven Constructors' Cups, Team Lotus must have known it was entering the 1994 season on a wing and a prayer, but with Herbert itching to be off to Ligier (and soon there on the advice of the team's financial administrators) a succession of indifferent replacement drivers means

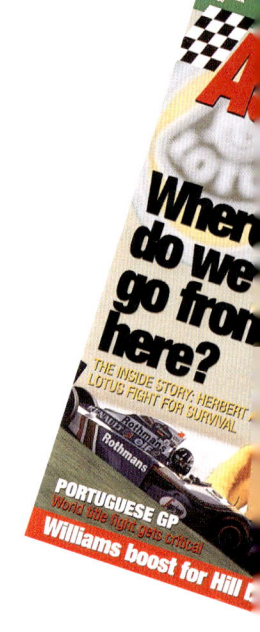

Formula 1 1994

TYPE 109

PICTURE DETAILS

Autosport September 1994

Model, Tameo, Italy, white metal, 1/43rd

Presspack, Mugen Honda.

Stickers, Komatsu, printed in Japan.

Stickers, Shionogi & Team Lotus

Steering wheel, 1994

Damaged front wing end plate, 1994

Poster, Mobil oil, 1994

it is hard to make a fair or accurate assessment of its final F1 design. Best to leave it as too little and too late – a sad final act for one of the truly great teams. The model shown is by an unknown hand, but to 1/43rd scale, and the press pack is one supplied by Mugen-Honda detailing the car's technical specification. It is accompanied by a number of sponsor stickers for Komatsu and Shionogi in Japan, and a steering wheel and damaged front wing end plate from 1994.

TYPE 111

Elise 1996

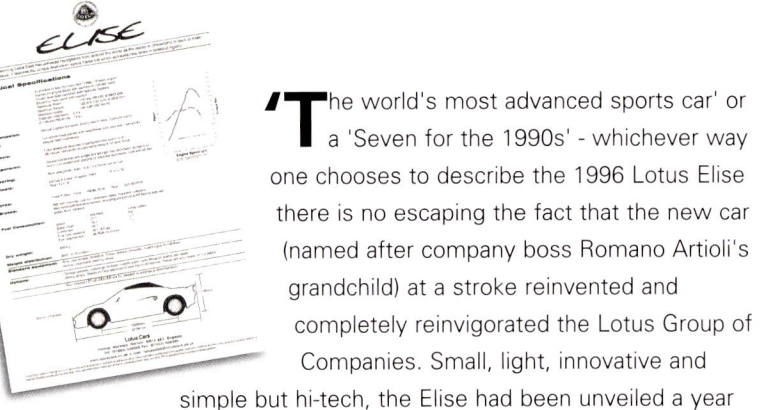

'The world's most advanced sports car' or a 'Seven for the 1990s' - whichever way one chooses to describe the 1996 Lotus Elise there is no escaping the fact that the new car (named after company boss Romano Artioli's grandchild) at a stroke reinvented and completely reinvigorated the Lotus Group of Companies. Small, light, innovative and simple but hi-tech, the Elise had been unveiled a year earlier at Frankfurt and was quickly heralded as a new breed of supercar. Unsurprisingly, it quickly amassed an array of awards for design and innovation, including Car of the Year from What Car?, Top Sports Car from BBC Top Gear Magazine, and Best Designed New Car from a poll of Car Magazine readers. More significantly, perhaps, the new Lotus also reached the finals of the prestigious Prince of Wales Award for Innovation - a first for the company - collecting numerous other trophies across Europe along the way. Featuring a futuristic-sounding yet practical and well-proven epoxy-bonded aluminium spaceframe chassis, the car was nevertheless conceived from the start to offer the most traditional hallmarks of so many classic Lotus sports cars, namely brilliant performance and outstanding handling for the enthusiastic driver. Managing director Rod Mansfield promised buyers the ultimate in driver satisfaction, and five years on it seems a fair assessment to say he and his company delivered. At the same time, with an all-up weight of only 690 kilogrammes and a correspondingly high

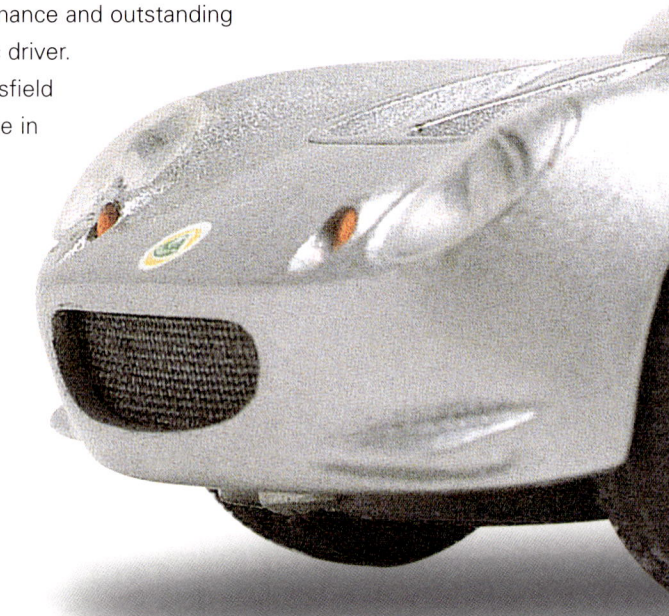

238

Elise 1996

power-to-weight ratio, the company sought to minimise weight rather than simply maximising power, doing so in order to improve prevailing braking, handling and steering responses whilst reducing overall fuel consumption and carbon dioxide emissions. Using a transverse-mounted Rover K-Series 1.8 litre quadvalve four, the Elise developed 118bhp in basic trim giving the car an effective 125mph potential with a 0-60mph time of around 5.5 seconds. At the same time, a finely-tuned independent suspension system, with upper and lower wishbones, co-axial coil springs and inverted monotube dampers, ensured that the new car could provide the handling to match. Just as importantly, it was affordable, an initial run of 700 new cars per year intended to sell in the UK at a base price of under £20,000. 'Elise is affordable and exclusive' said the publicity material handed out at Frankfurt, 'so there will [now] be many enthusiasts who will no longer have to dream of driving their own Lotus.' Much of that early publicity material is reproduced here, including

TYPE 111

PICTURE DETAILS

Model, Provence Moulage, France. 1/43rd scale resin painted silver.

Model, SMTS, GB, white metal, 1/43rd

Specification sheet, Elise 111s.

Specification sheet, Elise.

Adverts, Lotus dealers.

Advert, Elise 1998

Brochure, Lotus Cars, 1996

Promo-sheet, pre production, 1995

Promo sheet, Sport Elise 1997

TYPE 111

Elise 1996

the square green cover and a spread from the very first Elise brochure, 'Born to be wild', and a rare pre-production promotional sheet showing artwork of the nearly finalised car. Also shown are some later selling materials such as the German language Elise brochure and specification sheet (from 1999) and another translated into Italian. The high quality 4-page Elise brochure is also from 1999, shown here with the cover and inside spread from a square 6-page brochure called 'The Vision Realised' and another for the Sports Elise/Speedster Elise - both technically Type 111 cars.

The silver model is made by Provence Moulage in France to 1/43rd scale and of resin, while the yellow car is a white metal model to a similar scale made in Britain by SMTS. The third is by New Ray Co., and is of extremely poor quality manufacture given that it is apparently an 'official' product made under license from Lotus Cars. A recent Elise price list is also included here with several promotional photographs, two different

Elise 1996

TYPE 111

Elise specification sheets, and a number of advertisements for Lotus dealers and the 1998 model year. Somewhat rarer is this picture of a very late styling department pre-production model, or rather half of it. (Only half was actually made as it is difficult to handmake two halves identically, so the finished half is instead simply photographed against a mirror.)

Finally, the trophy is one awarded at the Lotus Driver Training Experience course, intended to help new customers get the most from their Elise. Very much in line, in other words, with Rod Mansfield's early forecast: that Elise would bring the true Lotus experience to the widest possible number of enthusiasts.

PICTURE DETAILS

Pre-production model, Lotus Cars 1995

Trophy, Lotus Driver Training Experience 2000

Brochure spread, Lotus Cars, 1996

Model, New-Ray Co. Ltd, China, die cast, 1/43rd

Brochure, 6-page, Lotus Cars.

Brochure / specification sheet, Germany, 1999

Brochure / specification sheet, Italian, 1999

Brochure, 4-page, Lotus Cars, 1999

241

Elise 340R 1999

The most extraordinary iteration so far of the Type 111 concept, the 340R – only 340 of which were built for sale, and 340bhp per tonne was the factory's original target – was always intended to be more than just a stripped down Elise although no attempt was ever made to persuade the public that it was in any way a whole new car. Featured heavily in Autocar during its development (the magazine carried a 'scoop' photograph of an early car on its cover in July 1996) the technical specification sheet and brochures reproduced here show it to be essentially the same machine but with a radically-reworked body which is more easily pictured than accurately described. (Indeed, Lotus simply called it 'the ultimate track-day machine'.) Despite the fact that all 340 cars were sold in advance, Lotus dealers not unnaturally used the car in numerous advertisements – a typical example being that reproduced here from the dealer Nelmes – and at Hethel the car even appeared on a Lotus Car computer mouse mat and numerous official promotional photographs. A central seat version of the car has also been produced, called the 'Track-Pack' version, it is ,unfortunately not a road legal car, so you won't see many on the road!

Elise 340R 1999

Lotus Sport Elise

PICTURE DETAILS

Autocar July 1996

Specification sheet / brochure, Lotus Cars, 1999

Mouse Mat, Lotus Cars, 1999

EVO magazine October 1999

Press photos / brochure sheets, Lotus Cars.

Advert, Lotus dealer Nelmes, Autocar, Sept 1999

TYPE 111

Lotus Sport Elise 1999

Further developments of the Elise, but not accorded a new type number, the Sport Elise and Exige are matching coupés, the former a track-only centrally located single-seater, the latter a productionised twin-seater version sharing almost the same 192bhp version of the 1.8 litre Rover K-Series but with a few nods – a very few nods – towards practicality and civilisation. Shown here is a plastic radio controlled 1/6th scale model made by Schumacher Racing of a racing Type 111, also a Lotus Sport race series transporter. Similar cars are portrayed on an offical Lotus Sport mug, on promotional postcards – one showing an incorrect race date after the series was delayed – and various promotional photographs and specification sheets. The car was also twice featured on the cover of Autocar (April and August 2000). The roadgoing version was launched at Brands Hatch on April 7th the same year – as per the invitation shown here – with various brochures and advertisements for the new car already being produced and rave reviews in the press, there will surely be much more seen about this car.

Exige 2000

TYPE 111

PICTURE DETAILS

Model, Schumacher Racing, plastic, 1/6th.

1/43rd scale Lotus Sport race series transporter

Mug, Lotus Sport.

Postcards, Lotus Sport, 2000

Photo sheet, Lotus Sport.

Photos, Lotus Sport.

Autocar, August 2000

Invitation, Exige launch, Brands Hatch April 7th 2000

Brochure/spec sheet, German

Brochure/spec sheet, Italian

Advert, Autosport July / August 2000

Brochure, 4-page, Lotus Cars, August 2000

245

TYPE 114

Esprit Racecar 1995

Developed along similar lines to the US-only Types 105 and 106, the Type 114 Esprit GT2 driven by former Lotus F1 driver Alessandro Zanardi was a strong challenger in the fiercely competitive GT field which, in the mid-1990s, included the McLaren F1, Marcos LM600, Ferrari F40 and a variety of different Porsche 911s. Running extremely light – very near the 900kg minimum – Zanardi shaved three seconds off successive laps whilst testing at Snetterton and at his Donington debut stunned several rivals by securing a provisional pole position. But here too, disappointment was waiting in the wings. Well ahead of his class and boxing clever with class above, Zanardi shuddered to a halt as his gearbox failed suddenly but completely. Zanardi, however, still thought it a 'fantastic racer, wet or dry', and the following race proved it with a fourth place overall and best in class. A specification sheet for the car is shown here, along with a photograph of the car and a poster by Lotus Cars 'Performance.' Also a model by SMTS, (a 1/43rd scale model from 1997 pictured assembled and in parts) and another by Provence Moulage of France.

GT1 1997

TYPE 115

Another near-900kg barnstormer, the Type 115 Elise was arguably the most innovative Lotus high performance road car to date. Eligible (as per the announcement reproduced here) for the 1997 FIA Endurance Championship and Le Mans 24 Hours, it also had the potential to be the most successful racing car from the company since Ayrton Senna's 1987 Type 99T. With painstaking attention to detail, widespread use of advanced lightweight composites, and a superbly engineered 550bhp V8 – detuned to 'only' 350bhp for the one street-legal example from the production run of eight – it was also the product of close cooperation between different departments at Lotus including engineering, design, racing and marketing. Just the thing for Mr Artioli to demonstrate what he called his company's 'advanced capabilities in these areas.' A high speed testbed, in other words, but also a useful advertising medium for a range of other Lotus products. The model, of resin painted yellow and black, is a 1/43rd scale model from FFI in France, whilst that shown in the Thai Airways livery is a 1/18th scale model from China which was also available as a road or racing car.

PICTURE DETAILS

Model, SMTS, white metal, 1/43rd, 1997.

Specification sheet & photo, type 114.

Poster, Lotus Cars Performance.

Model, Provence Moulage, France, resin, 1/43rd

Model, FFI, France, resin, 1/43rd

News release, Lotus GT1 Racer. 5th March 1996.

Press release, Lotus Cars, 1997

Model, Chrono, China, die cast, 1/18th

M250 Project 2002

Strictly speaking, only a concept car when it made its debut at the Frankfurt Motor Show in October 1999, the M250 coupé was nevertheless clearly always intended to be a pretty accurate representation of what the production car was going to be like. Indeed, styling chief Russell Carr admitted as much, telling journalists they would see the real thing within two years and it wouldn't look much different. 'Every detail of the body design,' he said, 'is there for a purpose. This car will set new standards in aerodynamic downforce.' Described, and with some justification, as a 'big brother to the Elise' by BBC Top Gear magazine, the new car and its still-secret bought-in 3.0 litre V6 (from the start a heavily reworked GM unit was the most popular choice) naturally made the covers of specialist motoring magazines around the world. One of these – from Britain's weekly Auto Express – is pictured here. A car quite pointedly devised to go head to head with the likes of the Porsche Boxster S and the TVR Cerbera – at the coupé's official launch there was already talk of a targa version being mooted for the near future – it uses a similar construction method to that employed on the ground-breaking Elise. Lightweight, hi-tech materials, a bonded chassis now of aluminium and carbon-fibre, and all the Lotus know-how necessary to take its starting weight down to just 1000kg – comfortably undercutting that of any rival. The transmission is a six-speed manual, and with all-independent suspension expectations are naturally high when it comes to the new car's roadholding and handling finesse. It also promises to be extremely quick, with an electronically limited top speed of

M250 Project 2002

155mph from the centrally-placed 250bhp V6, and a target time for 0-60mph of 'under five seconds.' Also shown is a specification sheet and styling dept drawing for the original concept car, a photograph of the car along with additional specification sheets in German and Italian, a set of three studio press shots of the car, and a Lotus Cars magazine advertisement for the entire Lotus range.

PICTURE DETAILS

Auto Express, November 1999

Specification sheet, Lotus style department

Specification sheet & photos, German and Italian

Press photos, Lotus Cars, 2000

Advert, Lotus Cars, 2000

TYPE 118

Anthony Colin Bruce Chapman

"Our years of involvement in top-level motor racing have, I believe, coincided with the most technically interesting and demanding period in the history of the sport"

Few people would disagree with that statement from Colin Chapman, nor indeed with the suggestion that few if any motor industry innovators proved in the long run as successful as he did. Not just in winning races, but also in ensuring that the skills and technologies perfected on the circuit cascaded down into cars that we could all to some degree enjoy ourselves. The Chapman family motto said much about the man – Crescit sub pondere virtus (In adversity we thrive) – for Chapman's unremittting creativity was never more inspired than when his back was to the wall. Not all his innovations were ultimately successful, but the best of them still impress, his fertile imagination ranging widely over so many other aspects of road and racing car development.

The true monocoque racing car was his, as was the first sports car built entirely using glass-reinforced plastic. It was he who patented a workable process for vacuum assisted resin injection, and of course right up to his death he was working on his own pioneering system of 'active suspension'.

Such ideas produced innumerable winners for Lotus and in every significant class of circuit racing – not forgetting that it was Lotus too which helped the Sunbeam win the 1981 World Rally Championship – and even now his ideas feed back into the motor industry and at so many different levels.

The company he started still surprises industry watchers with Olympic medal-winning bikes and best-selling designs which redefine the very notion of a sports car.

PICTURE DETAILS

The Guardian Young Businessman of the year 1970.

Tankard for Winter trial 1950 ACB Chapman. (Mark 2)

Tankard for W.H + D.C.C Ibsley trial 1951, C.Chapman. (Mark 2)

BRDC Silver tray, "Colin Chapman CBE, for his achievement in winning five world championships in ten years".

Royal Automobile Club medal, "Presented to ACB Chapman OBE In recognition of five world championship victories by his cars", should say CBE.

BRDC Gold Star given to Colin Chapman 1978

Cover of Shell Teams in Racing, 1970 LOTUS

Poster by Brian Caldersmith, Australia, Lotus 50th anniversary golden jubilee celebrations, 1998

ESSO Petroleum Company Ltd Trophy, "To Colin Chapman designer of The World Championship & Indianapolis winning Lotus 1965".

1925-1982

PRESENTED
TO

C. B. CHAPMAN
O.B.E.

IN RECOGNITION OF FIVE
WORLD CHAMPIONSHIP
VICTORIES BY HIS CARS

Whilst it is true that in F1 a star that once burned so brightly is now lost from view, the team's record in this gruelling, unforgiving arena still bears comparison with the very best from any era.

79 victories, 107 pole positions, six World Driver's Championships, seven for the Constructors' Cup and victory at Indianapolis - it is an incredible achievement for a small company, all the more so given that Hethel at the same time managed to develop and manufacture such a truly mouth-watering line-up of road going cars as the Elite, Elan, Europa and Esprit.

The company's continued survival and success, of course, was largely down to Colin and, whilst Lotus has continued after its founder has gone, for many enthusiasts, things will never be the same.

ACBC

ACBC

1925-1982

'At a race meeting,' his wife Hazel once said, 'you could see why he loved it so much. He was there on the spot where it was all happening. He designed the cars and they would be built in six months or even less, and he would then become involved in personally testing them...he was in control of it all."

It was a golden era, for the sport, for the enthusiast. Colin Chapman made it happen, and in a way and from another place his legacy means he is still doing precisely that.

PICTURE DETAILS

The CBE medal, 1970

Brass wheel spinner ashtray, "Lotus world champions 1963, 1965 Indianapolis, ACBC".

Chrome wheel spinner ashtray, "1963, 1965, 1968 Lotus World Champion car constructors, presented to Colin Chapman."

The Ferodo Trophy "1965 ACB Chapman".

Cover of Shell Motorsport profile No. 46 Colin Chapman, 1969

POSTSCRIPT

BY PATRICK PEAL

A wise old man once told me that it's not the name that matters - it's the story that's told about the name. The origin of the Lotus name is not known – or at least not publicly known – but the brand means so much to so many people all over the world who appreciate the ultimate in driving satisfaction. Whether it's watching an evocative video of Moss, Clark, Peterson, Andretti or Senna, or simply thrashing an Elise on a track day, the Lotus brand stands for unmatched driving satisfaction.

Another wise man, who used to work for John Surtees, is now a professional wise man at Lotus. He once told me that in the 1960s and '70s every race engineer used to rush down to his local newsagent to scan the pages of Autosport after Lotus had unveiled its latest race car 'and find out what on earth Chunky is up to this time'. It was clear then and is clear now that true driving satisfaction is often the result of great lateral thinking, innovation and large helpings of inspiration. Once again the Lotus Elise is a classic example of all that is best about the brand. Since the very earliest days of the company, its marketing collateral including brochures, motor shows and advertisements has inspired generations of owners, future owners and would-be owners. One might remember the James Bond movies as being powerful and inspirational marketing tools too! With such motivation stimulated by the brand, a huge industry has built up creating accessories and merchandise, some authorised and a great deal both independent of and heartily disliked by the factory. Many organisations around the world have felt a virtual hand on their shoulder from Lotus lawyers pursuing unauthorised merchandise, and no doubt examples of such items are represented here. Nor is it always the main brand that led to some great products like the Corgi 'James Bond' Esprit. In the heady days of Team Lotus domination, who remembers the 'Team Lotus Won Two One-Two' tee-shirt?

More recently, Chris Boardman and the LotusSport bike shot to prominence and gave Lotus a new sub-brand to develop. It led in turn to Lotus Motorsport, and the current success story – the Elise, once more.

In all cases, the story each item has to tell is fascinating in itself – from pure opportunism to a fascinating expression of an individual's appreciation of the Lotus brand. During my almost 20 years at Lotus, I was constantly amazed by the passion and ingenuity of the creators of these items. It would be invidious to mention examples by name but there's a lot of choice. It clearly gives the author plenty of opportunity for Volume II at some point – and on the evidence of this book that would certainly be something to look forward to.

I first met William on a very wet and muddy field in Norfolk more than 10 years ago. He impressed me with his vision and determination, which led him around the world before he completed what I believe is the finest record of the Lotus marque. This book is another 'must have' for anyone who feels the slightest thrill at the mention of Lotus and who enjoys the aura of the name expressed crudely, enthusiastically, illogically, comically and with great passion in the pages of this book. It has made me retreat to my box of Lotus treasures – which hasn't seen the light of day for some time – and has re-awakened many happy memories through each item. The name is powerful – the products tell the story.

INDEX

A

AG Wood 16, 31, 35
AK Models 78
Addicot, Dizzy 34
Airfix 68,152
Alexan 194
Allen, Ray 112
Allington, James A 38, 48, 50
Allison, Cliff 24, 28, 36
A.M.R. 117
Andretti, Mario 129, 130, 136, 158, 160, 164, 166, 168, 174, 253
Angelis de, Elio 174, 188, 190, 197, 199, 200, 202, 204, 206
AP Borg & Beck 67, 167
Arciero 'Brothers' 46
Artioli, Romano 215, 238, 247
Arundell, Peter 49
Asahi 64, 164
ATC Models 64
Atkinson Acorn 30
Atlas 52
Auto-Kits 15, 84
Avengers 62

B

Bailey, Julian 224
Baker, Stanley 21
Baldersmith, Brian 85
Balding & Mansell 31
Baldwin 134
Bandai 30, 77, 78, 98
Bardahl 135
Barrett, Alan 122
Bartels, Micheal 224
Becker, Roger 228
Berry, John 19
Birdsall, Derek 16, 31
Boardman, Chris 234, 253
Bolster, John 22
Bond, Bev 121
Bond, James 253
Bonnet, Rene 94
Bonnier, Jo 46, 128
Brabham, Jack 54
Brack, Bill 136
Brisbourne, David 228
Bristol Plastics 32
Britax 67
Bueb, Ivor 22, 28
Bundy, 'Doc' 228
Borrows, Mike 234

C

Camel Team Lotus 78, 120, 175, 203, 208, 210, 213, 218, 222
Carr, Russell 248
Castrol 32, 231, 233
Challman, Bob 32
Chamberlain, Jay 27
Chapman, Stan 44
Cherry, Wayne 5
Clark, Jim 7, 36, 44, 51, 54, 56, 58, 62, 66, 74, 76, 79, 82, 86, 100, 103, 104, 203, 230, 253
Classic Car Kits 67
Classic Team Lotus 120, 141, 197
Cogy 188
Coles 17
Colins, Peter 224
Coombes, John 34
Cooper, John 21, 42
Copp, Harley 102
Corgi 24, 60, 64, 151, 164, 184, 233
Costin, Frank 20, 36
Costin, Mike 56, 66, 102
Courage, Piers 87
Cox 86
Crown Models 98
Currie, Adam 11

D

D.M. Modeles 80, 96, 98
Dasshin 106
Dean, James 21
DeLonghi 207
DeLoran, John 176, 184
Dernie, Frank 218, 222, 224
Diamond-X 83
Dinky 49,107
Don Safety Trophy 151
Donnelly, Martin 222
Ducarouge, Gerard 200, 202, 208, 218
Duckhams 113
Duckworth, Keith 66, 102
Dumfries, Johnny 202, 206

E

Eagle Cycles 235
Eaton, Bob 226
Ecclestone, Bernie 134
Eidai-Grip 161, 165
Entex 96, 119
Equipe Models 88
Essex Petroleum 175, 176, 188, 189, 191

F

F.F.I. 247
Ferguson, Andrew 99
Fittipaldi, Emmerson 124, 134, 138, 140, 142, 145
Fleischmann 86
Formula 1 Models 210
Foyt, A.J. 78
Frog 71

G

G.P.Models 47, 80
Gama 86
Gammons, Peter 13, 16
Geoghegan, Leo 85
George Berrige & Co 110
Getty, J.Paul 48
Giugiaro, Giorgetto 162, 214
Gold Leaf 87, 92, 99, 100, 104, 106, 127, 129, 138, 140, 142
Goodyear 167
Granatelli, Andy 118
Grand Prix Classics 107
Graphic Designers 26
Guisval 210
Gunze Sangyo 81
Gurney, Dan 46, 71, 78

H

H. Model 34, 39
Hadfield, George 141
Haig-McAllister 186
Hakkinen, Mika 224, 230
Harris, Ron 65
Hart, Brian 79
Hatton 95
Hawk 72
Hawthorn, Mike 36
Heller 106, 210
Herbert, Johnny 222, 224, 230, 232, 236
Hexagon 90
Hi-Fi 197, 202
Hickman, Ron 60, 108
Hill, Graham 38, 36, 54, 66, 82, 85, 88, 100, 102, 104, 120, 121, 128, 131, 135
Hobos 167

I

Ickx, Jacky 143, 154
Imai 46, 52, 83
I.M.C. 83
Imperial Tobacco 190, 201
Inca Plas 159
Ireland Innes 36, 50, 54

J

JAK 48
John Day Museum 53
John Player 93, 138, 141, 142, 147, 148, 152, 154, 158, 160, 166, 175, 177, 190, 197, 198, 201, 207, 208,
Joker 48
Jones, Parnelli 78
Jordan, Chuck 214
Joyce, John 86, 87
Justice, James Robinson 21

K

Kirwan-Taylor, Peter 29
Kogure 62
Komatsu 237
Kyosho 93

L

la Ilusion 175
Lamy, Pedro 23
Lawson, Mike 11
Lee, Leonard 29

Lincoln international 37, 59
Lister, Brian 21
Loctite 232
Lovely, Pete 135
Lucas, Peter 122
Lucky Strike 142
Lumsden, Peter 22

M

M.A.E 36, 55
M.D.C 72
M.P.C 119
MA Scale Models 52
Mainwaring, Rupert 222
Mansell, Nigel 174, 188, 190, 197, 198, 200, 202, 207, 208, 218
Mansfield, Rod 238, 241
Marsh Models 64
Martini 167, 169, 174
Matchbox 15, 123
Matthews, Tony 158, 161, 202
Merrikits 106
Micromax 207
Midlantic 23
Miles, John 64, 97, 106, 121, 128, 189
Mini-Racing 169, 171
Mitsuwa 52
Models Plus 129
Monitor Advertising 163
Monogram 77
Morgan, Dave 145
Moss, Stirling 24, 42, 43, 46, 50, 51, 64, 253
Munday, Harry 60
Murphy, Chris 230

N

N.G.K 167
Nakajima, Saturo 208, 212, 218
Nearn, Graham 17
Nichimo 123
Nikko 159
Nilsson, Gunnar 160
Nitto Kagaku 98
Norman Bros 27

O

O.Z.Wheels 225
Ogilvie, Martin 199
Oliver, Jackie 97, 104
Olympus 205
Onyz 213, 222
Otaki 26, 72

P

Page, Theo 28, 44
Penny 88
Peterson, Ronnie 143, 145, 154, 158, 166
Pilen 152
Piquet, Nelson 212, 218
Polistil 131, 154, 169, 171
Politoys 96
Prost, Alain 205
Provence Moulage 24, 46, 127, 147, 240, 246

Q

Quartzo 161

R

R.D.Marmande 28, 30, 43, 49, 50, 53, 55, 65, 73, 74, 77, 79, 113, 121, 125, 135
R.E.M 107
Rebaque, Hector 161
Renwall 59
Reutemann, Carlos 168
Revell 52, 59, 70
Richmond Hill Printing 15, 27, 31
Rindt, Jochen 91, 106, 120, 128, 131, 134, 138
Roadace 59, 70
Rominger, Tony 234
Roxy 236
Rudd, Tony 90
Russell, Jock 136
Russkit 53, 59, 83

S

S.M.T.S 71, 83, 98, 111, 117, 119, 181, 215, 227, 240, 246
Salvadori, Roy 34
Scale Racing Cars 88, 140, 167, 189, 191
Scalextric 48, 51, 83, 119, 159
Schackman 83
Schuco 77, 140
Schumacher Racing 244
Sears, Jack 86
Sellers, Peter 64, 79
Senna, Ayrton 202, 204, 206, 208, 211, 247, 253
Serrifer, Mike 11, 13
Sharp, Hap 60, 86
Shelford, John 72
Shell 215
Shionogi 237
Simpson Racewear 202
Spence, Mike 62, 74, 76
Spooner, Colin 214
Stabo 50
Stacey, Alan 38
Steel, Anthony 21
Stevens, Peter 178, 214
Stewart, Jackie 66, 74, 121
Strombecker 46, 50, 70, 72, 155

T

Tada 106
Tallaksen 24
Tameo 205, 207, 213, 219, 230, 233
Tamiya 86, 161, 210, 225, 230, 233
Tandem 159
Taylor, Roger 137
Taylor, Simon 119
Telsalda 60
Temple Press 95
Tenariv 87, 101
Terry, Len 38, 82
Testors 71
Texaco 145
Thai Airways 247
Thorpress Litho 110
Tissot 197
Tojeiro, John 21
Tokyo Plamo 72
Tomica 152
Tomy 230
Trimmer, Tony 144

Tsukuda 152
Turmer, Micheal 44, 48, 87, 99, 100, 104, 127, 232
Tyrrell, Ken 73

U

U.P.C. 77, 101
UDT Laystall 54

V

Valvoline 167
Van Herpene, Eugene 187
Vandervell, Tony 36
Vermillio, Bernard 144
Vitesse 15

W

Walker, Dave 124, 138
Walker, Ian 64
Walker, Rob 42, 51, 55, 104
Warner, Graham 64
Warr, Peter 53 ,199 ,205 ,218
Warwick, Derek 222
Weiss, Sam 24
Western Models 165, 175, 176
Wheatcroft, Tom 44, 59, 104
White, Stuart 5
Whitfield, June 21
Whitmore, John 67, 68
Williams, Frank 230
Winklemann, Roy 134, 203
Winterbottom, Oliver 150
Wright, Peter 196, 224

Y

Yamada 60
Yodel 147
Yonezawa 35, 147
Yoshikawa, Shin 77

Z

Zakspeed 117
Zanardi, Alessandro 232, 246
Zee Toys 140

ACKNOWLEDGEMENTS

Many of the images in this book were accumulated whilst working on our previous book, so we would like to offer my thanks to all the people who helped on the making of THE LOTUS BOOK, I'm sure you know who you are, thank you all again.

SPECIAL THANKS

Our biggest thank you must go to Clive and Hazel Chapman who have continued to offer there invaluable help and support during the making of this book. They have never hesitated in allowing us access to their collection of Lotus history and without them the book would just never have happened.

Thanks also to both Graham Arnold and Patrick Peal. Both ex Lotus employees and die hard Lotus enthusiasts who, we are pleased to say, were happy to contribute some of their reminiscences.

The majority of the models in the book come from the collection of Jim Marsden in Boulder, Colorado, USA. Jim has one of, if not the largest collection of model Lotuses and related items in the world. His help and patience during the hours spent working in his home were truly admirable.

The other people who have offered their time and asistance by allowing us to delve through their collections for inclusion in the book are, Simon Hadfield, Wolfgang Reichert, Jim Bennett, Dennis de Hoog and Mark Plechaty.

BIBLIOGRAPHY

The majority of the information in this book, especially the facts and figures relating to the cars, have come directly from the files and press releases of Group Lotus and Classic Team Lotus. For much of this I have to thank, in particular, Clive Chapman at Classic and Dawn Mainwaring, Alastair Florance and Andrew Davis at Group.

As with all matters relating to Lotus, production fact and figures on the cars have always been shrouded in mystery, it was certainly no different dealing with all the associated items. Therefore many of these details and specifications are open to question, although some people are undoubtedly going to disagree with certain facts, I can only say, we tried!

Many other publications have been consulted and used as cross reference material during the course of producing this book. These include: Colin Chapman's Lotus (Haynes); Colin Chapman, The Man and His Cars (PSL); Lotus File (Temple); Lotus, All The Cars (Aston); Lotus Elan (Osprey); Lotus Seven (MRP); Lotus, a Formula One Team History (Crowood); The Lotus Elite (PSL); The Lotus Europa (RB Publications); The Original Lotus Elan (MRP); The Story of Lotus (MRP); Team Lotus, the Indianapolis years (PSL); The Third Generation Lotuses (MRP); Theme Lotus (MRP); The Brooklands Books Series.

Many of the items included in this book are part of the extensive range of Classic Team Lotus. For information on these and other collectables available, phone or fax Classic Team Lotus on; Tel: 01953 601621 Fax: 01953 601626